REEDS YACHT BUYER'S GUIDE

REEDS

YACHT BUYER'S GUIDE

A COMPREHENSIVE GUIDE
TO YACHTS FROM 20-40 FEET

Compiled by Fred Barter

ADLARD COLES NAUTICAL

Published 2004
by Adlard Coles Nautical
an imprint of A&C Black Publishers Ltd
37 Soho Square London W1D 3QZ
www.adlardcoles.com

ISBN 0-7136-7050-9

A CIP catalogue record for this book is available from the British Library.

A&C Black uses paper produced with elemental chlorine-free pulp,
harvested from managed sustainable forests.

Typeset in 9pt Palatino
Printed and bound in Spain by Graphycems

Designed by Fred Barter ARCA

Note: While all reasonable care has been taken in the publication of
this book, the publisher takes no responsibilty for the use of the
methods or products described in the book.

Contents

REEDS

Introduction

Welcome to this first edition of the *Reeds Yacht Buyer's guide.*

When I was asked to compile this book I had no idea just how complex the task would be. However it has finally made it to the printer and I hope into your expectant hands.

A few words on what we set out to do. The first section covers information on those sailing yachts which are currently in production. The second covers popular yachts which are no longer produced but are available on the used-boat market. The new yacht information has been collected from the yacht builders' brochures and through contact with their agents. I have made the presentation of information as consistent as possible but where data is missing it is because it was not supplied. Some builders' wanted to show VAT included in their standard price, some did not. Some preferred not to show a price at all and in these cases we have used (POA) Price on application.

If you are thinking of buying a new or used boat then please use this reference book as a place to start. Your next step is to contact the brokers or agents and get more information, brochures etc. If you are interested in a used boat, please ask a surveyor to check her condition before you buy.

Boat buyers

If you are a boat buyer and would like more extensive information on any of the boats in this book, I can arrange for this to be sent to you. If you are interested in a boat that is not included, I may have the information available. Please email:

info@reedsyachtbuyersguide.co.uk

Boat builders

If you are a boat builder, broker or agent and would like to be included in future editions. Please email:

fbarter@reedsyachtbuyersguide.co.uk

May you always have at least a foot under your keel.

Fred Barter
September 2004

Boat Name	LOA	Page
Athena 38	38ft 5in	108
Bavaria 38 Match	39ft 8in	120
Beneteau 25	24ft 7in	31
Beneteau 40.7	40ft 2in	124
Beneteau Clipper 323	32ft 8in	61
Beneteau Clipper 373	36ft 9in	91
Beneteau First 211	21ft 6in	18
Beneteau First 260	25ft 6in	34
Beneteau First 27.7	29ft	46
Broadblue Catamaran 38	38ft	102
Catalina 320	34ft 3in	70
Catalina 36 mkII	36ft 4in	87
Catalina 400	40ft 6in	127
Channel 27	26ft 9in	41
Channel 31	30ft 9in	53
Com-Pac 23/3	23ft 9in	26
Com-Pac 25	25ft	32
Com-Pac 27/2	29ft.7in	48
Cornish Crabber 22 Gaff Cutter	22ft	21
Corsair 24	24ft 5in	28
Corsair 28	28ft	43
Corsair 36	36ft	82
Crabber Pilot Cutter 30	39ft	111
DazCat	32ft 5in	60
Dragonfly 920	30ft 2in	50
Dragonfly 1200	39ft 4in	115
Dufour 34	34ft 9in	74
Dufour 40	39ft 4in	116
Dufour Classic 36	36ft 1in	83
Elan 31	30ft 2in	51
Elan 333	32ft 9in	63
Elan 37	37ft	94
Elan 40	40ft	123
Etap 21i	21ft 6in	19
Etap 24i	26ft 3in	38
Etap 26i	27ft 8in	42
Etap 30i	30ft 7in	52
Etap 32s	32ft 3in	59
Etap 34s	34ft 10in	75
Etap 37s	36ft 11in	92
Etap 39s	39ft 7in	119
Event 34	33ft 9in	66
Europa TS 230	23ft 2in	24
Feeling 36	36ft 5in	88
Feeling 39	38ft 4in	107

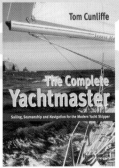
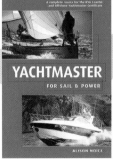

Yachts currently out of production

Boat Name	LOA	Page
Anderson 22	21ft 9in	131
Atlanta 26	26ft	147
Barbican 33	32ft 8in	169
Bavaria 32	33ft 9in	173
Bavaria 37	37ft 10in	181
Beneteau 35	34ft 9in	169
Catalac 12m	40ft 10in	152
Catalina 34	34ft 6in	176
Cobra 700	23ft	135
Cobra 750	25ft	142
Compac 23 (Finistere)	23ft 11in	138
Compromis 858	28ft 6in	155
Contessa 26	25ft 6in	144
Contessa 32	32ft	167
CR 310	31ft	163
Dufour Arpege	29ft 6in	160
E-Boat	21ft 10in	132
Elan 295	30ft 2in	160
Etap 24i	26ft 4in	150
Etap 26	25ft 5in	152
Fairey Fisherman	27ft 5in	175
Feeling 1040	34ft 4in	176
Feeling 356	34ft 7in	143
Folkboat (modified)	25ft	137
Foxhound	23ft 9in	137
Foxterrier	22ft 1in	133
Frances	34ft 3in	175
Freedom 21	21ft 8in	131
Freedom 33	33ft	170
Gemini (Cat)	33ft 6in	171
Golden Hind	31ft 6in	165
GibSea 284	28ft 6in	156
Great Dane 28	28ft	153
Hallberg Rassy 29	29ft 2in	157
Hanse 292/301	29ft 6in	158
Hanse 311	31ft	163
Hanse 315	31ft	164
Hanse 341	33ft 11in	174
Harrison Butler Cyclone II	25ft 9in	145
Hunter 701	23ft	136
Hunter Ranger	26ft 6in	155
Hunter Sonata	22ft 7in	134
Hurley 22	22ft	133

The yachts in this section are all currently in production. We have tried to give an accurate factual description of the boat: information comes from the builders' brochures.

An index size tab is printed in red at the top right hand corner of the right hand page. The entire 'New Boats, section is marked as an index tab in red on the left hand pages.

The name and length of boat are as described in the builder's brochure. The information is presented in ascending order of size.

The main photograph
is usually of the boat at sea.

The smaller pictures
show details of the interior.

When available, a profile drawing of the boat is included with a drawing of the interior layout.

The Specification box gives dimensions as supplied in the builders' brochures. These were not always consistent in their form of presentation. Where information is missing it is because it does not appear in the original brochures.

The Price guide is exactly what it says, a 'guide'. It is based on the price of a standard boat with no extra options. Prices also change with alterations in the currency exchange rate.

Please contact the agent or broker for the most up-to-date details.

Name and length of boat

LOA: 22ft - 28ft

The Hawk 20 is a unique boat she may also seem expensive. But she does have have some special features: self-righting, unsinkable and very quick. Stable and light enough to plane. The boat is built to a high quality standard. She is easily trailed behind the average family car. There is good stowage space with port and starboard amidship lockers. The buoyancy compartments are under the seats. The engine, which can be swung clear of the water when not in use, sits forward of the rudder so that the propwash gives good manoeuvrability under power. She can be left on a mooring as the cockpit is self draining. A steering compass is conveniently located just under the mast on a bulkhead which can easily take any other instrumentation.

Specification

LOA: 20ft / 6.10m
LWL: 17ft 9in / 5.19m
Beam: 7ft 5in / 2.26m
Draught: (Board up) 9in / 0.23m
Draught: (Board down) 4ft 3in / 1.30m
Mainsail: 140 sq ft / 13sq m
Jib: 80ft / 7.44m
Spinnaker: 255ft / 23.69m
Total weight (without motor): 1,800lb / 816kg
Ballast (included in above): 865lb / 320kg
Tilt back trailer: 706lb / 320kg
Design category: C

Contact:
Reid Marine,
Reid Street,
Christchurch,
Dorset BH23 2BT.

Tel: 01202 483333
Fax: 01202 470103
email: peter@reidsteel.co.uk

Price guide: 13

Hawk 20 - *20ft*

The **Hawk 20** is a unique boat she may also seem expensive. But she does have have some special features: self-righting, unsinkable and very quick. Stable and light enough to plane. The boat is built to a high quality standard. She is easily trailed behind the average family car. There is good stowage space with port and starboard amidship lockers. The buoyancy compartments are under the seats. The engine, which can be swung clear of the water when not in use, sits forward of the rudder so that the propwash gives good manoeuvrability under power. She can be left on a mooring as the cockpit is self draining. A steering compass is conveniently located just under the mast on a bulkhead which can easily take any other instrumentation.

Specification

LOA: 20ft / 6.10m
LWL: 17ft 9in / 5.19m
Beam: 7ft 5in / 2.26m
Draught: (Board up) 9in / 0.23m
Draught: (Board down) 4ft 3in / 1.30r
Mainsail: 140 sq ft / 13sq m
Jib: 80ft / 7.44m
Spinnaker: 255ft / 23.69m
Total weight (without motor): 1,800lb 816kg
Ballast (included in above): 865lb / 3.
Tilt back trailer: 706lb / 320kg
Design category: C

Contact:
Reid Marine,
Reid Street,
Christchurch,
Dorset BH23 2BT.
Tel: 01202 483333
Fax: 01202 470103
email: peter@reidsteel.co.uk

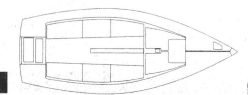

Price guide: £16,600 inc

Horizon Cat - 20ft

The Horizon Cat has been designed as a weekender for a cruising couple. The heritage of the boat is the famous Cape Cod shoal-draught cat-rigged boats that plied Nantucket during the 1900s. They were known for their seaworthiness and ease of handling. Her wide beam provides intitial stability and as she rises to her chine the underbody shape becomes sleek, narrow and easily driven to windward. There are two settee /quarter berths with storage bins under. Shelves with backrest bins line the hull for the length of the main cabin. A ten-gallon nylon water tank is located under the starboard settee. Four opening cat's eyes' ports provide the main cabin with lots of light and air. Teak doors, fiddles and a teak/holly sole give the boat a rich traditional decor. The port galley counter encloses a small ice box while the starboard galley counter provides storage under the sink and a hand-pump water spigot. When preparing meals the counters can be joined with an insert to form a continuous seven-foot work top supporting a single-burner, self-contained Butane stove.

Forward of the bulkhead is the head, with an optional privacy curtain, portable toilet, port and starboard vanities, storage bins and hamper. A lift hatch is located overhead for ample ventilation.

Specification

LOA: 20ft
LWL: 17ft 9in
Beam: 8ft 4in
Draught:
(Boards up) 26in
Draught:
(Boards down) 60in
Displacement: 2500lbs
Ballast: 600lbs
Sail Area: 205sq ft

Contact:
Clearwater Yachts
Unit 1
17 Ladbroke Close
Woodley
Reading
RG5 4DX
Tel: 0118 9698800
email:
clearwater@fsmail.net
www.Com-PacYachts.com

Red Fox 200 - 20ft 3in

The Red Fox is a mini-category C cruiser. She can be easily trailed and launched. Her twin asymetric dagger boards considerably enhance her performance. She comes in two versions, the 200S sports day sailer and the 200 cruiser which has slightly more room down below.

A third cruiser option comes with twin keels, the Red Fox 200T. The prototype Red Fox was launched in 1991 and her success is partly due to a continuous programme of improvement. She has a surprisingly generous amount of space and second hand boats when they appear on the market go very quickly. Large windows and an overhead hatch make the saloon light and airy. There are ventilators over the galley and the heads. The head is a moulded unit, easy to clean and smart. There are ample stowage lockers with easy to clean surfaces. There is a double berth forward. Because she draws so little you can walk around before she settles to make sure there are no nasty surprises underneath.

A lot of thought went into the design of these boats, and they will do well as day racers or as camping weekenders.

Specification

LOA: 20ft 3in / 6.17m
LWL: 20ft 0in / 6.10m
Beam: 8ft 2in / 2.50m
Draught: (Boards up) 0.8in / 0.20m
Draught: (Boards down) 2ft 11in / 0.9(
Draught twin keel: 2ft 3in / 0.70m
Displacement: (200S) 2200lbs / 99
Displacement: (200) 2550lbs / 1,16
Sail Area: 201sq ft / 18.70 sq m

Contact:
Select Yachts
Rock, Wadebridge,
Cornwall PL27 6NT
Tel: 01208 862666
email: Info@selectyachts.co.uk
www.SELECTYACHTS.co.uk

Price guide: £22.207 inc V

Pippin 20 - 20ft 8in

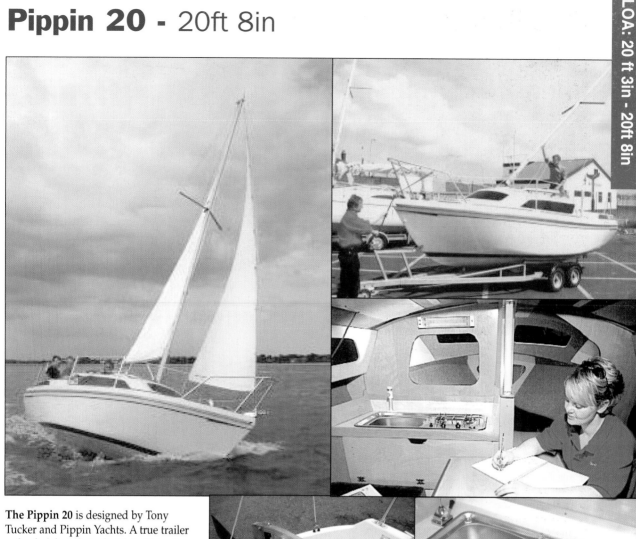

The Pippin 20 is designed by Tony Tucker and Pippin Yachts. A true trailer sailer, hand made in the United kingdom. Trailerability provides the key to economical yachting. With the lowest weight (850kg) in the 20 foot + sized boat range, the boat is capable of being towed behind the average family saloon (1800cc).

She has superb towing qualities, with the boat close to the road and the centre of gravity kept low by the ballast it is very stable. Easy towing opens up more opportunities, and sailing grounds throughout the UK, Europe and the Mediterranean are now possibilities. The boat has lots of internal space and comfortable full four berth accommodation. For additional insulation and appearance, the coachroof and interior walls are lined in carpet with inset beech panels.

There is full adult sitting headroom on all berths, including the forecabin. There is a fixed galley with room for sink and cooking stove. Ample storage space is provided below all berths, a locker for food, large storage area under the cockpit sole and two large lockers in the cockpit. She is designed for easy handling by both experienced and inexperienced alike. All necessary running rigging is led back to the cockpit.

Specification

LOA: 20ft 8in / 6.30m
LWL: 17ft 0in / 5.26m
Beam: 8ft 0in / 2.39m
Draught: (keel up) 1ft.3in / 0.38m
Draught: (keel down) 3ft 9in / 1.14m
Ballast: 441lbs / 200kg
Displacement: 1.874lbs / 850kg
Sail Area: 176sq ft / 16.4 sq m
Headroom: 5ft / 1.52m
CE Category: C

Contact:
Pippin Yachts Ltd
Enterprise Park
Endeavour Way
Sutterton
Boston
Lincs PE20 2JA
Tel: 01205 461212
Email: pippin-yachts.com
www.pippin-yachts.com

Price guide: £16.350.00

17

Beneteau First 211 - 21ft 6in

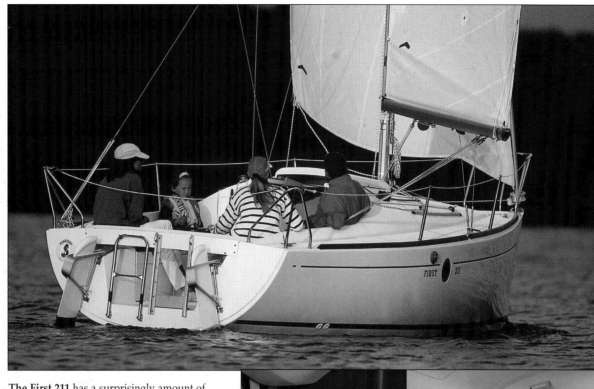

The **First 211** has a surprisingly amount of equipment for a boat of this size: a large cockpit with side lockers, wide side decks, an anchor well. The deck layout ensures optimum control for family sailing. The accommodation space is enhanced by the use of a structural beam integrated into the roof which makes a samsom post no longer necessary. The articulated hatch gives good standing height in the companionway.

The galley is fitted with a fresh water system and has generous additional locker space. The interior is fitted out in cherry wood finishes which go well with the 'Yacht Club' upholstery. There is a full anchor kit together with mooring lines and fenders. She is both fast and safe. The moulded deck and hull structure give optimum rigidity and the carefully positioned buoyancy foam ensure her unsinkability. She has a profiled cast iron lifting keel (350kg) for stabilty. Two lifting rudders give good control. She can be easily trailed and launched.

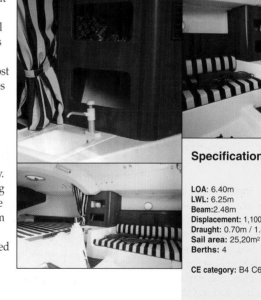

Specification

LOA: 6.40m
LWL: 6.25m
Beam: 2.48m
Displacement: 1,100kg
Draught: 0.70m / 1.80m
Sail area: 25,20m²
Berths: 4

CE category: B4 C6

Contact:
Ancasta International Boat Sales
Port Hamble
Satchel Lane
Hamble
Southampton SO31 4QD
Tel: 023 80 450 026
Email: Beneteau@ancasta.co.uk
www.ancasta.com

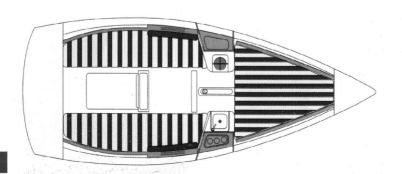

Price guide: £21.500

Etap 21i - 21ft 6in

The Etap 21i offers sleeping accommodation for 4 people. A roomy main cabin, functional corner galley and ample stowage space. The boat is easy to tow. The interior is stylish and finished in maintenance free pear laminated marine ply. The saloon contains two long sofas (each 2.00m x 0.60m) which are used as berths. The cushion covers are removable for cleaning.

Two stowage lockers complete with hinged covers are located under each sofa, while open stowage space is provided behind the backrests. The pear laminate saloon table stands on a removable leg; when not in use in the saloon, it can be stowed under the cockpit or even mounted and used in the cockpit. A 2-burner spirit hob is mounted on the solid galley unit, with a stainless steel sink and pump handle. The galley unit contains stowage space.

The open forepeak forms a very spacious double berth, with built-in plinth for mounting an optional sea or chemical toilet. If desired the cabin space can be closed off with an optional roller blind. Ample stowage space is provided under the berth.

When fitted with the 0.70m tandem keel the boat can be launched straight from the trailer.

Specification

LOA: 21ft 6in / 6.56m
LWL: 20ft 0in / 6.10m
Beam: 8ft 2in / 2.49m
Draught: 2ft 3½in / 0.70m
- 4ft 3in / 1.30m
Displacement:
2423lbs-2533lbs
/ 1150kg-1100kg
Mainsail:
167 sq ft / 15.50sqm
Jib: 91sq ft / 8.40sqm
CE Category: B/C

Contact:
Kiss Marine Solent Ltd
The Boatyard
Hythe Marina
Hythe Hants SO45 6DX
Tel: 02380 840 300
Fax: 02380 840 700

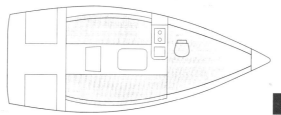

Price guide: £14.175.00 + VAT

Jeanneau Sun 2000 - 21ft 6in

The **Sun 2000** is a sailboat that unites tradition and innovation, tradition with a classic hull and colored gel coat. Innovation, a modern deck plan, plus an integral centreboard and telescopic rudder. She has a resin-infused deck. The boat has good stability for comfortable sailing. The cockpit is self-bailing, with port and starboard lockers. A folding swim ladder is fitted to the transom. The lifting tiller is removable.

The companionway has a removable entry door. In the saloon there is a stainless steel compression post and there are two opening ports. The furnishings are in teak with storage space under the seats. The forward berth is a double (6ft 3in x 4ft 7in) with storage under. The two aft berths are singles (6ft 7in x 2ft 7^1/$_2$ in) with storage under. Included in the comfort version are: Water tank, single burner gas stove, removable saloon table, 2 halogen spotlights, 1 circular roof hatch, 1 handpump, teak veneered floorboards, 70AH battery.

Specification

LOA: 21ft 9in / 6.64m
LWL: 20ft 4in / 6.20m
Beam: 8ft 4in / 2.55m
Draught:
11in - 5ft 2in / 0.30 - 1.60m
Displacement: 2756lbs / 1250kg
Sail area: 249 sq ft / 23.1sq m
Berths: 4
Engine: 10hp / 7.5kw
CE Category: C-5

Contact:
Sea Ventures Limited
Lymington Yacht Haven
Lymington
Hampshire SO41 3QD
Tel: 01590 672472
Fax: 01590 671924
email: sales@seaventures.co.uk
www.sea-ventures.co.uk

Price guide: £10.706 + V

Cornish Crabber 22 Gaff Cutter - 22ft

The Crabber 22ft has many features of the larger yachts built by Cornish Crabbers, whilst being able to be towed behind a 4x4 vehicle. Comfortably sleeps four. The forecabin with a pair of vee berths is divided from the saloon by a solid door in the main bulkhead. There is provision for a private toilet space mounted between them. There are storage bins below the berths. She also has a forehatch and vent in the deckhead. The saloon is dominated by the centreplate case with a solid double flap cabin table mounted on top. Wide berths run along both sides with stowage beneath them. The cabin also has a well-equipped galley. The raised coach roof allows more headroom and provides extra light. She can be supplied in a traditional varnished interior or a woodwashed and painted finish. The ingenious centreboard is designed to be raised or lowered single-handed and the canted bowsprit doubles as a pivot for raising and lowering the mast as well as saving money on marina berths. She has a powerful 1GM 10 inboard engine which deliver 9hp. She could be trailed behind a suitable vehicle but would probably need to be lifted by a boatyard.

Specification

LOA: 27ft / 8.23m
Length over deck: 22ft 0in / 7.81m
Length waterline: 20ft 8in / 6.29m
Beam: 8ft 3in / 2.52m
Draught: (plate up) 2ft 4in / .71m
Draught: (plate down) 5ft 0in / 1.50m
Displacement: 4480lbs / 2032kg
Sail area: 300 Sq ft / 27.87 Sq m
Berths: 4

CE category: B (under 12m)

Contact:
Select Yachts
Rock, Wadebridge,
Cornwall PL27 6NT
Tel: 01208 862666
email: Info@selectyachts.co.uk
www.SELECTYACHTS.co.uk

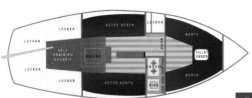

Price guide: £46.412 inc VAT

Viva 700 - 22ft 9in

The **Viva 700** and two layout options as shown below. Both are equipped with separate toilet compartments, galley, folding table and the choice of either 4 or 6 berths.

The heads compartment is complete with wash basin and space for sea or chemical toilet (optional extra). She has an attractive wood interior (choice of oak or mahogany) with high quality cabin lighting. The interior has a quilted lining and is fully upholstered in choice of materials. The saloon is lined with carpet. The galley area is equipped with a two burner hob, sink and cupboards. There is a large (40 litre) capacity fresh water tank with outside filling. There is a separate sea water system.

Standard equipment includes: jib and mainsail, with a single line reefing system, Stainless steel cleats, self tailing winches, Sheet rails with travellers, halyard stoppers, telescopic vang and safety railing. She is easily towable as a trailer-sailer and makes a comfortable family weekend cruising boat for the young family.

Specification

LOA: 7.30m
Beam: 2.50m
Draught: 0.30 / 1.35mm
Displacement: 1350kg
Internal ballast: 450kg
Keel weight: 80kg
Mainsail: 15.00m
Jib: 9.00m
Maximum persons: 6

Contact:
Wittey Marine Ltd
Unit 17
Haddenham
Business Park
Thame Road
Haddenham
Buckinghamshire HP17 8LJ

Tel: 01844 290890/344723
Fax: 01844 292431/347859
email: sales @ witteymarine.com

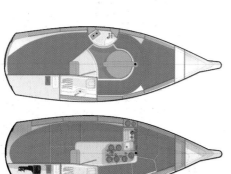

Price guide: £21.153 inc VAT

Yarmouth 23 - 23ft

The Yarmouth 23 was designed by David Freeman and Gordon Wyatt. The duo are famous for the Fisher range built by Northshore. The Yarmouth is an attractive traditional looking boat based on a typical shoal draught cutter. She comes in gaff and bermudan cutter versions. Those who are looking for a family friendly little ship will appreciate her many good qualities.

The interior below is cosy, with solid teak trim, ash bulkheads with the cabin sole in simulated teak and holly laminate. Both cabins are upholstered in fire retardant Airedale cloth. The heads compartment is fitted with a Jabsco sea toilet (with provision for a holding tank) and a corner handbasin. The galley has full standing headroom. A diesel fired ceramic hob is supplied and there is plenty of stowage for supplies, racks for crockery and a sink with hot and cold running water.

The yacht is trailerable and all the gaff rig spars lie within the hull's length. The hull sits on a wide keel and can be fitted with shore legs or bilge keels for drying moorings. The self-draining anchor well and cockpit are deep and add to the safety features of the design.

Specification

LOA: 23ft / 7m
LWL: 18ft / 5.5m
Beam: 7ft 6in / 2.28m
Draught: 2ft 11in / 0,89m
Mainsail: 155 sq ft / 14.4sq m
Foresail: 63 sq ft / 5.92 sq m
Jib: 52 sq ft / 4.82 sq m
Topsail: 34 sq ft / 3.2 sq m
Displacement: 2.5 tons
Ballast: 1 ton

Contact:
The Yarmouth Boat
Company Ltd
The River
Yar Boatyard
Saltern Wood Quay
Yarmouth
Isle of Wight
PO41 0SE
Tel: 01983 760521

Price guide: £48.255.00

23

Europa **TS230** - 23ft 2in

The Europa TS230. This versatile, comfortable 23ft cruiser racer makes an ideal first yacht for either club racing or family cruising. It's large cockpit is self draining with a removable tiller. It is ideal for all the family or a racing crew.

There is a GRP companionway cover with plexiglas washboards. There are large starboard and port lockers. The transom has a swim ladder and outboard bracket. The interior is both comfortable and spacious, with a dedicated galley area. In the saloon there are 2 opposite berths (1.98 x 0.76m) with cushions and storage lockers under. A table and overhead light is supplied. A drawer and storage is located under the companionway. The galley offers a gimballed, single burner stove and sink opposite, with stowage above and below. The cabin consists of a V berth forward (1.78 x 1.84m) with cushion and storage lockers under and a chemical toilet below. there are two settee berths running into two quarter berths aft.

The boat makes the ideal trailer sailor. With it's round bilge and internal ballast, it slides easily onto a trailer making launching and recovery of this versatile yacht simple.

She has a sparkling performance with an easily handled rig, including a self-tacking jib.

Specification

LOA: 7.05m/
LWL: 6.30m /
Beam: 2.54m /
Draught: (Boards up) 0.30 /
Draught: (Boards down) 1.45m /
Max headroom: 1.45m/
Displacement: 1100kg /
Ballast and keel: 405kg/
Berths: 4
Engine: 8hp outboard

Contact:
Europa Yachts Ltd
The Boat House
Shore Road
Warsash
Hants SO31 9FR
Tel: 01489 482045
Fax: 01489 482049
www.europayachts.com

Price guide: £17,745.00 inc

Parker 235 - 23ft 5in

The Parker 235 is a lifting keel trailer sailer. The builder has over twenty years of experience of this type of craft. The keel can be raised from the cockpit and she can dry out on mud sand or gravel. With keel lifted the boat has a twelve inch draught.

There is a large comfortable cockpit with safe side decks, forward anchor well deck and access to large forward bow locker. Within the cockpit there is situated a large port side stowage locker, outboard motor well in the cockpit floor, with hull aperture to allow the outboard engine to be raised when the craft is drying out. All sail and keel controls are arranged from the cabin top winches and clutches for easier handling from the cockpit. Included in the cockpit is a transom folding boarding ladder and provision for fitting a standard saloon table. There is easy access to a light and spacious interior having a head clearance in the saloon of 5ft 5in. This practicable lay-out is comfortable for four people living aboard. There is an aft thwartship double berth, stowage lockers and two large saloon berths with stowage lockers below. There is a central toilet compartment, hand basin, water pump and electric flush chemical toilet leading to a large forward locker. On the starboard side is the central galley area comprising of a sink, crockery drainage bin, single (Gaz) hob unit, below there is a large cool locker and above the worktop area are storage shelves for cutlery/crockery and equipment.

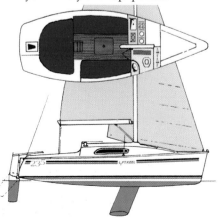

Specification

LOA: 23ft 5in / 7.4m
LWL: 20ft 9in / 6.32m
Beam: 8ft 5in / 2.56m
Draft: (keel up) 12in / 0.30m
(keel down) 4ft 6in / 1.37m
Displacement total: 1380kg
Keel Ballast weight: 330 kg.
Average kerbside weight: 1850kg
Headroom: 5ft 5in / 1.63m
Berths: 4
Sail Area:
Main/Headsail 270sq ft
Asymmetric: 343sq ft

CE Classification:
C (estimated
VPS 113 degrees)

Contact:
Parker Lift Keel Yachts Ltd
61 Horseshoe Lane
Kirton
Boston Lincs
PE20 1LW
Tel: 01205 722697
Fax: 01205 723549
www.parkeryachts.co.uk

Price guide: £22.000 inc VAT

Com-Pac 23/3 - 23ft 9in

The **Com-Pac 23/3** is a trailerable boat. She has 4 adult sized berths, with 3in cushions. There is plenty of storage, under the cockpit and berths. She has an unusual hide-a-way galley with plenty of storage, a stainless steel galley sink and a two burner alcohol stove with a cutting board. There is storage for a portable head. The interior is finished in teak with a holly cabin sole. There is a portable bulkhead mounted dining table and a 11 gallon water tank-filled from the deck. There is a large divided chain locker. Included in the standard specification are 6 polished opening portholes, anodized genoa track with sliding blocks.

Electrical package includes navigation lights, cabin lights, switch panel, battery box, stainless steel sternrail stanchions and vinyl coated lifelines. There is a stainless steel bowsprit with teak insert and built-in anchor roller with anchor storage capability. There is a cockpit mounted manual bilge pump and a portable bulkhead mounted dining table.

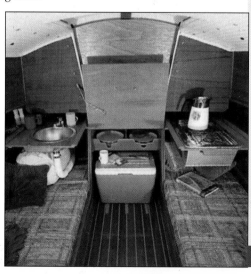

Specification

LOA: 23ft 11in
LWL: 20ft 2in
Beam: 7ft 10in
Draught: 2ft 3in
Displacement: 3000lbs
Ballast: 1340lbs
Sail area: 250 sq ft
**Mast height
above waterline:** 30ft

Contact:
Clearwater Yachts
Unit 1
17 Ladbroke Close
Woodley
Reading
RG5 4DX
Tel: 0118 9698800
email: clearwater@fsmail.net
www.Com-PacYachts.com

Price guide: £64.595.

Jeanneau Sun Odyssey 26 - 24ft 1in

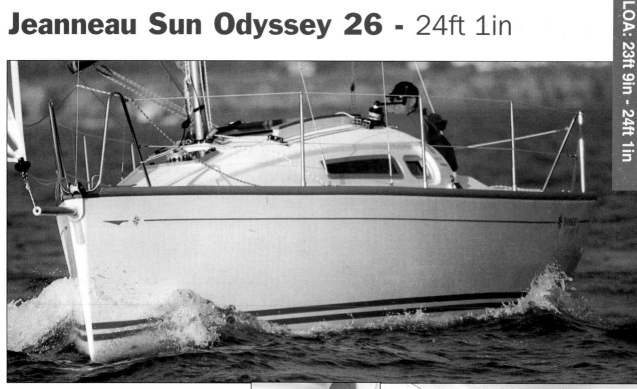

The Sun Odyssey 26 has a spacious open plan layout with good headroom (6ft decreasing gradually to 5ft as you go forward). There are two settees big enough to accommodate up to six people, with stowage under. The saloon table sits on top of the centreboard case. On top of the V berth a hinged shelf can also be a backrest for someone sitting at the head of the table. The berth is large (6ft 4in x 4ft 2in) The aft cabin is generous with a large bunk running athwart and measuring 6ft 10in x 5ft. There are two opening ports and a hanging locker. The galley has good stowage for a weekend away. There is a semi-gimballed two-burner gas hob. A coolbox is tucked away under a small chart table to port. The heads compartment is quite large for a boat of this size. There is reasonable stowage beneath the basin with good access to seacocks. There is a wet hanging area.

The boat would suit a small family. She should be great fun to sail and would appeal to both first time buyers and those trading down from bigger boats.

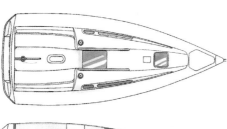

Specification

LOA: 24ft 10in / 7.59m
LWL: 22ft 2in / 6.7m
Beam: 9ft 8in / 2.97m
Draught:
Twin keel: 3ft 11in / 1.2m
Lifting keel: 2ft 3in - 5ft 6in / 0.7 - 1.7m
Displacement: 6063lbs / 2700kg
Sail area: 312 ft² / 29 m²
Ballast: 2071lb / 940kg
Berths: 4/5
CE Category: B (5 crew) C (6 crew)

Contact:
Sea Ventures Limited
Lymington Yacht Haven
Lymington
Hampshire SO41 3QD
Tel: 01590 672472
Fax: 01590 671924
email: sales@seaventures.co.uk
www.sea-ventures.co.uk

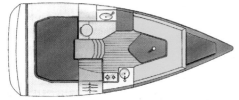

Price guide: £28.380 + VAT

27

Corsair 24 - 24ft 5in

GREG SMITH

The Corsair 24 trimaran is the Perfect Weekend Racer/Cruiser --compact, easily trailerable, and ideal for cruising and racing. It is tough, lightweight, sporty, exceptionally fast, responsive and safe to sail. The Corsair 24 incorporates innovations that make it especially exciting and fun, as well as affordable to own. With its roomy cabin and optional cruising amenities it is also a highly mobile pocket cruiser. But it's the amazing performance—with 20-knots plus speed capability—that sets the Corsair 24 apart. So well designed, even in the toughest conditions you only need a crew of three (or less) to obtain top racing performance. Spacious decks and nets give everyone plenty of room to spread out. With the optional bowsprit installed, the Corsair 24 can fly an easy-to-handle asymmetrical spinnaker for exhilarating performance on a yet higher plane.

Specification

LOA 24ft 5in / 7.3 m
LWL 23ft 7in / 7.2 m
Beam (overall) 17ft 11in / 5.5 m
Beam (folded) 8ft 2in / 2.5 m
Draught (hull only) 1ft 0in / 0.3 m
Draught (board down) 4ft 8in / 1.4 m
Weight 1,690 lbs. / 816 kg.
Berths 4
Engine 5hp o/b
Sail area:
Mainsail 243 sq.ft. / 23.35 sq.m
Jib 122 sq.ft. / 10.94 sq.m
Asym. 570 sq.ft. / 46.10 sq.m
Screacher 243 sq.ft. / 30.44 sq.m

Based on an original design by Farrier Marine Inc
Builder: Corsair Marine Inc USA
Dealer MacGregor Yachts Int Ltd
Ponsharden, Falmouth TR11 2SE Cornwall UK
Tel: 44 (01326) 379471
Fax 44 (01326) 379472
Email info@macgregoruk.com
www.macgregor.uk.com

Price guide: £32.700

Ranger 245 - 24ft 6in

The Hunter Ranger 245 is a category B Offshore yacht. She comes with twin or fin keels. The rig is fractional with self-tacking jib - easily managed by one person. Although a compact boat she has full standing headroom and is easy to sail short-handed. The cockpit is spacious but safe with high coamings and bridge deck. To increase the space further whilst in port, the tiller hinges up and the mainsheet is clipped to the pushpit.

Below decks the boat is spacious with plenty of stowage and full length shelves. The forward berth provides plenty of space for two adults. Optional windows either side of the forehatch increase the natural light in the saloon. The galley has a gimballed two-burner hob/grill with room for an optional oven. Six adults can comfortably sit around the table. The heads compartment has plenty of space for a wet locker and hand basin. The upholstery throughout the boat is plush and the cushioning is thick with a raised forward edge. The aft cabin has a double berth under the cockpit.

Specification

LOA: 24ft 6in / 7.47m
LWL: 21ft 0in / 6.40m
Beam: 8ft 9in / 2.67m
Draught: 3ft 1in - 4ft 6in / 0.94 - 1.36m
Displacement: 4945lbs / 2248 kg
Sail area: 250ft² / 2323m²
Max headroom: 6ft
Berths: 4

CE category: B Offshore

Contact:
Select Yachts
Rock, Wadebridge,
Cornwall PL27 6NT
Tel: 01208 862666
email: Info@selectyachts.co.uk
www.SELECTYACHTS.co.uk

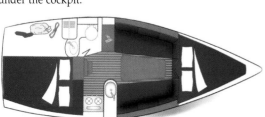

Price guide: £40.664 inc VAT

Ronautica Ro 265 - 24ft 6in

Introduced in 2004, the new RO 265 has all the advantages of a larger yacht. The modern interior is finished in a warm cherry coloured wood, and the joinery is designed with rounded forms for safety. There are 8 portlights. The companionway has anti-slip material integrated into the steps.

Headroom in the saloon is 185cm. There is a large foldable saloon table and a chart table with easy access to navigation instruments. The galley is equipped with a 2-ring cooker, sink and plenty of lockers and drawers for appliances, dishes and cutlery. An ice-box is included. The forward cabin has a double berth with storage shelves. The aft cabin has a large double berth with spacious lockers and storage shelves. The heads compartment has a headroom of 180cm, wash basin with storage below, pressurised water supply and a shower with dedicated electrical bilge pump. There is also ample space for wet sailing gear. With wide appeal, this boat is just as suited to those on their first introduction to sailing, as to the experienced sailor looking to downsize.

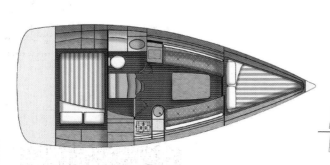

Specification

LOA: 7.48m
LWL: 7.18m
Beam: 2.98m
Draught: 156 / 165cm
Displacement: 2250kg
Ballast: 850kg
Mainsail: 18.8 m²
Genoa: 17 m²
Capacity:
Water: 80lt
Fuel: 70lt
Berths: 5+1
CE Category: B Offshore

Contact:
South West Yacht Brokers Grou
Atlantic Quay
Richmond Walk
Plymouth PL1 4LN
Tel: 01752 551991
Fax: 01752 551991
www.southwestyachts.co.uk

Price guide: £39.950

Beneteau 25 - 24ft 7in

The Beneteau 25: the ultimate in sportsboats. Class Winner of Cowes Week three years in a row! There is a European Class Association with active racing throughout the year in prime locations. A mini-Volvo 60 she is somewhat smaller but great value and exhilarating performance.

Faithful to the Beneteau One-Design spirit, the boat combines advanced technology with simplicity of construction. She was built using classic materials to ensure a long life, even under the toughest conditions.

The big cockpit makes crew manoeuvres simple and rapid. And for manoeuvres in port, there's a cunningly designed compartment under the cockpit, which houses the outboard motor, fixed to a pivoting bracket.

The Beneteau 25 European Circuit is particularly strong and regularly sees 25-30 competitors, and sometimes as many as 50 boats hit both the start and finish line within seconds of each other.

Specification

LOA: 24ft 7in / 7.50m
LWL: 22ft 2in / 6.74m
Beam: 8ft 4in / 2.54m
Draught: 5ft 2in / 1.58m
Displacement:
2.755lbs / 1.250 kg
Ballast: 1.124 lbs / 510kg
Sail area:
I: 29ft 10in
J: 8ft 6in
P: 30ft 10in
E: 11ft 11in

Contact:
Ancasta
International
Boat Sales
Port Hamble
Satchell Lane
Hamble
Southampton SO31 4QD
Tel: 023 8045 0000
Fax: 023 8045 5415
Email: hamble@ancasta.co.uk

Price guide: £14.773 + VAT

Com-Pac 25 - *25ft*

The American Com-Pac 25 is big for a twenty-five footer. The interior is in teak in a traditional style. She has accommodation for five, standing headroom, an L-shaped galley and a private enclosed head.

For the experienced sailor, she could be an ideal choice for those wanting to move up or scale down. Her midsize gives her easy handling with no sacrifice in creature comfort. With her eight foot six inch beam she is stable and comfortable. At the helm she's nimble and responsive and her underbody makes her fast, stable and closewinded.

On deck she has bronze opening ports and cleats, a heavy duty rigid vinyl rubrail with a stainless steel striker plate, midboom mainsheet traveller and all control lines led aft. An electric tilt motor bracket controlled from the cockpit makes handling the outboard motor an easy prospect. She has a stainless-steel bowsprit with a built in anchor roller. Below decks the atmosphere is traditional with teak and bronze fittings. The head gives complete privacy.

Specification

LOA: 25ft
LWL: 21ft
Beam: 8ft 6in
Draught: 2ft 6in
Displacement: 4,800lbs
Sail area: 308sq ft
Berths: 5

Contact:
Clearwater Yachts
Unit 1
17 Ladbroke Close
Woodley
Reading
RG5 4DX
Tel: 0118 9698800
email: clearwater@fsmail.net
www.Com-PacYachts.com

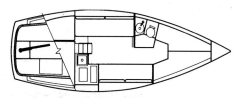

Price guide: £38.245

Fisher 25 - 25ft 3in

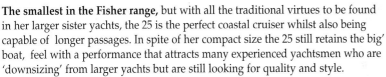

The smallest in the Fisher range, but with all the traditional virtues to be found in her larger sister yachts, the 25 is the perfect coastal cruiser whilst also being capable of longer passages. In spite of her compact size the 25 still retains the big' boat, feel with a performance that attracts many experienced yachtsmen who are 'downsizing' from larger yachts but are still looking for quality and style.

Unlike her bigger sisters, the Fisher has a transom stem (not canoe) and provides for a large and comfortable cockpit for working sails and relaxing. The 25, like all Fishers, can be steered from the tiller or from the comfort of the wheelhouse. The 'Tardis-like' interior, impressive by any standards for a 25 footer, can be fitted out with up to five berths.

This remarkable little yacht was first produced in 1975 and to date over 250 have been built.

Specification

LOA 25ft 3in
LWL 21ft 0in
Beam 9ft 4in
Draught: 3ft 9in
Displacement 4.5 tons
Ballast weight 2.1 tons
Sail Main 98 sq ft
Furling Genoa 131sq ft
Mizzen 44 sq ft

Contact:
Northshore Yachts Ltd
Itchenor, Chichester
West Sussex, PO20 7AY
Tel: 01243 512611
email: sales@northshore.co.uk
www.northshore.co.uk

Beneteau First 260 - 25ft 6in

The Beneteau First 260 Spirit has a long waterline length in relation to her hull. She also comes with a choice of hull colour as an option. Another unusual feature are her twin rudders which can be raised.

The interior is entered by a wide companionway hatch (in two pieces). Natural lighting comes from two large opening portlights and two small hull portlights. The saloon is a mixture of cherry wood and an ivory coloured moulded interior. Two settees are placed either side of the large table. One of the settees can be converted into a double berth. To port of the companionway, the L shaped galley is fully equipped with an ice box, sink and several lockers. The navigation area is to starboard. Forward of the saloon, a sliding door opens on to a completely independent head compartment with marine toilet, hanging locker to starboard and wash basin to port. A second sliding door gives access to the forward cabin with double bed, lockers and a large hatch for ventilation.

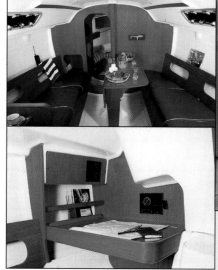

Specification

LOA: 7.70m
Hull length: 7.50m
LWL: 7.35m
Beam: 2.75m
Draught: 0.85 - 1.85m
Displacement: 2150 approx
Sail area: 36.20m2

CE Category: B4 - C5

Contact:
Ancasta International Boat Sales
Port Hamble
Satchel Lane
Hamble
Southampton SO31 4QD
Tel: 023 80 450 026
Email: Beneteau@ ancasta.co.uk
www.ancasta.com

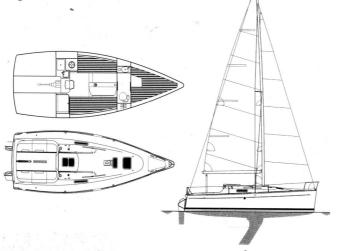

Price guide: £37.500

Sportina 760 - 25ft 6in

Sportina 760. The benefits offered by trailer/sailer yachts include significant savings on moorings, storage and maintenance. You can also take your boat to explore new sailing areas either around our costs or abroad. Popular demand for this type of craft has led to many innovations designed to provide a high comfort level - and sailing performance which compares very favourably with similarly - sized non-trailable boats.

This 25 footer, aimed at the family fast cruiser market has a retracting keel and rudder which allows her to take the ground flat and draws only 14 inches with the centreboard raised. Her unique one person mast raising and lowering system means that you can be ready to sail 45 minutes after arriving at your sailing area and can launch and recover the boat onto the trailer quickly and (with practice) easily.

Below deck a well-designed light and airy saloon offers 6ft 3 inches of headroom. The space also incorporates two double and one casual berth, a centre folding table, a separate heads compartment with room for wet gear, a galley space with a stainless steel sink with pressurized water and room for a cooker and refrigerator and masses of storage space. All furnishings and fittings are of outstanding quality and designed for live-aboard comfort.

The boat is offered with an inboard diesel engine and marketed as a complete package by the U.K. distributor, including trailer, sails. rigging, anchor lines, warps, boarding ladder, horseshoe lifebuoy and electronic speed and depth log.

Specification

LOA: 25ft 6in / 7.60m
LWL: 24ft 3in / 7.4m
Beam: 8ft 4in / 2.5m
Draught: (Min) 1ft 2in / 0.40m
Draught: (Max) 4ft 4in / 1.30m
Displacement: 5,070lbs / 2,300kg
Ballast: (keel) 287lb / 130kg
Ballast: (internal) 1,433lb / 650kg
Sail areas (main) 178ft² / 16.5m²
Sail areas (jib) 113ft² / 10.5m²
Sail areas (main)
178ft² / 16.5m²
Sail areas (genoa)
161ft² / 15.0m²
Engine: 10hp Beta

Max headroom: 6ft 2in / 1.88m
Berths: 4/6

Contact:
Ramsgate Yacht Sales Ltd
Smack Boys Home
36 Military Road,
Royal Harbour
Ramsgate Kent CT11 9LG
Tel: 01843 592973

MacGregor 26 - 26ft

The all new **MacGregor 26M** offers great sailing and powering at speeds of up to 20 miles per hour with a 50 hp outboard. The 26M sleeps 6 in generous berths, with full standing headroom, a galley and enclosed heads compartment. A walk through transom offers easy boarding, with a hinged steering seat that swings down for security.

Water ballast provides the self righting stability of a keel boat, with the security of being unsinkable. At 2600 pounds empty, and just under 8' wide the boat is easily towed behind many cars, and is the easiest to ramp launch and rig of any competing trailerable sailboats. MacGregor Yacht Corporation has built over 30,000 boats, and has dominated the trailer sailer market.

The new MacGregor 26M is the latest model, carrying on a 35 year tradition of affordable trailer sailing.

The price of £19,990 includes galvanized trailer, sails and VAT.

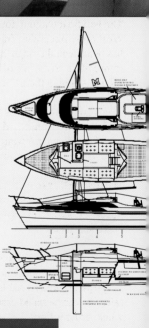

Specification

LOA: 7.87 m.
LWL: 6.915 m.
Beam: 2.29 m.
Draught: board up .3 m.
Draught: board down 1.75 m.
Engine capacity: up to 50 hp
Speed: 50 hp outboard up to 20 mph
Permanent Ballast: 136 kg.
Water Ballast: 533 kg.
Boat weight, less ballast: 1264 kg.
Sail area: Main:15.81sq. m.
Jib (100%):12.08 sq. m.
Main and jib: 27.89 sq. m.
Genoa: (150%) 9.14 sq.m.
Cabin headroom:1.83 m.
Fresh water capacity: 18.92 litres
Berths: 6

Dealer Information
MacGregor Yachts Int. Ltd.
Ponsharden, Falmouth TR11 2SE
Cornwall, U.K.
Tel: 44 (01326) 379471
Fax: 44 (01326) 379472
email: info@macgregoruk.com
www.macgregoruk.com

Price guide: £19,990.00

The Nordic Folkboat - 26ft

The Folkboat without doubt must be the success story of the sailing world. What other 26ft cruiser/racer can claim to have sold over 3000 worldwide, has twice won the single handed TRANSAT, been cruised single handed from Sydney to the Isle of Wight and back by a Grandmother, and have over 600 registered in the UK and Ireland?

Designed in 1942 she was the product of a competition held in Scandinavia. 58 designs were produced and the Committee made up of representatives of the 4 Scandinavian Countries selected the best parts from the top entries. So no one person can claim to have 'designed' the Folkboat.

The first 2000 or so were all constructed of wood but in 1975. A Dane Erik Andreasen, obtained permission for the boat to be built in GRP, and in 1977 he formed a company Folkebadeentralen which has produced over 1000 Folkboats in GRP.

The reasons for the Folkboat's success are many, but whether you are looking for a boat to cruise or to race the Folkboat fits the bill. With her 53% ballast ratio she is so stable that no reefing points are provided in the racing sails. She can be sailed easily single-handed and the maximum crew allowed when racing is three.

Specification

LOA: 25ft 9in / 7.64m
LWL: 19ft 9in / 6.0m
Beam: 7ft 5in / 2.20m
Draught: 4ft / 1.20m
Displacement: 4,750lb
Keel: 1040 kg
Sail area: 24sq m
(Main): 17 sq m
(Jib): 7 sq m
Engine: Outboard 2.2 hp - 6.0 hp

Contact
Folkboat UK Ltd
Riccarton House
Blacksmiths Lane
Thorley, Yarmouth,
Isle of Wight P041 OSS
Tel : 01983 760621
e-mail: folkboatuk2@aol.com

Etap 24i - 26ft 3in

The Etap 24i is built in Belgium and is unsinkable. The double skinned hull has enough bouyancy for it to stay afloat even if holed below the waterline.

For a boat of this size there is a suprising amount of space, although the headroom is restricted to 5ft 4$^1/_2$ in headroom under the main hatch. This tapers to 5ft 2in at the front end. There is enough space for perhaps two adults and two children to spend a period on board. The settee berths are 2ft wide and 6 ft 6ins long the aft ends intrude slightly under the cockpit. Incidentally you can get a view of the sea through the open transom from the settee.

There are two lockers under the berths. The forepeak berth (6ft 3in) is lit by an opening hatch. The galley is in two parts which can be joined together by using a door from the sink unit, to create a good work surface. The heads are fitted between the forward bulkhead and the vee-berth. There is space for wash bags and room for a holding tank. Opposite the head is a hanging locker with the door doubling as a table. It can be used in the saloon, the cockpit or as a chart table.

Specification

LOA: 26ft 3in / 8m
LWL: 24ft 0in / 6.7m
Beam: 8ft 2in / 2.5m
Draught: Tandem keel: 3ft 0in 0.85m
Fin keel: 4ft 11in 1.5m
Displacement: 3,524lbs / 1,600 kg
Ballast: 1,101lb / 500kg
Sail area: Mainsail: 196sq ft/ 18.2sq m
Headsail: 131sq ft/ 12.2sq m
Water: 11gal / 50l
Max headroom: 5ft 4$^1/_2$in / 1.64m
Berths: 4

Contact:
Kiss Marine Solent Ltd
The Boatyard
Hythe Marina
Hythe Hants SO45 6DX
Tel: 02380 840 300
Fax: 02380 840 700

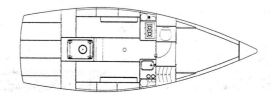

Price guide: £23.450 + VAT

Odin 820 - 26ft 9in

The Odin 820 is one of the new breed of dual purpose power sailers. She can be fitted with your choice of engine from 10hp up to a 70hp outboard giving the opportunity to change into power boat mode. The builders claims to offer a flexible fitout package. The boat has been designed in Germany with the hull moulded in Poland. Final fitting out is completed in Germany.

Owners are able to select from a longish list of options in the package. There is full headroom throughout the boat and enough space to accommodate six adults. Her cabin is partly covered with foam rubber fabric and is part timber lined. The interior is a moulded unit in hand-laid glass fibre construction, with a non-slip finish on the sole. The tabletop has fold-down sides. There are six berths with ample stowage under.

The heads compartment is fully lined with washbasin and space for a shower. Taps are available as standard with an electric pump. The fresh and grey water tanks each have a 12 litre capacity. The galley has space for a cooker and an icebox, and a sink with an electric pump comes as standard.

Specification

LOA: 8.2 metres
LWL: 7.6 metres
Beam: 2.5 metres
Draught: 0.3 - 1.45 metres
Weight empty: 1300 kilograms
Water ballast: 780 litres (approximately)
Centreboard ballast weight: 50 kilograms
Engine: From 10 - 70hp
Sail area:
Main: 15 square metres
Jib: 13.5 square metres
CE Certification Category: C

Contact:
Wittey Marine Sales
Unit 17 Haddenham Business Park, Thame Road
Haddenham, Buckinghamshire HP17 8LJ
Tel: 01844 290890
Fax: 01844 292431
Email: marinesales@witteymachinery.com

Price guide: £23.860

Hunter Channel 27 - 26ft 10in

The **Hunter Channel 27** is a solid stable Category B Offshore cruising yacht, easily handled and responsive, turning in speeds of up to 7 knots. Like her sister boat the Pilot 27, the use of layout of the available space is impressive making her an ideal family cruiser. The cockpit is well sheltered with no need to go forward except to pick up the anchor or a mooring. The interior layout gives good space and comfortable facilities which can easily accommodate six adults. With full standing headroom throughout and lots of stowage, she can take care of the crew for weekends and even longer. Her galley has a gimballed two burner stove and a modest workspace. The aft cabin feels big and has an 18in clearance under the cockpit sole. The chart table has ample room for navigational instruments and is well lit by an overhead light. The table is big enough for an Admiralty chart folded once. A screen separates the generous forepeak berths and the optional forward facing windows give additional light and visibility. The heads compartment is large, with a headroom of almost 6ft. It is well equipped and easy to clean. Stowage which can be used for wet gear is provided behind showerproof zip-up flaps.

Access to the engine is good by taking out the companionway steps and through a hatch in the aft cabin. The boat is aimed squarely at the family market.

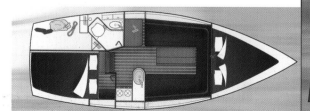

Specification

LOA: 26ft 10in / 8.18m
LWL: 22ft 6in / 7.15m
Beam: 9ft 2in / 2.80m
Draught: (Fin) 5ft / 1.540m
(Twin) 3ft 5in / 1.050m
Weight: (Fin) 5595lbs / 25
(Twin) 5708lbs / 2590kg
Sail area: 307sq ft
Berths: 6
CE Category: B

Contact:
Select Yachts
Rock, Wadebridge,
Cornwall PL27 6NT
Tel: 01208 862666
email: Info@selectyach
www.SELECTYACHTS.c

Price guide: £50,225. inc VAT

Hunter Pilot 27 - *26ft 10in*

The Hunter Pilot 27 offers comfort at sea. She is a Category B Offshore cruiser with the option of new generation twin keels with substantial bulbs to give exceptional stability plus the added ability to sit upright when the tide goes out.

The whole saloon deckhouse area is light and airy with outstanding views of the outside world. There is plenty of room for six adults and masses of storage space in the form of lockers and shelves. The large berths in the forward cabin can be arranged as two single or one double. In addition, there is a large double berth in the aft cabin and the table in the saloon can also be dropped down allowing an infill to form another double berth. The heads compartment is placed by the companioway so wet oilskins do not need to trailed through the saloon.

Specification

LOA: 26ft 10in / 8.18m
LWL: 22ft 6in / 7.15m
Beam: 9ft 2in / 2.80m
Draught: (Fin) 5ft / 1,540m
(Twin) 3ft 5in / 1,540m
Weight: (Fin) 5937lbs / 2693kg
(Twin) 6051lbs / 2745kg
Sail area: 290sq ft / 26.94sq m
Berths: 6
CE Category: B

Contact:
Select Yachts
Rock, Wadebridge,
Cornwall PL27 6NT
Tel: 01208 862666
email: Info@selectyachts.co.uk
www.SELECTYACHTS.co.uk

Etap 26i - *27ft 8in*

The Etap 26i, in common with all members of the Etap family, has a double skinned hull with enough buoyancy for it to stay afloat even if holed below the waterline.

The interior is stylish with steamed and sanded beech finishes with three coats of varnish. All furnishings have solid beech frames. The companionway has three curved aluminium treads covered in a non-slip finish. Headroom in the companionway area is 174cm.

The saloon contains two long sofas with an open forepeak, which can be used as a double cabin. There is a rotatable height-adjustable table located in the centre of the saloon. A panoramic window allows plenty of light, giving a spacious feeling.

Extra storage space is provided under the starboard sofa and a potable water tank is located under the port side sofa. Closed cupboards line the entire length of the saloon on both port and starboards sides. The galley is equipped with a two burner gas hob. Under the deep stainless steel sink is a large stowage space with a cutlery drawer and bin bag holder. The work surfcaces are finished in grey formica. A 75 x 60cm chart table is located on the starboard side. The heads is furnished with a washbasin fitted with a shower head and fed by a pressurized cold water supply. There is a large wet locker with drainage and cupboard above.

Specification

LOA: 27ft 8in / 8.25m
LWL: 23ft 5½in / 7.15m
Beam: 9ft 1½in / 2.78m
Draught: Tandem keel: 3ft 0in 0.85m
Fin keel: 4ft 11in 1.5m
Displacement: 5.066lbs / 2.325 kg
Ballast: 1,400lb / 500kg
Sail area: Mainsail: 240sq ft / 22.3 sq m
Jib: 84sq ft / 7.8sq m
Engine: 10hp / 7.35kW
CE Certification: B

Contact:
Kiss Marine Solent Ltd
The Boatyard
Hythe Marina
Hythe Hants SO45 6DX
Tel: 02380 840 300
Fax: 02380 840 700

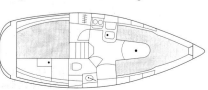

Price guide: £37.500 + VAT

Corsair 28 - 28ft

The Corsair 28, like all of its predecessors and current sisters, is an easily trailerable sport boat with its light weight and low profile. As with other Corsair trimarans, the transition from trailering to sailing takes about 30 minutes — the mast is raised or lowered using the installed winch on the trailer.

The Corsair 28 Centre-Cockpit and Corsair 28 Aft-Cockpit both have roomy, functional interiors with all the necessary amenities for comfortable cruising. The Corsair 28R is the super-high-performance version of either of these modes by virtue of its taller carbon fiber spar which is more efficient and powerful on the water and lighter on the trailer.

Although both basic models have excellent sleeping accommodation, the Corsair 28 Centre-Cockpit offers an aft cabin and V-berth as well as standard galley area with two-burner stove, stainless-steel sink, fresh water tank and pump, and an enclosed marine head. The Corsair 28 Aft-Cockpit model (interior shown) sleeps four (two in the V-berth and in each of two single main-cabin bunks), and is trimmed down in the accessories area for lighter weight and more speed potential.

Specification

LOA: 24ft 2in / 7.3 m
LWL: 23ft 7in / 7.2 m
Beam: (overall) 17ft 11in / 5.5 m
Beam: (folded) 8ft 2in / 2.5 m
Draft: (hull only) 1ft 0in / 0.3 m
Draft: (board down) 4ft 8in / 1.4 m
Mast length: 3ft 10in / 9.71 m
Mast height: 36ft 8in / 11.18 m
Weight: 1,690 lbs. / 816 kg.
Hulls: PVC foam core
Berths: 4
Aux. propulsion: 5hp o/b
Sail area: Mainsail 243 sq.ft. / 23.35 sq.m
Jib: 122 sq.ft. / 10.94 sq.m
Asym: 570 sq.ft. / 46.10 sq.m
Screacher: 243 sq.ft. / 30.44 sq.m

Based on an original design by: Farrier Marine Inc
Builder: Corsair Marine Inc

Contact:
MacGregor Yachts Int Ltd
Ponsharden
Falmouth TR11 2SE
Cornwall UK
Tel: 44 (01326) 379471
Fax: 44 (01326) 379472
www.macgregor.uk.com
info@macgregor.uk.com

Vancouver - 28ft

The Vancouver 28 is a direct descendant from the original Vancouver 27 - the design that started the Vancouver line. She is well balanced and will sail herself, making passagemaking an easier and less tiring task. She has a large carrying capacity without impeding her sailing performance.

This is a yacht suitable for a serious cruising couple with good sized sea berths, a wet locker adjacent to the companionway, a large chart table, good ventilation and easy access to all parts for maintenance. The forepeak is left open for sail stowage with access to the chain locker forward. On the centreline is the marine toilet, with a washbasin to starboard with storage under. A foot pump provides water to the washbasin. There are two single settee berths with lee cloths and storage under and outboard with upholstered back-rests. There are two full length storage lockers either side. Above the settee berths are bookshelves and lockers. A double flap table is on the centreline supported by the teak mast support post.

The galley has a stainless steel sink with fresh water foot pump to port with a two burner cooker with grill and oven with fail-safe on all burners. A galley crash bar is fitted. There is plenty of storage with purpose made drawers for crockery and cutlery stowage. There is a large oilskin locker aft of the galley. A large chart table is to starboard with stowage under for charts. Spaces for navigational instruments and electrical switch panel are outboard. The large quarter berth runs aft from the chart table, the head of which forms the navigator's seat.

Specification

LOA: 28ft / 8.54m
LWL: 22ft 11in / 6.99m
Beam: 8ft 8in / 2.64m
Draught: 4ft 3in / 1.30m
Displacement: 8,960 lbs
Sail areas:
Mainsail: 161sq ft / 14.96sq m
Cruising Yankee:
195sq ft / 18.01 sq m
Staysail: 85 sq ft / 7.90 sq m
Genoa: (optional)
44sq ft / 4.1sq m
CE category: A

Contact:
Northshore Yachts Ltd
Itchenor
Chichester,
West Sussex
PO20 7AY
Tel: 01243 512611
Fax: 01243 511473
email: sales@northshore.co.uk
www.northshore.co.uk

Price guide: £72.659 + VAT

Jeanneau Sun Odyssey 29.2 - 28ft 11in

The Sun Odyssey 29.2 has 3 different internal layouts. The interior teak woodwork is bright and modern in styling. Numerous opening deck hatches and ports offer light and ventilation in each of the three below-deck areas.

There are two double-berth cabins and the head has 5ft 8in standing headroom. The spacious saloon seats 6 adults. There is a toilet compartment with 1.74m / 5' 9" headroom. The L-shaped galley is well designed for comfort in harbour as well as offshore. A main feature on this boat is the separation between the saloon and the forward cabin to maintain privacy. The navigation table is forward facing with standing room of 5ft 9in. The portholes (side and front) are placed for maximum ventilation. There is lots of natural lighting provided through the deck hatch over the saloon area. For the best size versus cost value, the Sun Odyssey 29.2 offers above-average quality accommodation. It comes in two hull forms - keel version, or centerboard/double rudder. The spacious cockpit can accommodate an optional pedestal/wheel steering system for easier handling.

Specification

LOA: 28ft 11in / 8.80m
LWL: 25ft 3in / 7.70m
Beam: 9ft 9in / 2.98m
Draught:
Lifting keel: 2ft 6in - 5ft 3in
Deep: 4ft 7in / 1.40m
Displacement: 6063lbs / 2750kg
Main Sail area: 215sq ft / 20 sq m
Furling Genoa: 215 sq ft / 20 sq m
Fuel capacity: 12US galls / 45lt
Water capacity: 26US galls / 100lt
Berths: 6
CE Category: B (C) - 6 (8)

Contact:
Sea Ventures Limited
Lymington Yacht Haven
Lymington
Hampshire SO41 3QD
Tel: 01590 672472
Fax: 01590 671924
email: sales@seaventures.co.uk
www.sea-ventures.co.uk

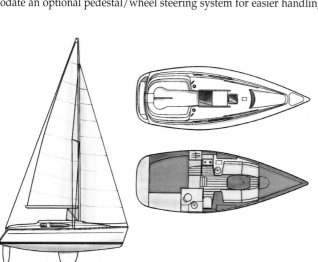

Beneteau First 27.7 - 29ft

The First 27.27 is described in her builder's brochure as a cruiser-racer and a boat designed to enjoy fast and easy sailing, upwind and downwind. With the hydraulic keel lifting system and rudder up she has a draught of only 0.62m, to enable the owner to explore shallow water coasts and islands.

She has a large double cabin aft and a double berth in the forecabin. Headroom under the sliding hatch is 1.76m and 1.60m throughout the rest of the boat. The saloon is roomy and functional with a separate heads compartment and sea toilet. In the head there is ceiling height of 1.60m, a hanging locker and an opening porthole. The chart table is 100 x 69cm with storage facility. There is a removable panel for navigation instruments. The galley has a stainless steel sink and a fresh water foot pump. The single burner cooker is gimballed. The lifting keel is contained in a case in the saloon which is out of sight when the keel is down.

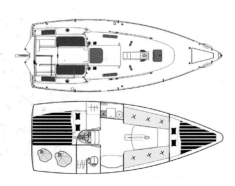

Specification

LOA: 29ft / 8.85m
LWL: 27ft 2in / 8.3m
Beam: 9ft 8in / 3m
Draught:
Keel up: 2ft / 0.62m
Keel down: 7ft / 2.15m
Displacement: 5842lbs / 2650kg
Main Sail area: 301sq ft / 28 sq m
Genoa: 237 sq ft / 22 sq m

CE Category: B

Contact:
Ancasta International Boat Sales
Port Hamble
Satchel Lane
Hamble
Southampton SO31 4QD
Tel: 023 80 450 026
Email: Beneteau@ ancasta.co.uk
www.ancasta.com

Price guide: £45.500

Sadler 290 - 29ft

The Sadler 290 has seven berths in 3 cabins, full standing headroom throughout, separate heads and combined shower cubicle, full chart table, large galley with ample surfaces, cooker and ice box. The forecabin has a double vee berth 2m long with storage under, hanging locker, cupboard and shelving, standing height 1.85m approx portlights, and door to saloon. The aft cabin, has a large double berth 2m long 1.5m wide, storage under and fiddled shelving around. Hanging locker, portlight, headroom 1.85m approx and door to saloon.

The L shaped galley is designed for safe use at sea. Work surfaces are treated with colour co-ordinated anti bacterial, high density 'polysurface'. There is a Stainless steel sink, mixer tap fed from the pressurized water system, 2 burner gas stove, and 60l ice box. A range of cupboards over and under the galley provide adequate storage for food, cutlery and utensils. The galley has 1.9m approx. headroom. Main saloon has seating for 7 to 8 persons on straight and L shaped settees surrounding large fiddled double drop leaf table. Open fiddled shelves behind the settees provide cavernous amounts of storage. Further storage is provided in a locker, wet locker, and under the settees. The L shaped settee converts to a large double berth.

There is full standing height throughout the saloon, ranging from 1.95m to 1.7m (approx). Heads are large and well appointed with sea toilet, sink and hand shower. There is a cupboard under the sink and shelving above.

Specification

LOA: 29ft / 8.84m
LWL: 25ft 11in / 7.90m
Beam: 10ft 8in / 3.26m
Draught: Deep fin: 5ft 8in / 1.73m
Shallow fin: 4ft 9in / 1.4m
Twin keels: 4ft 3in / 1.30m
Displacement: 10,500lbs / 4,763 kg
Ballast: 4,194lb / 2,229kg
Sail area: 470 sq ft / 43.7 sq m
Headroom: 6ft 3in / 1.90m

Contact:
Sadler Yachts Ltd
Ocean Quay Marina
Belvidere Road
Southampton SO14 5QY
Tel: 02380 237694
Fax: 02380 238627
Email: info@oceanquay.com
www.oceanquay.com

Price guide: £62.195 inc VAT

Com-Pac 27/2 - 29ft 7in

The Com-Pac 27/2 is another American yacht perhaps unfamiliar to our shores. Designed by Robert K Johnson she features bronze ports, bronze deck hardware and extensive use of teak which accents the white surfaces on the cabin sole and galley areas.

The saloon presents a comfortable and visually pleasing ambience. The interior provides 6ft 1in headroom. There are six berths, and a large enclosed head compartment with an optional hot water shower. The galley has loads of storage space which should satisfy the needs of a cruising family. Three large hatches and eight opening ports ensure ample ventilation and a bright airy atmosphere below. The cockpit is 6ft 10in with port and starboard lockers. There is also wet storage under the contoured helmsman's seat. Wide decks and cabin top provide plenty of room for sail handling.

Specification

LOA: 29ft 7in
LWL: 24ft 3in
Beam: 9ft 6in
Draught: 3ft 6in
Displacement: 6000lbs
Ballast: 2500lbs
Sail area: 380 sq ft
Mast height
above waterline: 35ft 8in
Fresh water: 50 gals

Contact:
Clearwater Yachts
Unit 1
17 Ladbroke Close
Woodley
Reading
RG5 4DX
Tel: 0118 9698800
email: clearwater@fsmail.net
www.Com-PacYachts.com

Price guide: £64.595

Legend 306 - 29ft 11in

The American **Hunter Legend 306** has many of the amenities of a bigger boat such as soft headliners, teak furniture and bulkheads high quality taps and hardware and a very good selection of fabrics included as standard. Two separate cabins and a spacious saloon contain a stylish galley including a two burner gimballed stove, an icebox, large sink and plenty of storage. She has a hot and cold pressure water system. The worktop fiddles double up as hand holds. She has a navigation station with electrical switchboard with water alarms, engine hour meter etc. The dinette can be converted to a double berth.

The forward cabin has a spacious vee berth with natural light and good ventilation. The aft cabin is wide and has ample clearance under the cockpit sole. The heads

compartment contains a stand up shower. Storage is generous and the space is easy to clean and maintain. The cockpit features wheel steering and a walk-through transom making boarding safe and easy. A retractable swim ladder is supplied as standard.

Specification

LOA: 29ft 11in / 9.12m
LWL: 26ft 11in / 8.19m
Beam: 10ft 9in / 3.28m
Draught: (Shoal or bilge) 3ft 10in / 1.7m
Draught: (Deep) 5ft 4in / 1.63m
Displacement: (Shoal) 7,150lbs / 3,246kg
Ballast: (Shoal or bilge) 2,500lbs / 1,158kg
Ballast: (Deep) 2,550lbs / 1,158kg
Mast height: 42ft 6in / 12.95m
Sail area: 400sq ft / 37.16m
Water: 40 gals
Fuel: 20 gals
Engine: Inboard diesel 18hp
Max headroom: 6ft 2in
Berths: 5
CE category: B

Contact:
Opal Marine
Camper and Nicholsons Marina
Mumby Road
Gosport, Hampshire PO12 1AH
Tel: 023 9258 3242
Email: info@opalmarine.com

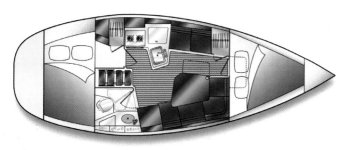

Dragonfly 920 - 30ft 2in

Dragonfly 920. Trimarans may look a bit high tech but sailing them is fun. The rig is no more complicated to handle than a conventional bermudan, and she can go very fast. The hulls slice through the water and the tiller in your hand gives you that magic contact that makes sailors smile.

Only two steps down lead you into the main cabin through a wide and clear companionway. Sturdy teak fittings combined with modern fabrics give an impression of quality. A folding table supported on the centreboard trunk gives plenty of room for six people to enjoy their meals. The functional galley is placed next to the companionway. A capacious locker is found under the cockpit sole, it slides out to provide ample storage for food etc. A hanging locker and switchboard is placed to port. The enclosable forward cabin has a good double berth and plenty of storage space. A hatch provides light and ventilation.

The boat is unsinkable. Each float contains three watertight compartments, any one of which is capable of keeping the entire trimaran afloat. The centre (main) hull incorporates a crash bulkhead in the forward section to prevent flooding in the event of major impact.

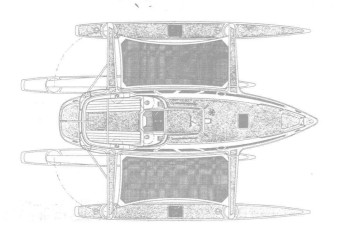

Specification

LOA: 30ft 2in / 9.20m
LWL: 28ft 8in / 8.75m
Beam: Max: 22ft 2in / 6.75m
Beam folded: 10ft 2in / 3.1m
Draught: Max: 5ft 3in / 1.60m
Min:1ft 6in / 0.45m
Mainsail: 32.8sq m
Furling Genoa: 22sq m
Displacement: 3960lb / 1800kg
Payload: 800kg

Contact:
Multihull Promotions
Sandpipers,
Smugglers Lane,
Bosham, Chichester,
West Sussex PO18 8QP
Tel: 01243 576533

Price guide: £71.750

Elan 31 - *30ft 2in*

The Elan 31 is built in Slovenia. The company has an international reputation for quality and design by Rob Humphreys. The Elan 31 has the looks of a boat built for performance with a long waterline and a deep and narrow keel.

Below decks the saloon is narrow with headroom of 5ft 9in. The finishing is of a high standard. There are two long settee bunks with a neat and strong table with two lifting leaves. Watertanks are located under the bunks. The galley is compact with a well insulated icebox. There is a large sink plus a drainer. The cooker is mounted low. The chart table is forward facing and has a comfortable seat. There is a small bookshelf and a bin for storage. The heads compartment aft of the chart table is well made and finished. It contains an unusually large wet hanging locker. In the forecabin there is a V shaped platform with sitting headroom. A large forehatch allows plenty of natural light into the space. The after cabin has a bunk which is well proportioned, 6ft 2in x 4ft 8in. There is some standing area. The boat is very much a performance cruiser racer and her interior dimensions are to be expected.

Specification

LOA: 30ft 2in / 9.20m
LWL: 26ft 9in / 8.21m
Beam: 10ft 5in / 3.20m
Draught: 6ft 1in / 1.85m
Displacement: 8.360lbs / 3.800kg
Sail area: 495 sq ft / 46 sq m
Capacity:
Water: 33gal / 150ltr
Fuel: 15.40 gal / 70ltr
Berths: 6
CE Category: B

Contact:
Elan Yacht Sales UK Limited
Swanick Marina
Southampton
Tel: 01489 885000
Fax: 01489 885509
email: sales@elanyachts.com

Price guide: £59.702 inc VAT

Etap 30i - 30ft 7in

The Etap 30i is unsinkable due to its double skinned structure. She is a comfortable ocean-going cruiser with a fast turn of speed.

The saloon contains two long settees which can be used as berths. A large table with a drop leaf to starboard is in the centre of the saloon. A panoramic window allows plenty of light, giving a spacious and airy feeling. The headroom is 185cm. The galley features a gimballed 2-burner gas hob. There is an opening porthole to provide ventilation. A heavily insulated 65 litre capacity coolbox is provided. The galley fittings are trimmed with solid beech.

A 75 x 57cm chart table with spacious chart storage is located on the starboard side next to the companionway. The switch panel is fitted with circuit breakers, a fuel gauge, voltmeter and a 12v electrical socket. A large storage cupboard is fitted under the chart table.

The front cabin is fully closable using two three-panelled sliding bulkheads. There is a double berth 195 x155cm. Closable lockers are fitted along the hull on both port and starboard sides. The aft cabin has a double skipper's berth 200 x 151cm. Ample headroom is provided under the cockpit lockers. A hanging locker and stowage lockers are fitted. Ventillation is provided by a ventilation grille and two opening portholes.

The heads compartment is situated to the starboard of the companionway. A spacious locker is mounted above the toilet. A marine toilet is provided and a septic tank can be installed behind the bulkhead as an option. The washbasin is fitted with a shower head and fed by a pressurized cold water supply. There is a capacious wet locker and drainage cupboards above and below the washbasin. An opening porthole provides light and ventilation.

Specification

LOA: 30ft 7in / 9.35m
LWL: 29ft 3½in / 9.32m
Beam: 10ft 4½in / 3.16m
Draught: 5ft 7in / 1.70m
3ft½in / 1.0m
Displacement: 7.709lbs / 3.600kg
Mainsail: 261 sq ft / 24.3 sq m
Engine: 19hp / 13.4kw

CE Category: B

Contact:
Kiss Marine Solent Ltd
The Boatyard
Hythe Marina
Hythe, Hants SO45 6DX
Tel: 02380 840 300
Fax: 02380 840 700

Price guide: £50.500 + VAT

Channel 31 - 30ft 9in

The **Hunter Channel 31** has both a deep fin keel or an alternative twin fin version. She has achieved CE Category A. With a 6ft headroom throughout she is well lit in her spacious saloon. The distinctive curved grab handles and the triangular saloon table impress you on entrance. It has good stowage including two spacious lockers and two drawers. The two settees are 6ft 3in long and 2ft wide. They would make good sea berths if fitted with leecloths. The L-shaped galley has a deep icebox and a better than average worktop with good deep fiddles. A two burner cooker with oven and grill is installed as standard. The excellent heads compartment, is to port of the companionway with ample space to move around. Foul weather gear can be stacked away in the locker. The outboard facing chart table has a hinged stool which takes up no space when not in use. The table is big enough to take a half-folded Admiralty chart. There is plenty of room for instruments.

In the forecabin two staggered single berths allow for sleep without feet colliding. It can be used as a double with its berth length of 6ft 7in. There is also a changing area and a hanging locker. The aft cabin has a very large berth (6ft 6in x 6ft 4in) so you can sleep in either orientation. If you choose tranversely, both occupants have sitting headroom. There is standing/changing space and good stowage including a large hanging locker and a deep shelf. The engine has excellent access via lift-off steps and removable panels in the aft cabin.

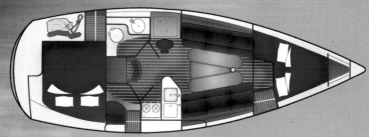

Specification

LOA 30ft 9in / 9.37m
LWL 26ft 8in / 8.13m
Beam 10ft 4in / 3.15m
Draft (Fin) 5ft 11in / 1.80m
Draft (Twin) 4ft 1in / 1.24m
Displacement 9,500lb / 4309kg
Sail Area 498 sq ft / 46.3 sq m
CE Category: A

Contact:
Select Yachts
Rock, Wadebridge,
Cornwall PL27 6NT
Tel: 01208 862666
email: Info@selectyachts.co.uk
www.SELECTYACHTS.co.uk

Price guide: £78.603 inc VAT

Global Midget - 31ft

The lines of the **Midget 31** have their origin in the classical form of the fishing boats from Lynaes, which is situated on the north coast of the Danish island of Seeland. For centuries this hull form has been considered ideal for boats in the open seas around Denmark. She is classified as Class A within the CE European Directives.

The boat has a sleeping capacity for six people in three cabins. Her aft sleeping cabins are both equipped with wardrobes. The interior layout comprises a spacious saloon with a U-shaped settee, two double quarter berths in separated aft cabins, a chart table, a galley and heads. In the saloon the table is height adjustable and supported on the mast column. It can also be utilised as an extra sleeping space by using a cushion supplied. The navigation area and chart table has ample space for instruments. The galley has a laminate worksurface, stainless steel sink with tap, electric pressurized water system, gimballed three burner gas-cooker with oven, cold box and lockers. The heads contain a marine WC, stainless steel sink with tap and mirror, wet locker with space for a heating unit.

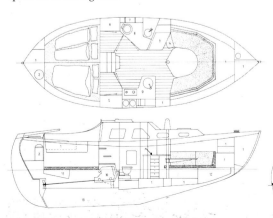

Specification

LOA: 9.55m
LWL: 7.80m
Beam: 3.10m
Draft: 1.35m
Displacement: 5.400kg
Ballast: 2.400kg
Sail area:
Main 21.30 sq m
Jib: 18.10 sq m
Genoa: 28.20 m
CE Category: A

Contact:
Global Yachts Ltd
Hamble Point Marina
School Lane Southampton SO3
Tel: 02380 456788
Email: info@global-yachts.co.u

Price guide: £75.594.0

Hanse 312 - *31ft*

The Hanse 312 used to be called the 315 but recently after some small changes the builder decided to rename her. She is fitted out in a combination of white laminate and warm red-stained mahogany faced marine ply.

The doors save weight by being made with a foam sandwich construction. The forward cabin is separated from the saloon by a door, and there is a large double berth (2m long) with a locker in addition to shelves above the berths. In the saloon there are two straight settees separated by a table with a single hinged flap. Shelves and lockers faced with rattan give the space a simple elegance. Under bunk lockers are limited by the water tank to starboard and the single battery to port. The ample chart table with its own seat, is positioned to port and has generous fiddles.

The galley is equipped with a two burner gas cooker and oven. Water is supplied with a pressure system.

The heads compartment has an unusual feature with a door that leads to an impressively large sail locker. The heads contains a marine-toilet with a holding tank system. A sink is supplied with a cold water electrical pressurized system.

The aft cabin is separated from the saloon by a door, inside there is a large double berth and hanging locker.

Specification

LOA: 31ft 0in / 9.45m
LWL: 26ft 6in / 8.07m
Beam: 10ft 6in / 3.20m
Draught: Deep fin: 5ft 9in / 1.75m
Shallow fin: 4ft 7in / 1.40m
Displacement: 8,509lb / 3,860kg
Ballast: 2,755lb / 1,250kg
Sail area: (main and 100% foretriangle)536sq ft / 49.80 sq m
Engine: 18hp Volvo diesel saildrive
Headroom: 6ft 2in / 1.88m

Builder: Hanse Yachts, Yachtzentrum Greifswald, Germany

Contact: Hanse Yachts UK Ltd
Chandlery Building
Hamble Point Marina
Hamble
Southampton S031 4NB
Tel: 02380 457008
Fax: 02380 458712
Email: south@hanseyachts.co.uk
www.hanseyachts.co.uk

Price guide: £54.990 inc VAT

55

Jeanneau Odyssey 32 - 31ft 5in

The Jeanneau Sun Odyssey 32. Has an almost plumb stem and her well disguised coachroof gives her a sleek modern appearance. The interior makes full use of an ample beam. Headroom is good with a minimum 6ft 1in. The saloon is open and bright with the galley set well aft. This is large for a boat of this size and extends under the cockpit. The galley has an icebox, and plenty of stowage. There is a two-burner cooker with oven. The navigation area has a forward facing chart table with a shallow chart drawer under. The heads compartment is set well forward. It is fitted with a shower tray serviced with an electric pump. There is an opening port for ventilation. The aft cabin has its bunk transversing the boat. It has good sized standing space with a large storage locker fitted with shelves. The cabin has two opening ports plus one fixed. The forecabin has 6ft 3in headroom with an exceptionally long bunk (7ft 6in) on the starboard side. The port side is 6ft 3in long. There are storage bins under the bunks and a hanging locker with shelves.

She will be a popular boat suitable for comfortable and fast coastal and offshore family cruising.

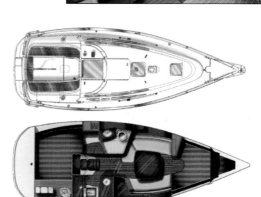

Specification

LOA: 31ft 5in / 9.60m
LWL: 27ft 11in / 8.52m
Beam: 10ft 9in / 3.30m
Draft: Deep keel: 4ft 11in / 1.50m
Lifting keel: 2ft 8in - 6ft 0in / 0.86
Displacement:
Deep keel:10009lb / 4540kg
Lifting keel: 10758lb / 4880kg
Sail Area:
Main: 294 sq ft / 27.3sq m
Spinnaker: 721sq ft / 67 sq m
Engine: 15hp

Contact:
Sea Ventures Limited
Lymington Yacht Haven
Lymington Hampshire SO41 3QD
Tel: 01590 672472
Fax: 01590 671924
email: sales@seaventures.co.uk
www.sea-ventures.co.uk

Price guide: £46.065 + V

Hallberg Rassy 31 - 31ft 7in

The Hallberg Rassy 31 is designed by Germán Frers. The interior is tastefully finished in selected mahogany with a two-component matt silk varnish.

The lighting is well positioned throughout. All upholstery is in high quality materials. There are curtains at the side windows and under the skylights. The floor is varnished teak. In the saloon are the galley and chart table, two sofas, two metres long and a stable table. There are lockers with louvered doors over the sofas with stowage under. The galley has drawers and a cutting board, cooker with oven and an openable window above. There is a double sink and insulated cool-box. On the opposite side there is a generous chart table with seat and drawers.

The white roof is accentuated with mahogany strips. Headroom is 1.86m in the saloon. The fore-peak has two berths 2.12m long, generous stowage above and below, and a door to the saloon. The aft cabin has a double berth, 2.25m at its widest point.

There is a folding door to the saloon and heads compartment. In the heads there is a built-in shower stall with teak grating. The marine toilet is robust. There is plenty of stowage space under the china basin.

This is a beautiful family cruising boat capable of offshore cruising.

Specification

LOA: 31ft 7in / 9.62m
LWL: 27ft 1in / 8.26m
Beam: 10ft 10in / 3.30m
Draft: Deep keel: 5ft 7in / 1.71m
Displacement: 9.920lbs /4.5t
Laed keel: 4410lb / 2.0t
Sail area: with working jib:
495 sq ft / 46.2 sq m
Engine: Volvo MD 2020
Water: 50.2 US gals / 190 lt
Fuel: 15.9 US gals / 60lt
Mast above water:
48ft 11in / 14.9m
CE Category:
A (Ocean)

Contact:
Transworld Yachts Ltd
Hamble Point Marina
School Lane, Hamble, Southampton SO31 4JD
Tel: 023 80 456069
Fax: 023 80 456406
Email: enq@transworld-yachts.co.uk
www.transworld-yachts.co.uk

Price guide: £74.000 + VAT

Nauticat 321 - *32ft 1in*

Nauticat 321. Nauticat's aim was to create a yacht with similar looks and the same high level of quality and performance as the Nauticat 39 and 515 but in a smaller size. The 321 has, since launching, been praised for her performance under sail. The boat can be specified with one of three different keel options and four different rigging alternatives. The 321 has two separate staterooms, a large head and shower compartment and a very cosy U-shaped settee which offers all-around visibility from the pilothouse. She offers two separate steering positions.

Each 321 is built to order and no two are the same; the prospective owner can have a great influence on the final fit-out. Internally the boat has an open plan look through the clever use of laminated beams and mini-beams disguised as framing for the fixtures. The navigation station is to starboard. The excellent galley is on the lower level with plenty of workspaces, an icebox and space for a microwave oven. There is plenty of stowage space. The heads compartment is opposite. It has full headroom and stowage for oilskins, and there is a shower-head. The owner might well choose to use the forecabin, with a length of 6ft 7in. There are lockers below and above and a large hanging locker. The aft cabin's double berth is 6ft 6in long by 5ft 10in wide. Maximum headroom is 6ft 6in. Engine, batteries and tank access is good. The cockpit is deep and secure with room for two or three people to sit around the binnacle. The wheelhouse gives good protection.

Note: All Nauticats are custom-built and this suggested layout can be, and usually is, altered in subtle ways to suit individual owners.

Specification

L.O.A: 32ft 10in / 10m
L.W.L: 27ft 3in / 8.30m
Beam: 10ft 8in / 3.24m
Draft:
(Shallow keel) 4ft 7in / 1.40m
(Fin keel) 5ft 3in / 1.60m
(Fin keel with bulb) 5ft 9in / 1.75m
Displacement:
6 tons / 13300lbs
Sail areas:
(All sails are optional)
550sq ft to 637 sq ft /
51.1m to 59.2m²
Ballast:
1.8 - 2.15 tons /
4000 -4300lbs
Fresh water capacity:
117 gal. UK / 440lt
Fuel capacity:
66 gal. UK / 250lt
CE Category: A

Contact:
Nauticat UK Ltd
Mariners House,
High Street, Hamble,
Southampton SO31 4JF
Tel: 02380 453900
Email: info@nauticatuk.co.uk

Price guide: £100.900

Etap 32s - 32ft 3in

The Etap 32s has a stylishly modern interior finish of selected mahogany treated with three coats of waterproof acrylic varnish. All furnishings have solid mahogany frames, and the floorboards are of maintenance free laminate with beech edging.

The companionway has three curved aluminum treads coated with a nonslip finish. Headroom in the companionway area is 190cm. The saloon contains two long sofas (each 2.00 m) which can be used as berths. A large table with two drop leaves and stowage for five bottles is located in the centre of the saloon. The panoramic window allows an ample supply of light into the saloon. Extra stowage space is provided under the starboard sofa and a 170 litre potable water tank is located under the port side sofa. The galley has a gimballed 2-burner gas oven. Underneath the two extra deep is a large stowage capacity with cutlery drawer and bin-bag holder. Worksurfaces are finished in grey Corian. An insulated 651t coolbox is provided. A 75 x 60cm chart table is located on the starboard side. The front cabin has a double berth and closable lockers are

fitted along the hull sides. The aft cabin has a double skipper's berth 200 x 157cm. Ample headroom is provided. The heads compartment has a traditional marine toilet. The washbasin is fitted with a shower head and is fed by a pressurized cold water supply. Headroom is 185cm.

Specification

LOA: 32ft 3in / 9.84m
LWL: 27ft 6in / 8.38m
Beam: 11ft 3in / 3.42m
Draft: keel: 4ft 11in or 5ft 11in / 1.50m or 1.80m
Displacement:
keel:8575lb or 8157lb / 3890kg or 3700kg
Sail Area:
Main: 293 sq ft / 27.2sq
Genoa: 297sq ft / 27.6 sq
Engine: 19hp / 13.4kW

Contact:
Kiss Marine Solent Ltd
The Boatyard
Hythe Marina
Hythe
Hants SO45 6DX
Tel: 02380 840 300
Fax: 02380 840 700

Price guide: £63.000 +VAT

Dazcat D10 Cruiser Racer - 32ft 5in

The Dazcat D10 is an exceptional sports catamaran, delivering outstanding performance and comfort. Class winner of the Round Britain Race 2002 (BEDAZZLED, skippered by owner Tony Cotton), the Dazcat D10 is available either complete and ready to sail or in kit form. Multimarine also offer 'open access boatbuilding courses' to ensure you complete your boat to the required standards.

As well as racing standard performance, the D10 offers plenty of space for cruising, including a large galley, navigation station and saloon, twin double berths and one single and a separate and private heads compartment.

On deck she's very easy to sail single handed, with all controls leading to the cockpit. In addition, all instruments are interfaced, so course changes can be made from either down below or in the cockpit.

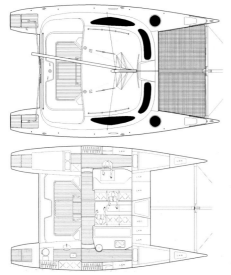

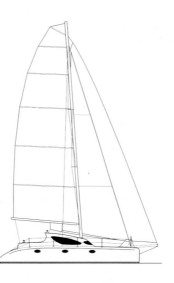

Specification

LOA: 32ft 5in / 10m
LWL: 31ft 10in / 9.7m
Beam: 20ft 8in / 6.3m
Draft: Shoal: 18in / 0.450m
Deep: 3ft 7in / 1.1m
Displacement: 5511lb / 2.500kg
Sail area: 700 sq ft / 65sqm

Contact:
Multimarine Composites Ltd
Foss Quarry, Millbrook, Torpoint, Cornwall PL10
Tel: 00441752 823129
Email: Darren@Dazcat.co.uk
www: multimarine.co.uk
www: dazcat.co.uk

Price guide: £ on application

Beneteau Océanis Clipper 323 - *32ft 8in*

The Océanis Clipper 323 has an ingeniously designed interior layout featuring spacious accommodation and generous stowage space. She has two large cabins, a built-in hanging locker, a convertible optional saloon, and a heads and separate shower stall. There is 2m headroom almost everywhere.

Each area contains several hull and roof hatches or ports, making a total of 3 hatches and 10 ports (5 of them opening) which provide excellent light and ventilation. There are multiple storage areas, along with a proper chart-table, lockers and a bottle holder beside the galley. The galley has headroom of 1.90m. There is a laminated work surface with moulded fiddle rail. The saloon has a headroom forward of 1.75m and aft 1.95m. There are two fore and aft settees. The saloon table has a bar box and flaps. There is stowage under the settee to port. The chart table is to starboard facing forward it has moulded fiddle rails. There is a 12 function instrument console with circuit breaker.

The aft head has headroom of 1.82m, a moulded unit, shower compartment with an electric shower drainage pump. The compartment contains an oilskin locker. The owner's aft cabin has headroom of 1.83m and a double berth 2.05 x 1.90m. There is a hanging locker and wooden shelving along the length of the hull.

Specification

LOA: 10.00 m
LWL: 9.72 m
Beam: 3.26 m
Light displacement (approx.) 3837 kg approx.
Max Engine Power: (Hp) 18 Cv / Hp
Fuel tank capacity: 75 lt
CE Certification: B6/C8/D10

Contact
Ancasta International Boat Sales
Port Hamble
Satchel Lane
Hamble
Southampton SO31 4QD
Tel: 023 80 450 026
Email: Beneteau@ancasta.co.uk
www.ancasta.com

Price guide: £60.000

61

Najad 331 - *32ft 8in*

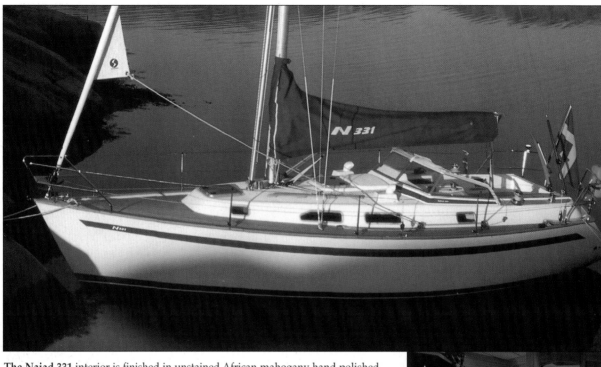

The Najad 331 interior is finished in unstained African mahogany hand polished and varnished to a satin finish. The spacious saloon has two settees surrounding the saloon folding table which is equipped with bottle storage. The settees can be used as two additional berths. There are shelves and cupboards above the settee backrests. The companionway steps can be removed for easy access to the engine. Headroom is approx 1.86m.

The L-shaped galley is located amidships allowing free passage between the cockpit and the saloon. The galley is separated from the saloon by a bulkhead. There is a stainless steel twin sink with a pressure system for cold fresh water. The stove is gimballed with twin burner and oven. The work top over the cooker can be stowed when not in use. There is a large work area in laminate, easily cleaned. An insulated icebox is included.

The Aft cabin has a comfortable and wide double berth, hanging wardrobes and shelves for storage. Headroom 1.67m. The forward cabin has two wide full size berths and a spacious hanging wardrobe to port. Headroom approx. 1.77m. The navigation area is located amidships to starboard. There is a forward facing navigation table with stowage for charts.

The heads compartment is amidships to starboard. It has white laminate bulkheads and a large washbasin built into the worktop. The sole is designed as a shower tub. There is a mirror on the inside of the door and an opening porthole and ventilator to the cockpit.

Specification

LOA: 32ft 8in / 9.98m
LWL: 26ft 8in / 8.14m
Beam: 10ft 8in / 3.26m
Draught: 5ft 6in / 1.70m
Alternative Draught: 4ft 11in / 1.50m
Displacement: 5.3t / 5,300kg
Bolted lead keel: 2.1t / 2100kg
Mast height above waterline: 49ft 11in / 15.2m
Sail Areas: Cruising 538sq ft / 50.0sq m
Semi-full batten main 285sq ft / 26.5 sq m
Working jib 110% 258sq ft / 24.0 sq m

Contact:
Najad UK
Hamble Point Marina
School Lane
Hamble
Southampton SO31 4NB
Tel: 02380 455 555

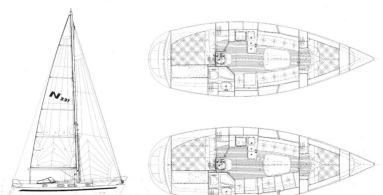

Price guide: 134.500

Elan 333 - *32ft 9in*

The Elan 333 is designed by New Zealander Rob Humphreys. She is the second smallest in a range of up to 45ft. The interior has a feeling of space. Headroom is 1.83m.

Ergonomically U shaped settees are to port and starboard.There are water tanks under the seats and a foldable saloon table with bar and stowage compartment. There are lockers and shelves above the backrests along the hull on both sides. The L-shaped galley has a headroom of 1.78m. The cooker is gimballed and has a two rings and an oven. The double sink has a pressurized water system. There is a well insulated cool box. Lockers and cupboards for dishes and cutlery are above and under the worktop.

The navigation station has headroom of 1.78m. With a good sized chart table 750 x 650mm. There are drawers under the table and a stowage compartment under the navigator's seat. The forward (headroom 1.70m) and aft cabins (headroom 1.79m) have double berths. The head and bathroom has a wet locker with drainage to the shower bilge.The washbasin has a pressurized tap. There are stowage lockers under the sink with access to the seacocks. The diesel engine has easy access, and there is a 77lt fuel tank.

Specification

LOA 10.45m
LWL 9.99m
Beam 3.46m
Draft (standard) 1.90m
Draft (shoal) 1.50m
Ballast 1.570kg / 1550kg
Displacement 5200kg
Engine 19hp
Water capacity 177lt
Fuel capacity 77lt
Mainsail 33,00 sq m
Genoa 33,40 sq m
Spinnaker 94,50 sq m
Design CE category A

Contact:
Elan Yacht Sales UK Limited
Swanick Marina
Southampton
Tel: 01489 885000
Fax: 01489 885509
email: sales @elanyachts.com

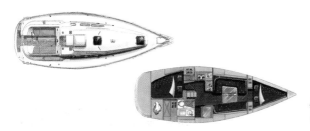

Ronautica RO 340 - 32ft 9in

The RO 340. This Spanish built Yacht is part of a range recently introduced to this country. They offer a range of yachts from 26ft to a 40 ft (12 metre) luxury 'Blue Water' Sport Cruiser.

The 340 is finished throughout in a warm coloured wood giving a light and pleasing interior. Curved edges give a comfortable and safe environment. There are 7 portlights and 2 hatches. The saloon has a headroom of 1.98m. There is a large folding table and the bench is convertible to an extra bed. The chart table is generous with easy access to navigation instruments. The galley is equipped with a 2-ring cooker and grill. With plenty of lockers and drawers for cutlery and dishes. An ice-box is provided. Headroom in the galley is 1.95m.

There are two cabins with an option for a three cabin version. The forecabin has a headroom of 1.95m and a double berth. The aft cabin has headroom of 1.95m with a double berth. The heads compartment has a marine toilet with pressurized water to the wash basin and shower unit. There is space to store wet sailing gear.

The RO 340 will appeal to people looking for a performance boat that handles easily and offers comfortable accommodation for up to six people.

Specification

LOA: 32ft 9in / 10.00 m
Hull Length: 9.8 m
Hull Beam: 3.25 m
Displacement 4000 kg
Ballast: 1600kg
Engine : Volvo dieselSD
Fuel capacity: 75lt
Water: 200lt
CE Certification: A

Contact:
South West Yacht Brokers G
Atlantic Quay
Richmond Walk
Plymouth PL1 4LN
Tel: 01752 551991
Fax: 01752 551991
www.southwestyachts.co.uk

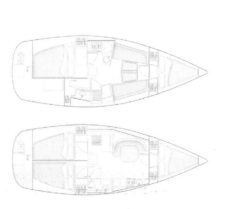

Price guide: £72.980.

Parker 335H - *33ft 5in*

The Parker 335. Parker Yachts specialise in lifting keel boats, and the Parker 335 is their largest version. In 1995 she won the RYA Yacht of the Year design award. She is a powerful offshore cruiser.

The saloon contains a settee berth on the portside with a navigator's chart table/stowage and folding seat. There is stowage under the seat with shelves and cupboards. There is a folding table in the centre with a fire extinguisher under. The galley to port of main companionway has laminated worktops and teak edged laminates. There is a stainless steel pedestal sink with a hot and cold water mixer tap. A failsafe cooker is supplied with oven and hob and an insulated cool locker with lid.

The forward cabin has standing headroom, and a large double berth with stowage under. There is a hanging locker with shelves on the hull sides. Doors lead separately to the saloon on port and the heads compartment on starboard. A GRP moulding is used for the heads including a stainless steel hand basin with pressurised hot and cold water, trigger shower tap, toiletry cupboards, wet clothes locker, marine toilet, holding tank and toilet pump out system. The lifting keel enables entry to shallow and drying harbours or beaches.

Specification

LOA: 33ft 5in / 10.21 m
LWL: 28ft 6in / 8.72 m
Beam: 10ft 6in / 3.23 m
Draft: Keel down: 6ft 2in / 1.88 m
Keel up: 2ft 1in / 0.64 m.
Displacement: 9.490lb / 4.302 kg
Ballast 2650lb / 1200 kg.
Sail area: 570sq ft / 53 sq m
CE Classification: B Offshore

Contact:
Parker Lift Keel Yachts Ltd
61 Horseshoe Lane
Kirton
Boston
Lincs PE20 1LW
Tel: 01205 722697
Fax: 01205 723549
www.parkeryachts.co.uk

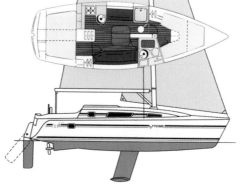

Event 34 - 33ft 9in

The Event 34 is a hand-built boat from Slovenia, offered at a production boat price. Her builders use the very best hardware and the joinery is in solid wood. The Adria Event Shipyard, part of a very large industrial group, is situated in a small, but beautifuly diverse country on the southern 'Sunny' side of the Alps, which stretches down to Adriatic Sea. Their yachts can be found all over the world.

Designed to embrace safety, with a well planned interior space, good sailing capabilities and ease of sailing in all weather conditions. This provides comfortable cruising comfort for six people and yet she can be easily handled by a single person. The interior is carefully designed, down to the smallest detail. A wide selection of high quality materials and upholstery fabrics are available.

The layout is enhanced by an luxury saloon with the functionally designed L-shaped galley. The galley is fitted with all modern conveniences: double sink, gas stove, cool box and plenty of storage. There are a lot of handholds and places to brace yourself during sailing. The vessel may be built to have two or three separate cabins each of them with spacious double berths.

Specification

LOA: 10,35 m
Hull length: 9,99 m
LWL: 8,80 m
Beam: 3,45 m
Draft: 1,80 m
Ballast: 1880 kg
Displacement: 5100 kg
Engine: Volvo Penta MD2030 21kW/29PS
Water tank: 210 lt
Fuel tank: 75 lt
Mast height: 12,85 / 11,50 m
Main sail: 26.sq m
Genoa: - furling 34.sq m
CE category: A

Contact:
Wittey Marine Ltd
Unit 17 Haddenham
Business Park, Thame Road
Haddenham, Bucks HP17 8LJ
Tel: 01844 290890
Email: marinesales@witteymachinery.com

Price guide: £72.244

Hallberg Rassy 34 - 33ft 9in

The Hallberg Rassy 34 is certified by Germanischer Lloyd and delivered with a CE Certificate for category A (unlimited ocean voyages). The accommodation is finished in mahogany.

There is full headroom throughout the boat and there are skylights, opening portholes and ventilators. In the saloon there are two sofas, to starboard 2.16m long. The port side is L-shaped and 1.84m, with lockers above and stowage below. The galley is on the port side with an opening window and there are two extra deep double sinks. There is ample stowage room, chopping board, drawers and a waste bin. The chart table is to starboard. In the forward cabin there is a generous double berth 2.03m long and 2.04m wide at the widest part. On both sides there are lockers above and stowage below. There is a door leading to the saloon. The aft cabin has a spacious hanging locker and there are two opening portholes. The heads compartment has a china wash basin with stowage above and below.

The watertight shower stall has a teak grating. There is a robust manual pump toilet.

This yacht is a classic Swedish style cruising vessel with comfortable medium to heavy displacement.

Specification

LOA: 33ft 9in / 10,28 m
Hull length: 30ft 10in / 9,40 m
Length water line: 28ft 6in / 8.69 m
Beam: 11ft 3in / 3,42 m
Draft: 6ft 1in / 1,85 m
Displacement: 11.650lbs / 5.3t
Lead keel: 4.650lbs / 2.1t
Engine: Volvo Penta MD2030 21kW/29PS
Water tank: 67 US gals / 255 lt
Fuel tank: 41 US gals / 155 lt
Mast height: 50ft 4in / 15.35m
Sail area: 592 sq ft / 55 sq m

Contact:
Transworld Yachts Ltd
Hamble Point Marina
School Lane, Hamble SO31 4JD
Tel: 023 80 456069
Fax: 023 80 456406
Email: enq@transworld-yachts.co.uk
www.transworld-yachts.co.uk

Legend 33 - 33ft 9in

The Legend 33 is built by Hunter Marine of America. One of the latest of the new Glenn Henderson designed cruisers, the new Hunter Legend 33 is a combination of comfort and performance in a very affordable package.

The underbody of the 33 mirrors Henderson's other Hunter designs in the recent 41 and 44-foot models, bringing the beam well aft to provide interior space, but not sacrificing performance.

The deck is wide and workable without intrusions. The cockpit can hold a crowd under sail or at the dock, but is also set up to sail easily single handed. The overhead arch allows for a convenient sage attachment point for the optional traveler and bimini. Accommodation includes a large, aft master stateroom with plenty of storage and headroom. There is a double berth and excellent ventilation. The forward vee berth guest cabin is private.

Entertaining or fortifying the crew is easy in the large saloon. The galley is complete with Corian® counter, a two-burner cooker, icebox and a deep, single basin stainless steel sink. There is a removable rubbish bin, and a refrigerator and freezer are also available. Even the non-skid dishware is included. The heads compartment includes a shower and marine sanitation device.

Specification

LOA: 33ft 6in / 10.21 m
Hull Length: 33ft 01in /10.08 m
LWL: 29ft 05in / 8.97 m
Beam: 11ft 06in / 3.51 m
Draft: (Shoal or Bilge) 4ft 06in / 1.37 m
(Deep) 5ft 06in / 1.67 m.
Displacement: 11,016 lb / 4,997 kg
Ballast (Shoal) 3579 lb / 1623 kg.
(Deep) 3459 lb / 1569 kg.
Mast Height: (Standard) 46ft 7in / 14.20m
(Furling) 51ft 11in / 15.80 m
Sail Area: - 625ft 2in / 58.06 sq m
(Furling) 542 ft 2in / 50.35 sq m
Standard cabin: Sleeps 6
Headroom: 6ft 4in / 1.93 m
Fuel tank capacity: 25 gal. / 95 lit
Water capacity: 50 gal. / 189 lit
Holding tank capacity: 25 gal. / 95 lit
Water heater: 6 gal. / 23 L
Aux power: (Volvo) 19 HP 14.2 KW
CE Classification: A

Contact:
Opal Marine
Camper & Nicholsons Marina
Mumby Road
Gosport
Hants PO12 1AH
Tel: 02392 583242
Fax: 02392 581028

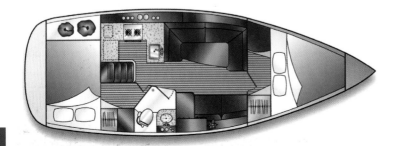

Price guide: £ on application

Ovni 345 - 34ft

The Ovni 345. Ovni range are a French company called Alubat. Founded in 1973, it has successfully followed a niche strategy - concentrating on building primarily lifting keel, aluminium yachts. Alubat is now Europe's leading, if not only, aluminium production boat builder offering a range of monohull lifting keel and monohull ultra light displacement fin keel boats.

The Ovni range of production built lifting keel aluminium yachts (34' to 58') remains the key product of the company. Each boat can be customised according to the wishes of the owners and can be unique in its internal layout/design. The 2 cabin version has a conventional fore and aft arrangement. 1 forward cabin, 1 aft cabin, 1 aft head. There is a manual lifting keel, hydraulic rudder lifting system, battery charger and load distributor, and holding tank. The Ovni 345 is a multi chine lifting keel aluminium yacht, with oak interior. Standard equipment includes 30hp engine, mainsail, furling genoa, wheel steering, electric anchor windlass.

The Ovni 345 is also available in a three cabin version, shown below with two aft cabins.

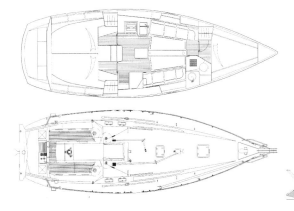

Specification

LOA: 11.48m
LWL: 10.93m
Beam: 9.10m
Draft: with centreboard down: 2.10m
with centreboard up: 0.58m
Displacement:
7.000 kg
Ballast: 2.900 kg
Sail Area:
Mainsail: 27.50 sq m
Genoa: 39.50 sq m

Contact:
North Sea Maritime Ltd
PO Box 5539
Southend-on-Sea
Essex SS1 3TE
Tel: 01702 584 584 **Fax:**
Fax: 01702 584 821
Email: info@northseamsritime.com
www.northseamaritime.com

Catalina 320 - 34ft 3in

The **Catalina 320** is an American yacht. The company that builds her has had great success creating conservative family cruisers. Designed for volume production and selling at a competitive price, the company's first design the Catalina 22 has sold well over 15,000 and is still in production.

The Catalina 320 is based on a high performance and high volume hull design. Over 800 have been built since her launch in 1993. She is said by the builders to track well under power or sail, to be light on the helm and that motion and heeling are gentle and predictable. Carrying the deck beam well aft has created space for a large cockpit with wide coamings. The decks are wide and moulded with non-skid surfaces.

Catalina have had a reputation for conservative yachts but they have also searched for radical ways to increase the internal space below. The interior is bright and easy to keep clean, finished in a combination of teak and hardwoods. The galley is a custom moulded unit with integral backsplashes, halogen lighting and a cedar panelled hanging locker. The aft cabin has an athwartships double. There is a double and single berth in the saloon and a double in the forecabin.

Specification

LOA: 34ft 3in / 10.44m
LWL: 28ft 0in / 8.53m
Beam: 11ft 9in / 3.58m
Draft: (Fin) 6ft 3in / 1.91m
(Wing) 4ft 4in / 1.32m
Ballast: (Fin) 4000lbs / 1814kg
(Wing) 4400lbs / 1996kg
Approximate weight: (Fin) 11.300lbs / 5126kg
(Wing) 11.700lbs / 5307kg
Engine: Diesel 3 cylinder 27hp
Sail area:
(100% foretriangle) 521sq ft / 48.40 sq m

Builder: Catalina Yachts USA
Contact:
Windward Yachting, Northney Marina
Northney Road, Hayling Island, Hampshire PO11 0N
Tel: 0870 350 1920.
Email: info@windwardyachting.co.uk
www.windwardyachting.co.uk

Price guide: £59.100 + VAT

Vancouver 34 - 34ft 3in

The Vancouver 34 is every inch an offshore cruiser. The interior accommodation is designed for use at sea, for long periods if required; the boat has good sea berths but still has a comfortably furnished saloon for relaxation when in harbour.

In the saloon there is a single settee berth to port, a wardrobe forward with hanging space plus shelves. To starboard is a dinette convertible to a double berth with bookshelf and two lockers outboard. There is a twin leafed table on the centreline around the teak mast support post. The galley has twin stainless steel sinks with foot pump and a hot and cold mixer tap, a gimballed gas cooker with two burners, grill and oven with fail-safe on all burners. There is ample stowage for crockery, cutlery, cooking utensils and food. A galley crash bar is fitted. A large drained ice box is situated under the forward end of the quarter berth. In the navigation area there is a large chart table to starboard with stowage for charts under and plenty of space for instruments outboard.

The quarterberth runs aft from the chart table with stowage under. The berth is long enough to allow the navigator to sit at the head of the berth using it as a seat, whilst someone is sleeping on the berth. A removable backrest is provided. In the forecabin there is a V berth arrangement providing two good length single berths with infill to form double. There is a dressing table with mirror in the cabin together with a hanging locker and access forward to the chain locker. There is a large opening perspex hatch above. The heads has a marine toilet with hinged down lid. The floor has a teak grating over the shower tray.

Specification

LOA: 34ft 3ins / 10.44m
LOW: 27 ft 6ins / 8.38m
Beam: 10 ft 6ins / 3.20m
Draught: 4 ft 9ins / 1.44 m
Ballast weight: 6,000 lbs 2,722 kgs
Displacement: 14,000 lbs 6,350 kgs
Mast height: 46ft 6ins 14.18 m
Sail area:
Mainsail: 243 sq ft / 22.57 sq m
Yankee: 244 sq ft / 22.67 sq m
Staysail: 103 sq ft / 9.57 sq m
Genoa: (optional) 435 sq ft / 40.41 sq m

Contact:
Northshore Yachts Ltd
Itchenor, Chichester
West Sussex, PO20 7AY
Tel: 01243 512611
email: sales@northshore.co.uk
www.northshore.co.uk

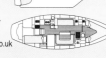

Vancouver 34P - 34ft 3in

The Vancouver 34P As her name suggests, is the Pilot version of the Vancouver 34, she shares all the same cruising attributes but with a pilot-house configuration.

There is an interior piloting position so that watches can be kept without sitting outside in the elements. From the saloon, the crew can enjoy 360 degree vision in the seated position and the yacht benefits from vast amounts of additional accommodation space as a result. There is a spacious central galley, two separate double cabins, space to fit an optional generator, water maker, fridge and freezer plus all the navigational instruments that may be required. As with all Vancouvers the oilskin locker is adjacent to the companionway and there is a full sized chart table. All the sail handling controls are led aft to the cockpit and the self tacking staysail makes sailing her that much easier. The cockpit has three large lockers giving plenty of stowage space for the dinghy, fenders, warps and spare sails.

Specification

LOA: 34ft 3ins / 10.44m
LOW: 27 ft 6ins / 8.38m
Beam: 10 ft 6ins / 3.20m
Draught: 4 ft 9ins / 1.44 m
Ballast weight: 6,000 lbs 2,722 kgs
Displacement: 14,000 lbs 6,350 kgs
Mast height: 46ft 6ins 14.18 m
Sail area:
Mainsail: 243 sq ft / 22.57 sq m
Yankee: 244 sq ft / 22.67 sq m
Staysail: 103 sq ft / 9.57 sq m
Genoa: (optional) 435 sq ft / 40.41 sq m

Contact:
Northshore Yachts Ltd
Itchenor, Chichester
West Sussex, PO20 7AY
Tel: 01243 512611
email: sales@northshore.co.uk
www.northshore.co.uk

Price guide: £122.438 + VAT

Fisher 34 - 34ft 4in

The Fisher 34. Over 100 Fisher 34's have been built since her introduction into the range in 1978. Built with all the virtues and traditional features of the original Fisher concept, the 34 has evolved in design over the years to the modern version of the MK III sloop built today.

With the sloop rig, double doors open into the cockpit to create a spacious feel. The traditional ketch rig is available as an option. The 34 can sleep up to 6 comfortably. The spacious forecabin has two single length berths with a double berth infill panel. The double aft quarter cabin is set under the wheelhouse, again with a full length double berth.

The U shaped saloon seating area converts to another double berth for additional space if required. The saloon area is truly spacious with plenty of stowage and a full dinette /seating area. Large opening portholes create a light and airy interior.

The galley on the starboard side has generous work surfaces with stainless steel sinks, top opening ice box which can convert to an optional refrigerator and a two burner cooker with both grill and oven.

Aft and to port is a modern spacious heads compartment with shower, all designed for easy care. The wheelhouse, as with all Fishers, is a distinctive and practical feature of the 34. The internal helm position provides a safe and warm environment to sail in poor weather or out of season. Under sail, the Fisher 34 handles beautifully, better in fact than many 'conventional' yachts but when power is needed there's more than sufficient in the 75 h.p. engine.

Specification

LOA 34ft 4in
LWL 29ft 10in
Beam 11ft 3in
Draft 4ft 11in
Displacement 11.5 tons
Ballast weight 4.75 tons
Sail area: Main 270 sq ft
Furling Genoa 360f sq ft

Contact:
Northshore Yachts Ltd
Itchenor, Chichester
West Sussex, PO20 7AY
Tel: 01243 512611
email: sales@northshore.co.uk
www.northshore.co.uk

Price guide: £142.890 + VAT

73

Dufour 34 - 34ft 9in

The Dufour 34 was voted unanimously as European Yacht of the Year in 2003 in the 10 to 12m category. This title was awarded by a panel of 11 editors of European yachting magazines from the UK, Norway, Sweden, Denmark, Germany, France, Switzerland, Austria, Greece, Italy and Spain.

The boat also impresses down below. She offers 6 people the pleasure of living on board as pleasantly at sea as in harbour. She features an impressive navigation area, with storage space behind the navigator. The galley is compact and has a synthetic stone worktop. There are opening ports over the galley and the chart table. The saloon is large, with attractive wood panelling and plenty of stowage, probably better than average. There are two closed lockers with louvre slats and bookcases. There are well-positioned handrails everywhere. The heads compartment and is fitted out with a moulded lining including basin and stowage units. There is a large wet weather locker behind the toilet itself. The shower sump has an electric drain.

The optional cabin arrangements are shown below. The forecabin has plenty of room, but the height is limited. The Dufour 34 is a performance yacht, and is said to be delightful to handle, being quick and responsive. The interior is practical, particularly for offshore conditions.

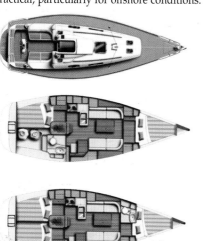

Specification

LOA: 33ft 9in / 10.30m
LWL: 29ft 11in / 8.9m
Beam: 11ft 5in / 3.50m
Draught:
Standard: 4ft 7in / 1.43m
Deep: 6ft 4in / 1.95m
Displacement:
10,340lbs / 4,690kg
Ballast ratio: 32%
Water: 58 gal / 265 litres
Fuel: 22 gal / 100 litres
Berths: 6

CE category: A (Ocean)

Contact:
Portfolio Marine
Beacon Quay
Torquay
Devon TQ1 2BG
Tel: 01803 380506
Fax: 01803 380507
Email: info@portfolio-marine
www.portfolio-marine.co.uk

Price guide: £62.723 + VAT

Etap 34s - 34ft 10in

The ETAP 34s has a stylishly modern interior finish of mahogany treated with three coats of waterproof acrylic varnish. All furnishings have solid mahogany frames, with co-ordinated sofa cushions and curtains. The floorboards are of maintenance free laminate with beech edging. Stainless steel inspection hatches provide easy access to the keel bolts and sea valves etc.

The companionway has four curved aluminum treads coated with a nonslip finish. Headroom in the companionway area is 190cm. The saloon contains two long sofas (each 2 m) which can be used as berths. A large table with two drop leaves and stowage for five bottles is located in the centre of the saloon. Extra stowage space is provided under the starboard sofa and a 170 litre potable water tank is located under the port side sofa. The galley has a gimballed 2-burner gas oven. Worksurfaces are finished in solid Corian. An insulated 651t refrigerator is provided.

A 97 x 58cm chart table is located on the starboard side. The front cabin has an asymmetric double berth and closable lockers are fitted along the hull sides. The aft cabin has a double skipper's berth 205 x 158cm. Ample headroom is provided under the cockpit floor. The heads compartment has a traditional marine toilet. The washbasin is fitted with a shower head and is fed by a pressurized cold water supply. Headroom is 190cm.

Specification

LOA: 31ft 5in / 9.60m
LWL: 27ft 11in / 8.52m
Beam: 10ft 9in / 3.30m
Draught: Deep keel: 6ft 1in
Displacement:
Deep keel:11013lbs
Sail area:
Main: 294 sq ft / 27.3sq m
Spinnaker: 721sq ft / 67 sq m
Engine: 15hp

Contact:
Kiss Marine Solent Ltd
The Boatyard
Hythe Marina
Hythe, Hants SO45 6DX
Tel: 02380 840 300
Fax: 02380 840 700

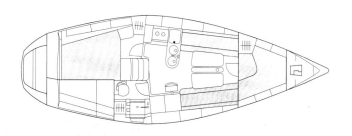

Hunter Mystery 35 - 35ft 2in

The Hunter Mystery 35 is a Category A Ocean cruiser. She has a long counter stern, gentle sheer and spoon bow. She reminds us with her spoon bow, low topsides, long cockpit and afterdeck, of the yachts of the 1940s and 50s. Inside she is very much of today. She has accommodation for seven adults. The builders allow for the customers choice of colour-cordinated interiors, and she gives a general feeling of comfort and quiet luxury. The interior is finished in cherry wood and the upholstery is deeply cushioned. The backrest of the port settee hinges up to form the pilot berth which can comfortably sleep an extra adult. The navigation table is large enough to take an Admiralty folio chart and is well positioned, sitting to starboard of the companionway. The saloon has a large table with a top-loading drinks cabinet and locker. The two leaves have high fiddles. The bunks have large lined storage bins.

The galley has made much of the available space, with good work surfaces, stowage and cooker installation. The heads compartment has the best headroom in the boat (6ft 2in). It contains a wet locker, washbasin, shower tray and good ventillation from two opening ports. The forecabin has good headroom (5ft 11in). Her beam allows no space for an aft cabin but there is room for a single quarter berth. She is a well designed boat for offshore work.

Specification

LOA: 35ft / 10.67m
LWL: 24ft 9in / 7.6m
Beam: 9ft 11in / 3.02m
Draught: 5ft 11in / 1.81m
Displacement: 10,000lbs / 4,5
Sail area: 576sq ft / 53.51 sq m
Berths: 5/6
Capacities:
Water: 33 gal / 150 litres
Fuel: 19.8 gal / 90 litres
CE category: A (Ocean)

Contact:
Select Yachts
Rock, Wadebridge,
Cornwall PL27 6NT
Tel: 01208 862666
email: Info@selectyachts.co
www.SELECTYACHTS.co.uk

Price guide: £89.693 inc VA

Jeanneau Sun Odyssey 35 - 35ft 3in

The Jeanneau's 'Sun' designation was first seen in 1980 with the Sun Fizz 40. Nowadays the brand is further divided into the cruising 'Odysseys' and the performance-orientated 'Sun Fasts'.

Inside the boat there is a secure companionway with dished steps. The saloon is large with plenty of grabrails. The interior is finished with a dark teak veneer which contrasts well with the vinyl panelled headliners, giving a light and modern ambiance. The saloon table can be expanded to seat six or more and can be raised to the deckhead. It can also be dropped down to form a double berth. The chart table is a reasonable size which slides on runners and it has a navigator's seat which is created with an infill board joined to the settee. Storage space for charts is available on a shelf. The L-shaped galley is large and there are two sinks with hot and cold water. There is a two burner cooker/oven. There is also a hatch to a large well-insulated icebox.

The heads compartment has a generous amount of space. Headroom is 6ft 2in (1.89cm), and the showering space is large. There is an access door to a vast amount of stowage space in the after end of the heads. The standard boat comes with a single aft cabin but a two cabin version is also available. Headroom in the forecabin is 6ft (1.83m). The bunk is well proportioned at 6ft 8in long (2.06m) by 4ft 9in (1.50m) wide. The space under the bunk is taken up by the water tank but there is plenty of space up forward.

Specification

LOA: 34ft 2in / 10.42m
LWL: 31ft 10in / 9.74m
Beam: 11ft 5in / 3.49m
Draught:
Standard: 6ft 0in / 1.85m
Displacement:
11.464lbs / 5.200kg
Sail area: 646 sq ft / 60 sq m
Berths: 5-9
Capacity:
Water: 68gal / 310ltr
Fuel: 28gal / 130ltr
Berths: 4/6
Headroom: 6ft 5in / 1.96m
Engine: Volvo 2030
CE Category: A

Contact:
Sea Ventures
Hamble Point Marina
Southampton SO31 4JD
Tel: 023 8045 5333
Fax: 023 8045 4966

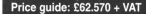

Price guide: £62.570 + VAT

Rustler 36 - *35ft 4in*

The Rustler 36 was designed by Kim Holman. All internal joinery is hand crafted in solid wood and teak faced ply. The cabin sole is of decorative marine ply. Lockers are edged with solid teak to give a rich and luxurious finish. Lockers above th waterline are lined whilst the bilges and remaining lockers, are finished in white gelcoat. Under berth lockers are sealed from the bilge.

In the saloon there is a shaped settee to port with double berth conversion. There is a settee berth to starboard. The central table, has room for six with full access around, even when fully extended and includes bottle stowage within. There are lockers to port and shelving to starboard behind the settees.

The galley has a functional U shape for safe use at sea. There is a fully gimballed cooker with oven and grill. An insulated icebox with Supercool electric refrigeration unit. Generous workspace with an extra lift-up flap.

The heads is a GRP self-contained white moulded compartment. Large amount of storage space. Full standing headroom, Fixed coachroof window with Lewmar Ocean hatch cover. Pressurised hot and cold water with shower. Shower tray electrically pumped out overboard

There is an athwartships chart table large enough for folded Admiralty charts. Large amount of chart stowage is accessed through the lift-up table top. Customised switch panel with circuit breakers.

In the forecabin there is full headroom and dressing space, two single berths which convert into a double when using infill, vanity unit, full length shelves port and starboard, split cushions to give access to locker space below berths, Lewmar Ocean hatch and Dorade vent. The practical sea going single quarter-berth with lee board and wet locker, converts to a double berth in harbour by dropping the lee board and setting the infill cushion.

In 1992 a Rustler 36 was bought by HRH The Princess Royal.

Specification

LOA: 35ft 4in / 10.77m
LWL: 26ft 11in / 8.08m
Beam: 11ft 11in / 3.35m
Draft: 5ft 6in / 1.67m
Ballast: 3.4 tons / 3.456 kg
Displacement: 7.5 tons / 7.623 kg
Sail Area:
Main: 258 sq ft / 24sq m
No 1 Genoa: 435 sq ft / 40.4 sq m
No 2 Genoa: 341 sq ff / 31.7 sq m
No 1 Jib: 209 sq ff / 19.5 sq m
Engine: Beta Marine 28 hp

Contact:
Rustler Yachts Ltd
Maritime Buildings
Falmouth Road
Falmouth
Cornwall TRiO BAD
Tel: 01326 310120
Fax: 013263i4092
Email: info@rustleryachts.com
www.rustleryachts.com

Price guide: £114.450

Nordship 35 - 35ft 5in

Nordship 35DS is a deck saloon cruising yacht with large T shaped cockpit, hand laid teak deck, and integral bathing platform. Both boat and equipment are built according to EU guidelines for CE Certification class A, Ocean.

The interior is well lit by numerous portlights and hatches. The standard specification of the boat includes hand laid teak side decks, cockpit sole and seating, sprayhood, stainless steel bowsprit with teak grating, hinged boarding ladder with 12KG Bruce anchor and 50 metre chain. There are cave lockers in the cockpit coaming, removable helm seats and a spinnaker boom mounted on mast. Autohelm ST60 Tridata, log/echo sounder, 2 burner cooker with oven, shower with electric pump out in heads, automatic bilge pump, stainless steel holding tank, 3 fire extinguishers.

The deck saloon is spacious and an owner can specify an open plan aft cabin to increase the sense of space. There is room for four people to sit in comfort on the 7ft 6in settee. A chart table is opposite 2ft 6in x 2ft. The galley is down a couple of steps and there is plenty of stowage and a two burner gimballed cooker. In addition there is a large 'fridge. The heads compartment has good hanging space for wet gear, the marine toilet faces inboard. The owners quarters are in the forecabin which has good headroom and space for two people to get changed in comfort. The aft double is a snug fit for two people although the bunk measures 6ft 3m. Stowage is good throughout the boat.

Specification

LOA: 35ft 5in / 10.80m
LWL: 28ft 6n / 9.32m
Beam: 11ft / 3.30m
Draught:
5ft 3in
Displacement: 13.404lbs / 6080kg
Sail area: 510 sq ft / 47.4 sq m
Capacity:
Water: 62.2gal / 280ltr
Fuel: 44gal / 200ltr
Berths: 5/6
Engine: Volvo MD 2030 28hp
CE Category: A

Contact:
North Sea Maritime Ltd
PO Box 5539
Southend on Sea
Essex SS1 3TE
Tel: 01702 584 821
Fax: 01702 584 821
Email: info@northseamaritime.com
www.northseamaritime.com

Price guide: £118.103

Legend 36 - 35ft 6in

The Legend 36 is an American boat and is a development of the very popular 356 model. Now named the 36 she has a wide beam, which is carried well aft to provide great space below. This space includes a cavenous sail locker which can swallow the asymetrical jib and a roll-up dinghy and still have room for more.

The large cockpit features a Whitlock™ steering system, fold-up tables and plenty of room to stretch out. An entertainment sized saloon is flanked by two private cabins. The saloon sole is in hardwood.

There is a well fitted-out galley, supplied with crockery, double stainless steel sinks, dual burners, a recessed rubbish bin, plentiful storage and a front loading refrigerator. There are accordion cabin blinds, carbon monoxide detectors and an automatic engine fire extinguisher.

The extra beam of the 36 is very evident in the aft cabin. It feels like a much larger boat. The heads compartment has a hot/cold pressurised water supply and is easy to clean. It contains a wash basin, shower unit, mirror and cupboard. The forecabin has a double berth with lockers to port and starboard. The 36 combines a lavishly comfortable interior with an easily managed performance hull. The boat provides good value for money.

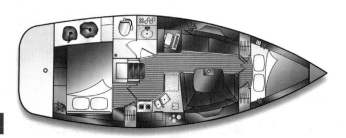

Specification

LOA: 35ft 6in / 10.82m
LWL: 30ft 7in / 9.32m
Beam: 12ft / 3.66m
Draught:
Shallow: 4ft 10in / 1.52m
Deep: 6ft 5in / 1.96m
Displacement: 13900lbs / 6318kg
Sail area: 721 sq ft / 66.98 sq m
Capacity:
Water: 75gal / 284ltr
Fuel: 38gal / 144ltr
Berths: 4/6
Headroom: 6ft 5in / 1.96m
Engine: Yanmar 27hp/20kw
CE Category: A

Contact:
Opal Marine,
Camper & Nicholsons Marina
Mumby Road, Gosport, Hants
PO12 1AH
Tel: 02392 583242
Fax: 02392 581028
www.opalmarine.co.uk

Price guide: £ on application

Southerly 110 - 35ft 6in

The Southerly 110 is the smallest of the Southerly fleet. The large saloon is very spacious and has generous seating with dinette facilities for six. This can convert to a double and a single berth for additional sleeping, if required.

The chart table is positioned within the raised pilot house to starboard, which provides good visibility. The interior styling of the Southerly 110 is finished to a very high standard with cherry joinery for a modern and warm feel. The large galley is a particular feature on a yacht of this size. Designed for comfortable living, there is good lighting for food preparation, ample work surface areas with stainless steel grab rail, and lots of storage space. Twin stainless steel sinks, an ice box with top access and a fully gimballed cooker with two burners, grill and oven are standard. The spacious aft cabin has a large double berth offset to starboard. There is plenty of storage including a mirrored vanity unit. A second door provides ensuite facilities.

The forecabin has a single berth to port that converts to a double for sleeping. An alternative layout with twin overlapping berths, shown below, is available as an option. Summing up the Southerly 110 features, she offers: a swing keel which enables a draught of 2ft 4in - 7ft 2in, twin rudders, accommodation for seven, spacious and light interior, raised pilot house, able to dry out in an upright position with a protected propeller, and a roomy aft cockpit with stern access.

Specification

LOA: 35ft 6ins / 10.82 m
LWL: 30ft 3in / 9.22 m
Beam: 11ft 10in / 3.57m
Draught: Keel up:
2ft 4in / 0.72m
Keel down:
7ft 2in / 2.18 m
Displacement:
15,016lbs / 6811 kg
Ballast weight:
4,455lbs / 2,205 kg
Keel weight:
2,310 lbs / 1.050 kg
Total ballast:
6,765 lbs / 3,255 kg
Sail area:
Mainsail:
264 sq ft / 22.53 sq m
Furling Genoa:
334 sq ft / 31.01 sq m
Tall rig option:
Mainsail:
290 sq ft / 27.00 sq m
Furling genoa:
316 sq ft / 29.40 sq m

Contact:
Northshore Yachts Limited
Itchenor, Chichester
West Sussex PO20 7AY
Tel: + 44 (0) 1243 510945
Fax: + 44 (0) 1243 511473
Email: sales@northshore.co.uk
website: www.northshore.co.uk

Price guide: £99.713 + VAT

Corsair 36 - 36ft

The Corsair 36 Trimaran is an American boat designed for the serious blue water cruiser. She features shallow draft with retractable daggerboard and rudder, aluminum rotating wing mast, carbon fibre bowsprit, and quality hardware.

The deck layout leads all control lines aft to the cockpit for ease of handling and control. The interior offers a functional spacious galley, pressurized hot and cold water, ample cabinet and storage space, curved settee with seating for six, head with vanity and sink and shower attachment. Forward is a spacious V berth with ample storage and lighting which sleeps two adults in unmatched comfort. Additional sleeping accommodations for two are in an under cockpit bunk or in a spacious aft cabin. Power is provided by a 15hp 4 stroke outboard with electric start. The standard sail plan includes a fully battened square top mainsail and jib with an optional asymmetrical spinnaker and screacher easily flown from the retractable carbon fibre bowsprit.

Specification

LOA: 36ft 0in / 11 m
LWL: 35ft 0in / 10.7 m
Beam: (overall) 25ft 7in / 7.8 m
Beam: (folded) 9ft 10in / 3 m
Mast: Length) 47ft 6in / 14.5 m
Auxiliary power:
15hp 4 stroke outboard

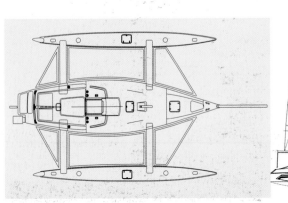

Dealer Information
MacGregor Yachts Int., Ltd.
Ponsharden,
Falmouth TR11 2SE
Cornwall, U.K.
Tel: 44 (01326) 379471
Fax: 44 (01326) 379472
email: info@macgregor.uk.com
www.macgregor.uk.com

Price guide: £ on applicati

Dufour Classic 36 - 36ft 1in

The Dufour 36 Classic is the best-selling boat in the Dufour range. Designed as a replacement for the Dufour 35 in 1999, the layout is based on two double cabins plus an option for three doubles with twin aft cabins.

The chart table is able to take a folded Admiralty chart, and there is a locker for pilot books. The galley which is linear is on the starboard side has a double-drainer sink and a large refrigerator, stowage is under the bench seat. The galley area is restricted if the twin aft cabin option is chosen. The heads compartment is a moulded GRP liner with a sink, toilet, locker and opening portlight. The saloon area has a good feeling of space. It is U shaped and has a comfortable bench type seat anda settee to port which continues around the forward bulkhead. Seating for six is comfortable with storage under the bench seat, plus a saloon cupboard and fiddled shelving. The twin after cabins have berths measuring 6ft 6in x 4ft. The fore cabin contains a double berth 6ft 6in x 3ft 9in. There is also room for a settee and hanging wardrobe. There is a very impressive use of space on a boat of these dimensions. This boat is very suitable for cross channel and longer trips in fair weather.

Specification

LOA: 36ft 1in / 11.02m
LWL: 30ft 1in / 9.18m
Beam: 12ft 4in / 3.77m
Draught: 5ft 1in / 1.80m
Shoal draught: 4ft 5in / 1.45m
Light displacement: 13,090lbs / 5.9 T
Keel weight: 3.528 lbs / 1.600 kg
Engine: 18/20hp
Fuel: 42 US gal / 160 lt
Fresh water: 90 US gal / 340 lt
Engine: 18/24hp
Sail area: 688 sq ft / 64 sq m
Berths: 7/8

CE category: A (Ocean)

Contact:
Portfolio Marine
Beacon Quay
Torquay
Devon TQ1 2BG
Tel: 01803 380506
Fax: 01803 380507
Email: info@portfoliomarine.co.uk
www.portfolio-marine.co.uk

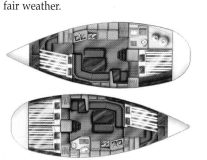

Price guide: £68.949 + VAT

Ovni 36 - 36ft 1in

The Ovni 36 is a multi chine lifting keel aluminium yacht with oak interior. Standard equipment includes : main sail, furling genoa, wheel steering, 40HP engine, electric anchor windlass, 1 aft cabin, 1 aft head, 1 forward cabin, manual lifting keel system, hydraulic rudder lifting system, battery charger and load distributor, holding tank, curtains.

The Ovni 36 standard version has 3 cabins and a single heads compartment. The boat is also available in a 2 cabin version with 1 heads compartment. In addition it is possible to semi-customise the interior of all Ovni yachts as the strength of the hull does not rely on the bulkheads for reinforcement. The navigation area has a chart table with plenty of stowage space. In the saloon there isa U shaped seating area. The galley is L shaped. The forward cabin has a double berth with lots of storage. See the website for further details: www.northseamaritime.com

Specification

LOA: 12.03 m
LWL: 9. m
Beam: 3.75 m
Draught: with centreboard down
With centreboard up: 0.55 m
Displacement:
7.500 kg
Sail Area:
Main: 27.5 m
Genoa: 41.5 m
CE category: A

Contact:
North Sea Maritime Ltd
PO Box 5539
Southend on Sea
Essex SS1 3TE
Tel/Fax: 01702 584 821
Email: info@northseamaritime.co
www.northseamaritime.com

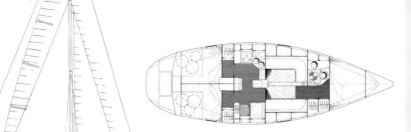

Price guide: £103.655 +

Starlight 35 Mk 2 - 36ft 1in

The Starlight 35 Mk2 has all interior woodwork in a choice of teak or American cherry-faced marine ply with a satin varnish finish, featuring a maple stripe in the door frames and in specific areas of the saloon and galley.

The saloon has settee berths port and starboard, lee cloths port and starboard saloon berths, shelves. lockers and bookcases outboard. The large saloon has drop-leaves and bottle storage. The galley is provided with a gimballed two-burner gas cooker with grill, oven and fiddles and pan clamps. There are 2 stainless steel sinks with pressurised hot and cold water supply and fresh-water foot pump. There is also a refrigerated ice box.

The navigation area has a chart table large enough to take a half admiralty chart, with ample stowage for charts and books. Instruments can be stored in the teak console.

In the forecabin there is a double berth, with insulated under berth stowage. There is full length shelving out-board and large shelf over the forward end, there is a wash basin with hot and cold supply, and a mirror on the bulkhead.

The heads compartment is aft and contains a marine WC and wash basin. Pressurised hot and cold water supply with shower with electric pump out. The aft cabin features a large double berth, hanging locker and seat. There is insulated under-bunk storage and a large full-length shelf with stowage bins along hull side, a mirror on the bulkhead, opening deck hatch, and a large opening port to cockpit.

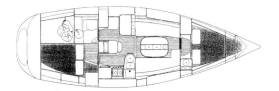

Specification

LOA: 36ft 1in / 11.00m
LWL: 28ft 8in / 8.75m
Beam: 11ft 6in / 3.51m
Draught:
Fin keel: 6ft 0in / 1.83m
Wing keel: 4ft 11in / 1.50m
Displacement: 15.227lbs / 6.907kg
Ballast: 5.600lbs / 2.540kg
Capacity:
Water: 45 imp gal / 205ltr
Fuel: 30 imp gal / 136ltr
Engine:
Beta Marine 28hp / 20.9kW
Sail area:
Main: 304sq ft / 28.20 sq m
Genoa: 447sq ft / 41.56 sq m
CE Category: A

Contact:
Rustler Yachts Ltd
Maritime Buildings
Falmouth Road
Falmouth
Cornwall TR10 8AD
Tel: 01326 310120
Fax: 01326 314092
Email: info@rustleryachts.co.
www.rustleryachts.com

Price guide: £124.500

Nauticat 35 - 36ft 3in

The Nauticat 35's Pilot house/Deck saloon distinguishes a Nauticat from other vessels. The visibility is unimpaired in all directions. The interior offers you both warm comfort and elegant taste. She has been designed for sailors who demand good sailing performance, but who would also like to have a comfortable and spacious pilothouse with an excellent view.

The forecabin has two berths with drawers and storage under the berths. There is a hatch overhead. The forward heads compartment has pressurised water, basin, marine pump type head and handshower, plus an overhead hatch. The aft heads has pressure water, basin and a handshower, mirror and an opening port. The straight galley provides ample counter space. There are double stainless steel sinks and a two burner gimballed gas stove with oven and flame guards, plus a pressurised water system. There is also a top-loading cool box. The extensive cabinetry contains plenty of drawers and lockers.

The helm station to starboard includes a large chart table with chart storage beneath the hinged top. Access to the engine room is through the pilothouse sole. The large raised U-shaped settee accommodates six people comfortably for dining or relaxing. The Owner's cabin is dominated by a double bunk on port side, a settee for two persons on starboard and a large lit wardrobe. There are drawers, storage under the berth, a door to the aft toilet and a full-length mirror.

Note: All Nauticats are custom-built and this suggested layout can be, and usually is, altered in subtle ways to suit individual owners.

Specification

LOA: 36ft 3in / 11.06.m
LWL: 29ft 8in / 9.05.m
Beam: 11ft 6in / 3.50.m
Draught: 5ft 5in or 5ft 11in / 1.65m or 1.80m
Displacement: approx. 16500 lbs / 7.5 tons
Headroom: 6ft 1in-6ft 5in / 1.84-1.
Ballast approx: 6000 lbs / 2.7 ton
Capacity: Fresh water: 103 gal / 4 Fuel: 73gal / 330.lt
Sails: (all sails are optional)
Sloop rig: 58.5 sq m
Main sail: 27.2 sq m
Genoa I: 40.5 sq m
Genoa II: 31.3 sq m
CE Category: A

Contact:
Nauticat (UK) Ltd
Mariners House
High Street
Hamble Southampton SO31 4JF
Tel: 02380 453900
Email: info@nauticatuk.co.uk

Price guide: £137.900

Catalina 36 mkII - 36ft 4in

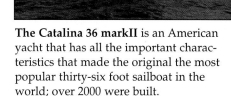

The Catalina 36 markII is an American yacht that has all the important characteristics that made the original the most popular thirty-six foot sailboat in the world; over 2000 were built.

The 36mk11 is built to be the same seakindly moderate displacement hull. The deck is the classic trunk cabin configuration designed by sailors, not stylists. The beautiful and functional aft cabin is complete with a large athwartship double berth, hanging locker and bureau. The owner's cabin forward is comfortable and well ventilated and has a private entrance to the head.

The Catalina 36 is renowned for its storage. The galley is a functional a functional U shape, with composite counter tops and sinks that are near the centreline for proper drainage underway. The large refrigerated ice box is aft and a dry food locker is forward. A gimballed, stainless steel LPG stove with oven is standard equipment. The main cabin can be arranged with a dinette or traditional table at your option.

Traditional table shown, a "U" shaped dinette is also available

Specification

LOA: 36ft 4in
LWL: 30ft 3in
Beam: 11ft 11in
Draught: Fin Keel 5ft 10in
Wing Keel: 4ft 5in
Ballast: Fin Keel: 6,000lbs.
Wing Keel: 6,600lbs.
Approximate Weight:
Fin Keel: 13,500lbs.
Wing Keel: 14,100lbs.
Engine: Diesel 4 cylinder 35 HP
Sail Area:
(100% foretriangle) 555 sq ft

Builder: Catalina Yachts USA
Contact: Windward Yachting,
Northney Marina
Northney Road,
Hayling Island, Hampshire
PO11 0NH
Tel: 0870 350 1920
Email: info@windwardyachting.co.uk
www.windwardyachting.co.uk

Feeling 36 - *36ft 5in*

Feeling 36. The Feeling 36 lifting keel offers two or three double cabins, with a large airy saloon, excellent chart table facing forwards and a good-sized galley and heads. The capacious starboard locker on the two cabin version can be accessed from the cockpit or via a door from the heads.

Feeling, world leaders in lift keel GRP yachts, are renowned for their innovative, large, light and airy cabins and superbly crafted joinery in beech and light cherry. Feeling yachts combine cruise anywhere versatility with excellent sailing and sea keeping performance. The entire range from 32 to 44 feet is designed to both offer fin or lift keel sailing giving unbeatable access to creeks, estuaries, harbours and even the French canal system, whilst still offering superb sailing performance.

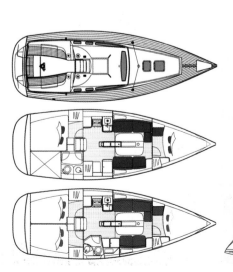

Specification

LOA: 36ft 5in
LWL: 35ft 5inin
Beam: 11ft 9in
Draught: 2ft 5in - 7ft 1in
Weight of lifting keel ballast: 2.380kg
Draught Fixed keel: 6ft 6in
Weight of keel: 1.975 kg
Sails area upwind: 68.40sq m

Contact:
Feeling Yachts Ltd
The Shipyard
Lymington
Hampshire SO41 3YL
Tel: 44 (0) 1590 647421
Fax: 44 (0) 1590 647446
Email: feelingyachts@berthon.co.uk
www.feelingyachts.com

Price guide: 110.000

Sweden 370 - *36ft 7in*

The Sweden 370 was introduced in 1993 by a builder who concentrates on high quality, producing between 25 - 30 boats a year.

The forward cabin has a double-berth with lots of stowage under. The moulded heads compartment is fitted between bulkheads. There is a shower drained by electric pump and a door both to forward cabin and the saloon. The saloon has a settee on both sides, a table with fixed mid section with storage and folding wings, cabinets and bookshelves above sofas on both sides. There is a L-shaped galley with Formica counter top 160 lt icebox in GRP with plexiglass dividers, drained to a separate sump. There is a gas stove with two burners and oven. There is a large navigation table with stowage and a moulded, detachable instrument panel for electronic equipment on hinges, separate chart stowage space above instrument-panel, and a navigation seat.

There is a large aft cabin with double berth on the starboard side, and a seat to port it also contains a wet locker and stowage space. There is a door to the main cabin, and shelves along hullsides, starboard and port.

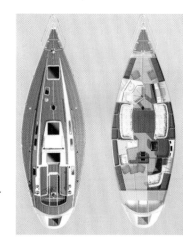

Specification

LOA: 36ft 7in / 1l,15m
LWL: 29ft 6in / 9,00m
Beam: 12ft 0in / 3,68m
Draft: 6ft 9in / 2,05m
Wingkeel: Option 5ft 7in / 1,70m
Mainsail: 334 sq ft / 31 sq m
Displacement:
15.2901bs / 6,950kg
Genoa: max 549 sq ft / 51 sq m
Ballast: (lead) 6050lbs / 2.750kg
Wingkeel: (Optional)
5ft 7in / 1.70m
Roller genoa:
135% 474 sq ft / 44 sq m
Spinnaker:
1227 sq ft / 115sq m

Contact: Sweden Yachts
Box 80, Angsv 5
S-44421 Stenungsund
Sweden
Tel: 00 46 303 77 06 40
Fax: 00 46 303 88 61 0
www.swedenyachts.se
Email: info@swedenyachts.se

Price guide: £ POA.

Nauticat 37 - *36ft 8in*

The **Nauticat 37** is a pilot house yacht. From the cockpit companionway there are steps, which lead down to the owners cabin. The helm to starboard includes a navigation table with a drawer for charts there is ample storage on the starboard side. The switchboard includes automatic fuses and one push button for the signal horn. Access to the engine room is through the pilothouse sole. The large raised U-shaped settee accommodates six people comfortably, storage is under the settee.

The boat has a forecabin with two V berths, with a large full-length illuminated hanging locker and shelves in the rear. There is a large hatch overhead. The forward heads are located by the fwd cabin. It has pressurised water, a basin, and a marine pump type head and shower, there is storage behind and underneath the basin. On the ceiling there is an overhead hatch and a Dorade vent. The guest cabin (optional) is located on the port side of the yacht. It has a comfortable wide berth. There is an openable skylight hatch for light and ventilation and a full height wardrobe. The aft heads compartment (optional) has pressurised water, a basin, and a handshower. The toilet is supplied with marine pump type head, holding tank and a pumpout fitting on deck. The galley has a large stainless steel double sink a two burner gimballed gas stove with an oven and flame guards. A pressurised water system is provided. There is also a toploading refrigerator 100 lt. The galley has also two opening hatches and a Dorade vent.

The owner's cabin is dominated by a wide centre double bunk. On both sides there are large lighted wardrobes. Drawers and storage are located under the berth. There are shelves beside the bed. Cabinets are located on starboard side. The reading lights are above the bunk and overhead lights are situated on the ceiling. On the port side there is a vanity desk with mirror. There are four windows in the cabin, which all are openable and two windows in the stern. The cabin also has one vent.

Note: All Nauticats are custom-built and this suggested layout can be, and usually is, altered in subtle ways to suit individual owners.

Specification

LOA: 36ft.8in / 11.23 m
LWL: 33ft.1in / 10.10 m
Beam: 11ft. 9in / 3.65 m
Draught: 6ft. 07in /
1.85 m
Displacement:
approx. 19200 lbs / 8.7 ton
Headroom:
from 6ft - 6ft 6in / 1.82 - 1.8
Ballast: 6700 lbs / 3 tons
Capacity:
Fresh water: 96 gal / 440lt
Fuel: approx. 88 gal / 350lt
Sails: (all sails are optional
Total sail area: 75.0 sq m
CE category: A

Contact:
Nauticat (UK) Ltd
Mariners House
High Street
Hamble Southampton SO3
Tel: 02380 453900
Email: info@nauticatuk.co.

Price guide: £169.900

Beneteau Océanis Clipper 373 - 36ft 9in

The Clipper 373 comes in alternative 2 or 3 cabin versions. They share the same forward cabin, both have a forward facing chart table and a large panoramic hatch above the saloon. The designers have managed to blend volume, comfort, and high performance. The slender hull, well-balanced sail plan and the standard deep keel, enhance upwind performance, give directional stability and helm balance when heeled. The new split-level deck layout of the Océanis 373 combines greater headroom with an elegant interior. The cunningly designed removable helmsman's seat simplifies access to the bathing platform, whilst the removable door step makes the companionway very practical. Unrivalled circulation is possible thanks to the brand-new, patented, steering wheel, which can be swivelled out of the way to clear the cockpit, still leaving all the instruments on the helm pedestal.

Beneteau is the largest yacht building company in the world. Over 4,000 yachts are built every year in seven factories. The latest design developments of the Océanis range concentrate on headroom, light and ventilation.

Specification

LOA: 11.25 m
Hull Length: 11 m
Beam: 3.75 m
Light displacement: (approx.) 6600 kg
Draught:
Standard deep: 1,90m
Shallow: 1,55m
Air draught: 15.50m
Sail Area: (sq m) 67
Max Engine Power: (Hp) 40
Fuel tank capacity: 115 lt
Water tank: 360lt
CE Certification: A8/B8/C12 (pending ratification)

Contact:
Ancasta International Boat Sales
Port Hamble
Satchel Lane
Hamble
Southampton SO31 4QD
Tel: 023 80 450 026
Email: Beneteau@ ancasta.co.uk
www.ancasta.com

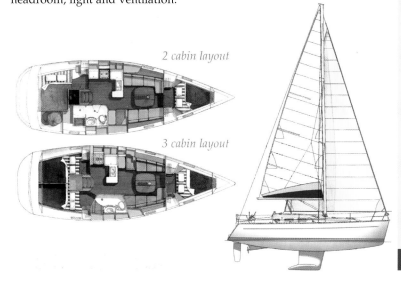

2 cabin layout

3 cabin layout

Price guide: £96.500

91

Etap 37s - 36ft 11in

The **ETAP 37s** has a modern interior finish in solid cherrywood and cherrywood laminate with an extra-hard surface. All furnishings have solid cherrywood frames, and the floorboards are of maintenance free laminate with beech edging.

Stainless steel inspection hatches provide easy access to the keel bolts and sea valves etc. The companionway has three curved aluminum treads coated with a nonslip finish. Headroom in the companionway area is 199cm. The saloon contains two long sofas (each 2m) which can be used as berths. A large table with two drop leaves and stowage for five bottles is located in the centre of the saloon. The panoramic window allows an ample supply of light into the saloon.

The galley has a gimballed 2-burner gas oven. Underneath the worktop there is a large stowage capacity with cutlery drawer and bin-bag holder. Worksurfaces are finished in solid Corian. An insulated 120lt refrigerated coolbox is provided.

A 61 x 77cm chart table is located on the starboard side. The front cabin has a double berth and a sofa. Closable lockers are fitted along the hull sides. Headroom is 5ft 11in.

The aft cabin has a double skipper's berth 2m x 1.5m. Headroom is 6ft 5in. The heads compartment has a traditional marine toilet. The washbasin is fitted with a shower head and is fed by a pressurized cold water supply. Headroom is 6ft 5in.

Specification

LOA: 36ft 11in / 11.26m
LWL: 32ft 6in / 9.90m
Beam: 12ft 7½in / 3.85m
Draught: 6ft 5in - 4ft 5in / 1.95 - 1.35m
Displacement:
14,427lb - 13.987lb / 6.550 - 6.350kg
Sail area:
Mainsail: 389 sq ft / 36.10sq m
Genoa: 427sq ft / 39.70 sq m
Engine: 28hp
CE Category: A

Contact:
Kiss Marine Solent Ltd
The Boatyard
Hythe Marina
Hythe, Hants SO45 6DX
Tel: 02380 840 300
Fax: 02380 840 700

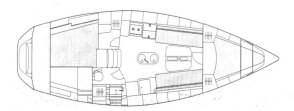

Price guide: £90.500 + VAT

Hanse 371 - 36ft 11in

The Hanse 371 is a value for money performance cruiser. Built in what used to be East Germany, these boats are fast, aimed at people who like to cruise, but if possible with a good turn of speed. With government grants and the reunification of Germany, the boats were also available at unbelievably low prices.

She is ideal for 2-6 member crews. The stylish saloon uses red-stained mahogany trim, finished in high gloss varnish, contrasted with white-painted bulkheads. The only interior mouldings are used in the forecabin aft cabin and heads. Otherwise the joinery is bonded to the hull, reinforced with frames and stringers. Overhead in the saloon there are removable panels. The L-shaped galley has a large ice-box and a two burner gas stove with an oven. There is a stainless steel double sink.

The saloon has a big U-shaped sofa with a table to starboard and two separate seats on the other side. The chart table has seating both forward and aft.

The forward cabin has a large double berth with hanging lockers. The aft cabin has a large double berth and space on the starboard side for either sail storage or an optional second cabin. Engine access is good.

Specification

LOA: 36ft 11in / 11.25m
LWL: 32ft 4in / 9.85m
Beam: 11ft 9in (3.59m)
Draught: Standard fin: 6ft 6in / 1.98m
Shallow fin: 5ft 6in / 1.69m
Centreplate: 3ft 5in /1 .05m
Displacement: 13,117lb / 5,950kg
Ballast: 4,950lb / 2,245kg
Sail area: (main and 100% foretriangle)
717sq ft / 66.61 sq m
Engine: Yanmar 3GM, 29hp
Headroom: 6ft 5in / 1.96m
Designer: Judel/Vrolijk
CE category: A

Contact: Hanse Yachts UK Ltd,
Chandlery Building Hamble Point Marina
Hamble Southampton S031 4NB
Tel: 02380 457008
Fax: 02380 458712
email: south@hanseyachts.co.uk
website: www. hanseyachts.co.uk

Price guide: £84.990 inc VAT

93

Elan 37 - 37ft

The Elan 37 is designed by New Zealander Rob Humphreys. The boat has a saloon with 1.9m headroom. There is a large ergonomically designed U-shaped settee with cushions and backrests on the starboard side and a centreline settee on the port side. There is a large folding saloon table which can also be an auxiliary double bunk as an option. There are lockers and shelves on both sides.

The forward cabin has a headroom of 1.78m. There is a double berth with storage under. There are two large hanging lockers. There are two aft cabins with double berths in each, and both have headroom of 1.9m. They have large hanging lockers.

The galley has a headroom of 1.8m. It has an L-shaped working top. The cooker is gimballed with 2 rings and an oven. There is a 12v refrigerator, and the double sink has a pressurized water system.

The navigation station has a chart table 70 x 60cm. The navigator's seat has storage under. There are bookshelves, lockers and drawers. There is a panel for navigation instruments with a voltmeter for batteries, fresh water and fuel.

The head has a wash basin with a pressurized water tap. The headroom is 1.8m. There are stowage lockers under the sink with access to the seacocks, and a wet locker with drainage to the central bilge which is behind the loo. The engine is easily accessible from all sides.

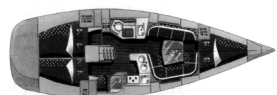

Specification

LOA: 11.33 m
Hull length: 11.16 m
LWL: 9.77 m
Beam: 3.65 m
Draught: 2.05 m / 2.30 m
Ballast: 2290 kg / 2190kg
Weight: 5900 kg
Engine: 29 HP
Water capacity: 200 lt
Fuel capacity: 125 lt
Mainsail: 37.40 sq m
Genoa: 43.00 sq m
Spinnaker: 108.1sq m
CE category A

Contact:
Elan Yacht Sales UK Ltd
Swanwick Marina
Swanwick
Southampton SO31 1ZL
Tel: 01489 885000
Fax: 01489 885509
email: sales@elanyachts.com

Price guide: £93.840 inc VAT

Fisher 37 - *37ft*

The Fisher 37 is the epitome of the large, powerful motor sailer. Over 140 have been built since her introduction in 1973. Over this period the interior layout and rig have evolved into what many owners today would say is the best motor sailer of its type.

Under sail, or powered by her massive 100 h.p. engine, this boat will take you safely and in comfort to any destination around the world. Fisher 37s have sailed more miles than any other in the range and her distinctive profile will be found in many of the oceans around the world, from the Arctic to the Antarctic. The sail plan has been well refined over the years and today the cutter ketch rig is standard, with bowsprit, giving powerful performance yet still being easy to manage.

Below deck the saloon and cabin areas are extensive. The 37 can sleep up to six with two full length single berths in the forecabin and a large double berth in the aft quarter. In the saloon the settee converts easily to a double berth when extra sleeping area is required. The wheelhouse provides much more than extra working space. There is a full length settee on the starboard side with stowages beneath it. To port there is a wet locker, settee and chart table. The whole wheelhouse area creates a second saloon with excellent all round visibility.

With the Fisher 37 an owner can be confident that every design detail has been developed over the years to create a yacht that can virtually be all things to all people — a pleasure to sail, powerful under motor, a long distance cruiser, or a comfortable liveaboard permanent home.

Specification

LOA: 42ft 6in
LWL: 37ft 0in
Beam: 12ft 0in
Draught: 5ft 3in
Displacement: 14 tons
Ballast weight: 6 tons
Sail areas:
Main: 265 sq ft
Furling Genoa: 443 sq ft
Staysail: 136 sq ft

Contact:
Northshore Yachts Ltd
Itchenor, Chichester
West Sussex, PO20 7AY
Tel: 01243 512611
email: sales@northshore.co.uk
www.northshore.co.uk

Price guide: £189.137 + VAT

Southerly 115 Series IV - 37ft

The **Southerly 115 series IV** has a deep draft of 2.48m (8'2")
with the keel lowered, this gives precise directional stability for
fast blue water passages. At the 'touch of a button' the swing
keel can be raised to give a shallow draft of just 0.71m (2'4"),
allowing you to explore shallow lagoons and inland waterways,
reaching places denied to most yachts. Since the original
Southerly 115 series l was introduced into the Southerly range
in 1983, she has outrivalled many yachts of her size.

The large saloon has dinette seating for six people. It can be
converted to a double berth and a single berth if required.
The galley has good lighting and views through the pilot
house windows. There are twin sinks, a top loading ice box
and a fully gimballed cooker, plus lots of storage.

The two large cabins have plenty of storage and ample headroom. The aft cabin has a large double bed. The forecabin has
twin overlapping berths with cupboards above and storage below.
The heads compartment is to starboardof thge companionway.
There is a shower, washbasin with pressurised hot and cold water.

The new twin rudder configuration, together with increased mainsail area provides
outstanding sailing performance and improved handling.

Specification

Length 37ft 0in
Waterline 29ft 2in
Beam 12ft 1in
Draught 2ft 4in - 8ft 2in
Displacement 4,750lb
Keel up: 2ft 4in
Keel down: 8ft 2in
Sail area 280 sq ft
Furling Main: 288 sq ft
Furling Genoa: 375 sq ft
Cruising Chute:
(Optional) 746 sq ft
Engine Yanmar 40hp

Contact:
Northshore Yachts Limited
Itchenor, Chichester,
West Sussex PO20 7AY
Tel: + 44 (0) 1243 510945
Fax: + 44 (0) 1243 511473
Email: sales@northshore.co.uk website:
www.northshore.co.uk

Price guide: £136.061 + VAT

Hallberg Rassy 37 - 37ft 2in

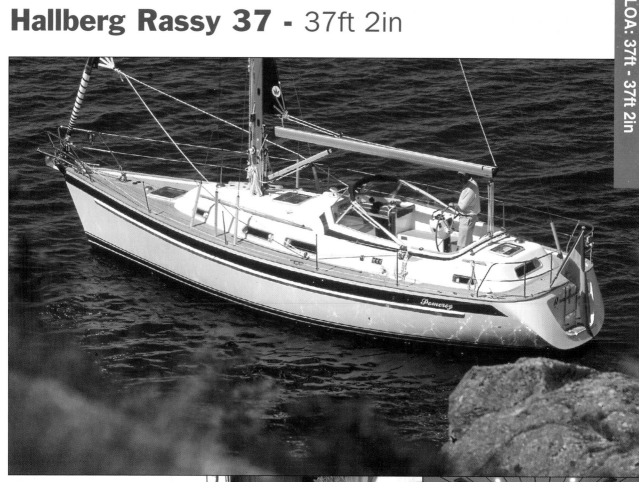

The Hallberg Rassy 37 is typical of what has become recognised as the Swedish style of cruising yachts. All the interior woodwork is in mahogany with a light matt silk finish.

The saloon has comfortable seating with an L-shaped sofa on the port side. The backrests are hinged so that the whole width of the berth can be used for sleeping. Headroom is 1.92m. The galley has a large work top with a fiddle all round. The double sink is extra deep. There is a two burner gas cooker with oven, and there is plenty of space for storage. The heads compartment is furnished with a china wash basin, teak grating and a shower unit. A cupboard and mirror are provided. The forward cabin has plenty of room for free movement. There are two generous berths with ample storage above and below with hanging lockers.

The navigation area has a spacious chart table and seat, and there are drawers and instrument storage. The aft cabin has a hanging locker on starboard and two comfortable berths. There is stowage room below and above, and a seat between the berths.

Specification

LOA: 37ft 2in / 11.32 m
Hull length: 33ft 6in / 11.16 m
LWL: 33ft 6in / 10.20 m
Beam: 11ft 8in / 3.55 m
Draught: 6ft 3in / 1.90 m
Displacement: 16.500lbs / 7.5t
Lead keel: 7.100lbs / 3.5t
Engine: Volvo Penta D2-55
Water capacity:
107 US gals / 400 lt
Fuel capacity:
91 US gals / 340 lt
Sail area:
744 sq ft / 69.1 sq m
Category CE A

Contact:
Transworld Yachts Ltd
Hamble Point Marina, School Lane, Hamble SO31 4JD
Tel: 023 80 456069
Fax: 023 80 456406
Email: enq@transworld-yachts.co.uk
www.transworld-yachts.co.uk

Price guide: £136.300 + VAT

Malo 36 - *37ft 3in*

The Malo 36, has a spacious saloon with sofa on starboard side and U-sofa on port side. The table has a flap towards the gangway. The back cushions are detachable when extra berths are required. There are various handrails, and headroom is 1.93 m. An L-shaped galley with double bowl sink with hot and cold pressurized water. The stove has two burners and an oven; it is electrically lit and has gimballed suspension, and there is a well-insulated refrigeration box (80lt). There is full headroom in the entire galley.

The navigation area is on starboard forward of the head. There is a large navigation table with drawers and room for charts.

The head is centrally placed, close to the companionway on the starboard side. The water mixer with hot and cold water is retractable. The shower tray empties via the electric drainage pump. The toilet connects with a holding tank that can either be emptied directly into the sea or pumped out through a connection on deck

The aft cabin consists of a double berth and contains ample stowing space. Two opening port lights one of which in the cockpit side, allowing ventilation. The forward cabin has a large full-length double berth and ample stowing space. There is a seat inboard of the lockers. Two opening port lights, a skylight and a dorade ventilator provide a light and well-ventilated cabin The skylight also serves as emergency exit. There is a ceiling light plus two reading lights.

Specification

LOA: 37ft 3in / 11.35m
LWL: 31ft 0in / 9.45m
Beam: 11ft 5in / 3.48m
Draught: 5ft 10 1/2in - 1.79m
Displacement: 16.976lbs / 7.7ton
Ballast: 6.834lbs / 3.1ton
Main sail: 333.7 sq ft / 31 sq m
Engine: Yanmar 40hp / 29.4kW
Water: 106 US gals / 400 lts
Fuel: 62 US gals / 235 lts

Contact:
Nordic Marine
Salterns Marina
Lilliput
Poole
BH14 8JR
Tel: 01202 700089
Fax: 01202 709072

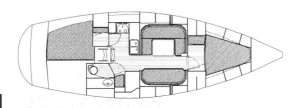

Price guide: £157.000

Jeanneau Sun Odyssey 37 - 37ft 4in

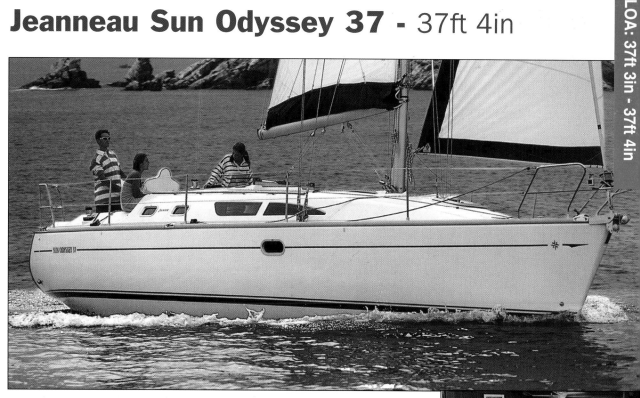

Sun Odyssey 37, designed by Jacques Fauroux, this yacht combines style, performance and comfort, typified by the smooth roof design and the new deck layout. The helmseats set out to the cockpit coamings provide the ideal position for steering. On the performance side, the keel/ballast ratio improves sailing stability, and the generous sail area keeps the boat moving well under all conditions. This new model is available with two interior layouts.

In the 2 cabin version, the layout is arranged around a saloon with an L shaped galley and a traditional chart table to port along with a very large washroom, while to starboard there is a comfortable aft cabin. The owner's cabin is located forward.

In the 3 cabin version, there is a classic layout of 2 aft cabins and the forward owner's cabin. The smooth lines incorporated in the deck layout show the latest in modern yacht design.

Positioning the helmsman on the cockpit coamings gives better visibility. There is greater stability from increased ballast. A larger sail area provides easy sailing in all conditions.

2 cabin version

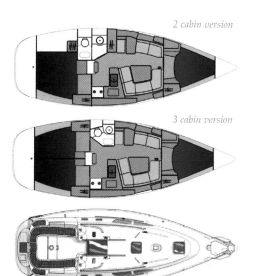

3 cabin version

Specifications

LOA: 37ft 4in / 11,40 m
LWL: 35ft 11in / 10,95 m
Beam: 12ft 1in / 3,70 m
Draught: Deep keel: 6ft 4in / 1,95 m
Shallow keel: 4ft 9in / 1,45 m
Displacement: 13779 lbs / 6250 kg
Cabins: 2 / 3
Engine: power maxi:
55 HP / 41 kW
Capacity:
Fuel: 36 US gal / 136 lt
Water: 85 US gal / 320 lt
Sail area:
729 sq ft / 67.8 sq m
CE Category: A

Contact:
Sea Ventures Ltd
Lymington Yacht Haven
Lymington
Hampshire SO41 3QD
Tel: 01590 672472
Fax: 01590 671924
Email: sales@sea-ventures.co.uk
www.sea-ventures.co.uk

Price guide: £71,749 + VAT

Najad 373 - *37ft 8in*

The Najad 373 is built in Sweden, where the builder has specialised in high-quality, medium to heavy displacement cruisers. The interior is handcrafted in unstained African mahogany, hand polished and varnished to a satin finish. Each boat is built to order, with the possibility of combining other fixed layout alternatives.

The spacious saloon has two settees surrounding the table, with bottle stowage in centre of table. The companionway steps can be removed for easy access to the engine room. The L-shaped galley is located amidships allowing free passage between the cockpit and saloon. There are stainless steel twin sinks, a pressure system for hot and cold fresh water, gimballed twin burner gas cooker with oven, well insulated ice box, 100 lt. incl. refrigeration unit, storage cupboards for plates, cups and glasses, cupboard under cooker for pans, etc, waste basket fitting under sink, and an opening porthole above the cooker.

The navigation area is located amidships. The table has stowage for charts and drawers. The heads compartment is amidships to starboard standing headroom approx. 1.85 m, with white laminated bulkheads. There is a large wash basin built into the worktop. The aft cabin has a double berth on the starboard side and a single berth on the port side. There are ample cupboards and a hanging wardrobe. The forward cabin has two wide full size berths, with a wardrobe and settee on the port side and cupboards on the starboard side.

Specification

LOA: 37ft 8in / 11.30 m
LWL: 32ft / 9.75 m
Beam: 12ft / 3.65 m
Draught: 6ft 3in / 1.90m
Alternative draught: 5ft 2in / 1.59 m
Displacement: 8,300 kg / 8.3 t
Bolted lead keel: 3,100 kg / 3.1 t
Headroom in saloon: 6ft 3in / 1.90m
Engine: Yanmar 4JH3-E
Capacity:
Water: 69 gal. / 315 lt
Hot water heater: 4.4 gal. / 20 lt
Fuel: approx. 40 gal. / 180 lt
Sail areas
Cruising:
705 sq.ft. / 65.5 m²

Contact:
Najad England, Hamble Point Marina
School Lane, Hamble
Southampton SO31 4NB
Tel: +44 2380 455 450
Fax: +44 2380 455 450
email: najadsales @btclick.com

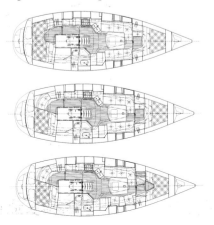

Price guide: 228.300 + VAT

Island Packet 370 - 37ft 10in

The Island Packet 370 is an American boat. It offers handcrafted cabinetry, rich oiled woods, and designer fabrics. Stowage throughout the yacht is exceptional, with 300 cubic feet of enclosed space available.

Numerous ports, hatches, and dorade vents provide the entire interior with abundant light and ventilation. The main saloon of the 370 provides for space and comfort. The large main dining table folds and stows against a bulkhead rack. A smaller removable table is available to add even more flexibility. There are full length port and starboard seating areas, and the port settee converts to a double berth. Generous storage is available under and outboard of the settees.

One of the notable features of the 370 is the versatility of the aft cabin. This multi-use area is unique. The desk area can be used as a vanity, a navigation station, or work station. The table top lifts to reveal a storage tray and a vanity mirror mounted on its underside. The open U design of the 370 galley has generous space, with plenty of storage available. An optional refrigerated drawer is offered and there are wide countertops with integral fiddles. The forward and aft cabins have large island berths, with plenty of elbow and headroom, hanging lockers and bureaus with deep drawers. In the heads compartment, a separate stall shower has folding acrylic doors and an electric sump drain. Ample storage is provided by the built-in vanity. Doors from both the forward state-room and the main saloon provide both utility and privacy.

Specification

LOA: 37ft 10in / 11.53m
LOD: 35ft 5in / 10.80 m
LWL: 31ft 0in / 9.45 m
Beam: 13ft 1in / 3.99m
Draught: 4ft 3in / 1.30m
Capacity
Fuel: 75 gal. / 284 lt
Water: 160 gal. / 605 lt
Headroom: 6ft 5in / 1.96 m
Engine: Diesel 56 hp / 42 kw
Sail areas:
Cutter rig: 814 sq.ft. / 75.62 sq.m
Sloop rig: 683 sq.ft. / 63.45 sq.m
Displacement: 21000 lbs. / 9,525 kg
Ballast: 8,400 lbs. / 3,810 kg
Cabins/Berths: 3/7

Contact:
Opal Marine,
Camper & Nicholsons Marina
Mumby Road, Gosport,
Hants PO12 1AH
Tel: 02392 583242
Fax: 02392 581028
www.opalmarine.co.uk

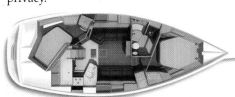

Broadblue Catamaran 38 - 38ft

Broadblue catamarans are rated to the highest level of the European Recreational Craft Directive: Category A (Ocean) and are built using Lloyds approved materials.

Both one-piece hull and deck mouldings are hand laid glassfibre, using powder-bound mat, biaxial woven rovings, isopthalic resin, and Kevlar reinforcement in high load areas. Below the waterline, the hulls are solid laminate, while the topsides and deck incorporate an end grain balsa core. The deck has an integrally moulded non - slip finish. The hull and deck join is fully bonded and protected by a substantial rubbing strake. Many of the structural bulkheads are of vacuum bagged foam core, and when the interior furniture is fully bonded in a light and stiff 'honeycomb' structure is created.

The Broadblue 38 is virtually unsinkable due to its water-tight bulkheads and buoyancy compartments fore and aft. The keels are integrally moulded and sealed off from the hulls forming a double bottom.

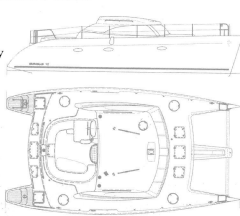

Specification

LOA: 38ft 0in
LWL: 34ft 6in
Beam: 17ft 5in
Draught: 3ft 3in
Air draught: 55ft 9in
Standard dry weight: 14330lb
Max recommended weight: 19290lb
Steering: Hydraulic
Engine: (FW Cooled)
2 x 20hp diesel
Battery capacity:
2 x 80 & 2 x 100 amp
Fuel tank: 68 gal
Water tank: 88 gal
Mainsail area: 276 sq ft
Genoa area: 417 sq ft
Cruising chute area: 1075 sq ft

Contact: Broadblue Catamarans (Sales) Ltd, Sea Lake Road, Oulton Broad, Suffolk NR32 3LQ
Tel: 01502 518002
email: sails@broadblue.co.uk
www.broadblue.co.uk

Price guide: £151.500 + VAT

Nordship 38 - 38ft

The Nordship 38DSC is a centre cockpit yacht, which means there is great scope to provide space for very large aft cabins.

Although she has a relatively narrow stern, the design provides 6ft (1.83m) headroom and a king-size double berth, a good hanging locker, plenty of stowage, two opening ports, an overhead hatch, and a window on each side.

Going forward, there is a 'lobby' to starboard between the after cabin and the saloon - a pair of seats (with shelving above and a heater below). This is separated by a locker which is removable to create an extra berth. It's an ideal place to sit down quietly for a tranquil moment. Opposite this space is the door to the walk-in locker - which, if not needed for stowage, can be converted to a second heads/shower. Opposite the galley, the main heads is a spacious compartment with a separate shower stall.

Amidships, the nav table is to starboard with duplicated controls. Further details include ventilated bunk tops, all-wood drawers and neatly-fitted joinery. The Nordship 38 is a blend of Scandinavian quality, and plenty of imagination.

Specification

LOA: 38ft 0in / 11.60 m
LWL: 32ft 0in / 9.75 m
Beam: 12ft 0in / 3.65 m
Draught: 5ft 10in / 1.78m
Displacement: 18.188lbs / 8.250kg
Ballast: 7.056lbs / 3.200kg
Sail areas: (main and 100% foretriangle)
695 sq ft / 64.61 sq m
Engine: Volvo D2 55hp saildrive
Headroom: 6ft 5in
CE approved category: A

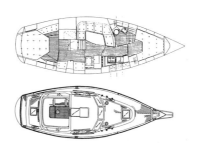

Contact:
North Sea Maritime Ltd
PO Box 5539
Southend-on-Sea
Essex
SS1 3TE
Tel/fax (01702) 584 821
E-mail info@northseamaritime.com
www.northseamaritime.com

Vancouver 38 - 38ft

The Vancouver 38, an ocean cruiser, has huge volumes. The fresh water tanks take approximately 100 gallons (450 litres) while the fuel tank's capacity is approximately 80 gallons (365 litres), and the boat is just as accommodating in other areas.

The large cockpit has deep coamings for security and wide comfortable seats. A deep locker is fitted to starboard and a large lazarette aft for stowage. Down below there are two double cabins and a large, luxuriously fitted-out galley. The forward heads are vast with an excellent shower space and there are plenty of hanging lockers and storage spaces. The big chart table in the saloon provides space around it to mount any amount of navigational instruments and good stowage under its hinge tip lid for chart stowage. The tall cutter rig providing 865 sq ft (80.36 sq m) of sail area powers the yacht along even in the lightest winds.

All in all, the yacht is worth serious consideration as an ocean cruiser. In the forecabin there are two full length single berths with an infill to make a double. The infill will stow between the berths to form a seat. There are GRP storage bins under the berths. A separate heads compartment is en suite with the forecabin. It has a teak shower grating with an electric pump out. In the saloon is a dinette dining table which can be reduced to coffee size when not in use. The galley is to starboard. It is fitted with a two burner gimballed cooker, and an ice box (convertible to a refrigerator).
The navigation station is aft, with plenty of space for instruments and chart stowage. The aft cabin is to port and has a large double berth. there is an emergency escape hatch to the cockpit. A separate toilet compartment is aft, complete with shower, washbasin and pressurised hot and cold water.

Specification

LOA: 38ft 0in / 11.58 m
LWL: 30ft 5ins / 9.27 m
Beam: 12ft 0ins / 3.66 m
Ballast weight:
3,718 kgs / 8,198 lbs
Displacement:
10.151 kgs / 22,378 lbs
Draught: 1.70 m / 5 ft 7 ins
Sail areas: Main:
300 sq ft / 27.87sq m
Yankee:
480 sq ft / 44.60 sq m
Staysail:
105 sq ft / 9.75sq m

Contact:
Northshore Yachts Ltd
Itchenor
Chichester
West Sussex PO20 7AY
Tel: 01243 512611
Fax: 01243 511473
email: sales@northshore.co.uk

Price guide: £169.618 + VAT

Vancouver 38P - 38ft

The Vancouver 38 Pilot is similarly conceived to the 34 Pilot. With the comfort and security of a raised deck saloon, everyone - the skipper included - can shelter from the elements while still enjoying 360 degree views. The sailing performance is excellent with the same rig as the Vancouver 38 but with a self tacking staysail for convenience.

The interior volume for a 38 footer is vast, with three double sleeping cabins - all large, two heads compartments, and a large galley with space for every modern convenience. It can be finished in a choice of timbers and tailored to the owner's exact requirements. There are spaces to fit any manner of optional equipment including generator, watermaker, fridge and freezer. The Vancouver 38 Pilot is not a motor sailer but a powerful sailing yacht built for long distance cruising.

The Deck saloon seating provides excellent vision through the pilothouse windows, which are 10mm thick toughened glass. To port is a dinette with a settee that can be used as a sea berth with the lee cloth. The table unfolds – coffee size to dining size – by use of hinged flaps and will extend across to the helm seat by addition of a leaf. Forward of the dinette are stowage bins and there are cave lockers behind the seat backs.

To starboard is the chart table with adjustable helmsman's seat giving excellent views forward. A console is provided to mount instruments and there is plenty of space to stow books and charts. There are stowages under the sidedeck and aft to starboard is a large oilskin locker and access steps to the aft heads and cabin. The aft cabin is to port and has a large double berth.

Specification

LOA: 38ft 0in / 11.58 m
LWL: 30ft 5ins / 9.27 m
Beam: 12ft 0ins / 3.66 m
Ballast weight:
3.718 kgs / 8,198 lbs
Displacement:
10.151 kgs / 22.378 lbs
Draught: 1.70 m / 5 ft 7ins
Sail areas:
Main: 300 sq ft / 27.87sq m
Yankee: 480 sq ft / 44.60 sq m
Staysail: 105 sq ft / 9.75sq m

Contact:
Northshore Yachts Ltd
Itchenor
Chichester
West Sussex PO20 7AY
Tel: 01243 512611
Fax: 01243 511473
email: sales@northshore.co.uk

Price guide: £191.705 + VAT

Legend 386 - 38ft 3in

Hunter Marine's new 386 is an American boat described by the builders as an evolutionary boat. Comfort, convenience and liveability is what the 386 is designed to offer.

Abundant natural light streams in from the Hunter signature windshield as well as the many fixed and screened ports. Entertaining the family is easy with the enlarged salon complete with a convertible dinette and facing settee. Storage is plentiful as is electronic space at the integrated nav-station. A Corian® covered, full-service galley comes complete right down to the dishware. The private forward stateroom includes an ensuite vanity with sink and storage as well as plenty of hanging locker space and drawer storage. Aft, you'll find the master stateroom with a huge Queen berth and more storage. Privacy is enhanced by the dual access head that offers a Corian® covered vanity, electric marine head and shower stall all wrapped in a complete glassfibre shell for easy cleaning and maintenance.

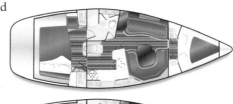

Specification

LOA: 38ft 3in / 11.66 m
Hull: 37ft1in / 11.30 m
LWL: 32ft 0in / 9.75 m
Beam: 12ft 7in / 3.84 m
Draught: (shoal) 5ft 0in / 1.53 m
(deep) 6ft 6in / 1.98 m
Ballast: (shoal) 5,900 lbs./ 2,679 kg
(deep) 5,495 lbs / 2,495 kg
Displacement: (shoal)16,000 lbs./ 7,264
(deep)15,595 lbs. / 7,080 kg
Mast Ht: 59ft 6in / 18.14 m
Sail Area: (actual) 811sq ft / 75.34 sq m
Headroom: 6ft 6in /1.98 m
Capacity:
Fuel: 30 gal. / 114 lt
Water: 75 gal. / 284 lt
Holding tank: 35 gal./ 132 lt
Engine: Diesel aux power
(FWC)40 hp / 29.6 kw
CE Classification: A

Contact:
Opal Marine
Camper and Nicholsons Marina
Mumby Road
Gosport, Hampshire PO12 1AH
Tel: 023 9258 3242
Email: info@opalmarine.com

Price guide: £ on application

Feeling 39 - 38ft 4in

Feeling 39. Feeling are world leaders in lift keel GRP yachts and are renowned for their innovative, large, light and airy cabins and superbly crafted joinery in beech and light cherry. Feeling yachts combine cruise anywhere versatility with excellent sailing and sea keeping performance. The entire range from 32 to 44 feet is designed to both offer fin or true lift keel sailing giving unbeatable access to creeks, estuaries, harbours and even the French canal system, whilst still offering superb sailing performance.

The Feeling 39 offers outstanding accommodation and volume for her size. The option of a second heads in the forward cabin and the offset saloon with longitudinal galley give the Feeling 39 the space of 40 footer but with the ease of handling of a 36 footer. She can accommodate eight.

Specification

LOA: 38ft 4in / 11.70 m
LWL: 32ft 7in / 9.2 m
Beam: 13ft 2in / 4.02 m
Capacity:
Water: 350 lt
Fuel: 145 lt
Air draught: 55,38in
Tonnage: 16,62 tx
Sail area: 80,80 sq m
Draught:
Fin keel: 6ft 7in / 2.0 m
Lift keel:
2ft 3in - 7ft 3in / 0.70 -2.20 m
Weight of fin keel:
(cast iron) 2.915 kg
Weight of ballast: - lift keel
(cast iron) 3.590 kg
Displacement:
fin keel 7.150 kg
Displacement:
lift keel 7.825 kg
Berths: 8

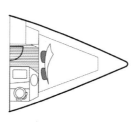

Contact:
Feeling Yachts Ltd
The Shipyard
Lymington
Hampshire SO41 3YL
Tel: 01590 647421
Fax: 01590 647446
Email: feelingyachts@berthon.co.uk
www.feelingyachts.com

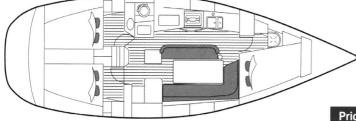

Athena 38 - 38ft 5in

The Athena 38 is described by its builders as a French catamaran that combines style with practicality. Beauty in the shape of the hull, the sun shade and the aft skirt, and intelligence in its design which makes handling, berthing, mooring and storage easy.

This catamaran is also designed so that everyone in the crew can take part in the best moments of a cruise; the functional helmsman's cockpit for navigation, a spacious cockpit for sun bathing and very convenient steps at the rear of the floats providing the best possible access for all kinds of recreation on the water. The high tech materials, the build quality and the choice of high quality fittings make the boat an especially safe and pleasant vessel in which you can sail in all weathers.

The high level of Fountaine Pajot build standards can be seen below decks on the Athena 38. The large friendly saloon with its well equipped chart table and galley, is provided with very large storage and refrigerated spaces. There is an extensive worktop, 2 stainless steel sinks, and an oven with three burners. The private areas in the well insulated hulls feature 4 light and airy cabins.

There is optimum use of space for king size beds and there are 2 independent toilets in the corridors with built-in showers.

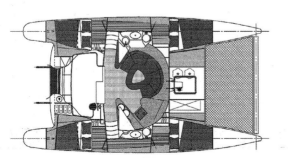

Specifications

LOA: 38ft 5in / 11,60 m
Beam: 20ft 1in / 6.3 m
Draught: 3ft 1in / 0.95 m
Displacement unloaded: 5.5 t
Main sail area: 538 sqft / 50 sq.m
Genoa area: 376 sq ft / 38 sq.m.
Engines:
Twin 18hp diesel
Capacity:
Fuel: 40 gal / 180 lt
Water: 80 gal / 360 lt

Contact:
Multihull
International Ltd
Birdham Yacht Club
Suite 1
Lock Lane
Birdham
Chichester PO20 7BB
Tel: 01243 512 111
Fax: 01243 513 111
email: info@multihull.co.uk

Price guide: £150.000 inc VAT

Nauticat 38 - 38ft 9in

The Nauticat 38 is known as a 'sailor's motorsailer' due to her exceptional perform-ance under sail. In the forecabin there are two berths with reading lights and ample storage under. A large translucent hatch is provided. The forward heads compart-ment contains pressurised water, basin and handshower. with storage behind and underneath the basin. Opposite the toilet is a large hanging locker. The aft heads has a spacious toilet with pressure water, basin, and handshower. The toilet is supplied with a septic tank and a pumpout fitting on deck.

In the saloon there is a large U-shaped settee providing comfortable seating for up to six people, convertible to a luxurious double bunk. Outboard is cabinetry, bookshelf and space for a TV and radio. Large stowage compartments are under the seats. The galley opposite the main saloon features a two-burner propane stove with oven (gim-balled), and flame guards. There are double stainless steel sinks with flush-fitting counter. there is ample space for dishes, provisions. There is one Dorade vent and one hatch.

In the pilothouse the visibility is unimpaired to all directions through the aluminium framed safetyglass windows. The pilot-house features a steering position with full instrumentation, compass, depth sounder etc. There is an extra large chart table with storage under and the engine controls are at the helms-man's fingertips. Ventilation is provided by two hatches overhead, and two sliding doors, on port and starboard.

The completely private aft cabin is large, airy and exception-ally comfortable. It has a large double berth to starboard and a single to port. In addition there are two windows in transom four openable windows. A full-size wardrobe with shelves, en suite head.

Note: All Nauticats are custom-built and this suggested layout can be, and usually is, altered in subtle ways to suit individual owners.

Specification

LOA: 38ft 9in / 11,80 m
LWL: 30ft 4in / 9,25 m
Beam: 11ft 2in / 3,40 m
Draught: 5ft 11in / 1,80m
Displacement: approx. 24200lbs / 10,0 tons
Headroom:
Fore and aft cabin: 6ft 0in / 1,82 sq m
Pilothouse and saloon: 6ft 1in / 1,86 m
Ballast approx:
6800 lbs / 3.1tons
Capacity:
Fresh water:
88 gal. UK / 400 lt
Fuel:136 gal. UK / 620 lt
Sail areas: (all sails are optional)
A = Ketch rigged without bowsprit: 64,2 sq m
B = Ketch rigged with bowsprit: 70.1 sq m
C = Ketch rigged with bowsprit and double (cutter) headsails: 84,6 sq m
CE approved category: B.

Contact:
Nauticat (UK) Ltd, Mariners House
High Street, Hamble,
Southampton SO31 4JF
Tel: 02380 453900
Email: info@nauticatuk.co.uk

Price guide: £176.900

Nauticat 39 - 38ft 10in

The **Nauticat 39** is built to an uncompromising design, and performs well both under sail and power. The Nauticat 39 has good visibility forward from the deep and safe cockpit and the pilothouse, which allows a panoramic view from both the inside steering station and saloon area.

The boat offers spacious accommodation including two separate state cabins backed up with a third cabin in the middle of the boat, a spacious galley and excellent internal and external stowage facilities. Interior construction is of satin varnished solid teak and teak faced marine plywood, except the galley and toilets, which are finished in light laminates with teak trim. There is wall-to-wall carpeting in the pilothouse. The forecabin has two V berths, with storage under the berths and a hatch overhead. The forward heads has pressurised water, a basin and shower. On the ceiling an overhead hatch and a Dorade-vent.

In the galley there is a toploading refrigerator. Extensive cabinetry for storage. The galley has also two opening hatches and a Dorade-vent to provide light and ventilation.

The pilothouse distinguishes a Nauticat; the visibility is unimpaired through the safetyglass windows. From the pilothouse there is a companionway to the cockpit and there are steps which lead down to the owner's stateroom. The helm station to starboard includes a large chart table with chart storage beneath the hinged top. Access to the engine room is through the pilothouse sole. The large raised U-shaped settee accommodates six people comfortably for dining or relaxing. Storage is under the settee.

Note: All Nauticats are custom-built and this suggested layout can be, and usually is, altered in subtle ways to suit individual owners.

Specification

LOA: 38ft 10in / 11.85 m
LWL: 32ft 2in / 9.80 m
Beam: 11ft 6in / 3.50 m
Draught: 6ft 3in / 1.90m
Displacement: approx. 19800lbs / 9.0 tons
Headroom:
Fore and aft cabin:
6ft 1in - 7ft 6in / 1,86 - 2.28m
Pilothouse and saloon:
6ft 1in - 6ft 3in / 1,85 - 1.90m
Ballast approx:
6600 lbs / 3 tons
Capacity:
Fresh water:
97 gal. UK / 440 lt
Fuel: 88 gal. UK / 400 lt
Sail area: (all sails are optional)
(mainsail + genoa 1) 76.1 sq m
Mainsail: 34.7 sq m
Genoa: 1 41.4 sq m
Jib; 35.8 sq m
CE approved category: A.

Contact:
Nauticat (UK) Ltd
Mariners House
High Street
Hamble
Southampton SO31 4JF
Tel: 02380 453900
Email: info@nauticatuk.co.uk

Price guide: £ 171.950

Cornish Crabber Pilot Cutter 30 - 39ft

The Pilot Cutter 30 is available with either a Gaff or Bermudan rig and featuring a pivoting bowsprit which aids the raising and lowering of the mast as well as reducing berth charges. The Pilot Cutter handles with ease in all conditions.

As with all Cornish Crabbers, the Pilot Cutter 30 is built to individual requirements with an impressive range of features fitted as standard. The airy interior with luxurious seating has 5/6 berths and a superbly designed and equipped galley, which includes a fridge, gimballed two burner cooker with oven and grill, fitted plate and cup rack and a pressurised water system. The private toilet and shower means living aboard the Pilot Cutter for longer sea passages is a more civilised experience. A well proportioned navigation station with chart storage is situated starboard of the companionway steps. A generous double V-berth provides comfortable accommodation for two adults.

A Yanmar 3GM30 28hp diesel engine provides more than enough power to provide outstanding performance and the sight of the Pilot Cutter in full sail says all there is to say about the magic of sailing.

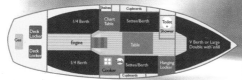

Specification

Pilot Cutter Gaff
LOA: 39ft 0in / 11.88 m
LOD: 30ft 0in / 9.14 m
LWL: 25ft 9in / 7.85 m
Beam: 9ft 6in / 2.89 m
Draught: 3ft 6in - 5ft 3in / 1.07 - 1.60 m
Displacement: 6.25 tons / 6.35 tonnes
Sail area: 600 Sq ft / 55.74 Sq m

Pilot Cutter Bermuda
LOA: 35ft 6in / 10.82 m
LOD: 30ft 0in / 9.14 m
LWL: 25ft 9in / 7.85 m
Beam: 9ft 6in / 2.89 m
Draught: 4ft 6in / 1.37 m
Displacement: 7.0 tons / 7.12 tonnes
Sail area: 566 Sq ft / 52.6 Sq m

Contact:
The Select Yacht Group
Rock, Wadebridge
Cornwall PL27 6NT
Tel: 01208 862666
Fax: 01208 862375
email: Info@selectyachts.co.uk

Price guide: £102.992 inc VAT

Lavezzi 40 - 39ft

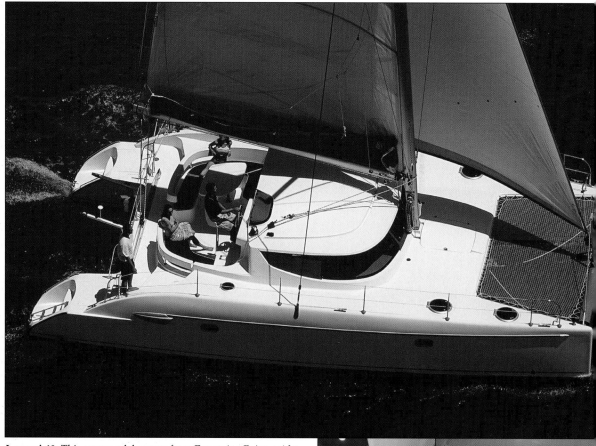

Lavezzi 40. This new model comes from Fountaine Pajot, said to be the world's leading builder of cruising catamarans.

The saloon and cockpit open on to each other with a large sliding door and window making for good ventilation and easy use of the galley whether you wish to eat inside or outside.

The centrally-accessed cockpit features a rest area close to the helm station as well as a dining area. The helm station has a deflector, protecting the person at the helm. The galley is on the port side, which leaves a lot of space for the table and bench seating, with enough room for 8 people. The saloon of the catamaran has spacious cupboard space in the galley and for the chart table. The instrument panel has been incorporated into a user-friendly display. Wood is used extensively inside the saloon, to give it a warm atmosphere and an overall finish of high quality.

To avoid noise levels in the cabins, the engines have been installed in the aft holds which are independent from the cabins. They can be accessed easily for maintenance purposes without any noise or unpleasant odors in the cabins. The beds are extra-wide (2m x 1.40 -1.50m) compared to other boats of the same size. The white ceilings contribute to the overall impression of light and volume.

Each cabin is ventilated with a forward-facing overhead hatch and sidescuttle, both of which can be opened.

Specifications

LOA: 39ft / 11.90 m
Beam: 21ft 40 / 6.50 m
Draught: / 3ft 60 / 1.10 m
Light displacement: 6.2 T
Sail areas:
Main sail: 592sq ft / 55 sq m
Genoa: 376.75sq ft / 35 sq m
Standard engines: 2 x 18 hp / 2 x 13.23
Capacity: Fuel - approx 250 lt / 66 US g
Water: approx 2 x 280 lt / 2 x 73.9 US ga

Contact:
Multihull International Ltd
Birdham Yacht Club
Suite 1
Lock Lane
Birdham
Chichester
West Sussex PO20 7BB
Tel: 01243 512 111
Fax: 01243 513 111
Email: info@multihull.co.uk

Price guide: £180.000 inc VAT

Sweden 390 - *39ft*

The 390 was introduced in 1991 by a builder with a high reputation for quality and customer service. The forward cabin, has a double-berth utilizing the full width of the cabin. The heads compartment is fitted between bulkheads. and there is a shower drained by electric pump. It has a door both to the forward cabin and saloon. The saloon has an L-shaped sofas on both sides, a table with fold-down wings and built-in bar in a fixed mid section. There are cabinets and bookshelves above the sofas on both sides.

There is an L-shaped galley with Formica counter top 160 lt icebox in GRP with plexi-glass dividers, which drains to a separate sump. The large navigation table has good stowage. There is a moulded detachable instrument panel for electronic equipment, plus extra chart stowage space above the instrument-panel. The adjustable navigation seat has stowage space underneath. In the starboard aft cabin there is a wide single bed with stowage under, and a wet locker. In the port cabin there is a double bed, seat with stowage under, a wide hanging locker and stowage shelf with doors along the hullside. There are doors from the main saloon to each cabin.

Specifications

LOA: 39ft 0in / 11.88 m
LWL: 31ft 6in / 9.60 m
Beam: 12ft 7in / 3.87 m
Draft: 7ft 4in / 2.25 m
Displacement: 16,800lbs / 7.600 kg
Ballast: (lead) 7000lbs / 3.150 kg
Mainsail: 35 sq m
Furling Genoa: 52 sq m
Jib: 43 sq m
Spinnaker: 137 sq m
Water capacity: 380 lt
Fuel capacity: 150 lt
Engine: 40hp

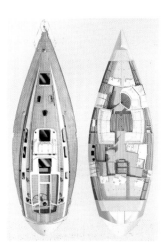

Contact: Sweden Yachts
Box 80, Angsv 5
S-44421 Stenungsund
Sweden
Tel: 00 46 303 77 06 40
Fax: 00 46 303 88 61 0
Email: info@swedenyachts.se
www.swedenyachts.se

Salona 40 - 39ft 3in

The **Salona 40** is built in Croatia. She has three cabins. The interior is finished in mahogany or cherry. The saloon has a U-shaped seating arrangement, with a single seat to starboard. The saloon table is moveable and has a locker for storage. The galley is equipped with a a two burner cooker and oven. There is a double sink with hot and cold water and a 135 lt refrigerator.

There is an option for a single heads compartment next to the fore cabin, or for an additional second heads situated in the central saloon cabin. The navigation area is on the starboard side.

There are two aft cabins, both have double berths with large hanging lockers. The forward cabin has a double berth with hanging lockers.

Specifications

LOA: 11.99m
Beam: 4m
Draught: 2.0m - 2.5m
Displacement: 7.500 kg
Ballast: 2.800 kg
Mainsail: 46 sq m
Genoa: 60 sq m
Water capacity: 500 lt
Fuel capacity: 260 lt
Engine: 40hp
Berths: 6-7

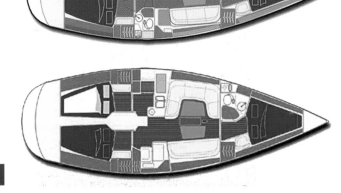

Contact:
Wittey Marine Ltd
Unit 17 Haddenham
Business Park
Thame Road
Haddenham
Bucks HP17 8LJ
Tel: 01844 290890
Fax: 01844 292431
Email:
sales@witteymarine.com

Price guide: £99.285 + VAT

Dragonfly 1200 - 39ft 4in

The Dragonfly 1200 is a Swing Wing Ocean Cruiser built in Denmark. She is a unique, high quality cruising trimaran. Designing a folding trimaran of this size requires great attention to the forces that are applied to the superstructure - such as main bulkheads and the position and attachment of the swing wings.

The designer has chosen a centre cockpit to fulfil the structural demands and because it provides excellent living accommodation. The engine, tanks and other equipment are all close to the centre for better performance. The main cabin offers the best Danish furniture design using laminated solid teak wood trim. To save weight the bulkheads are foam-sandwich construction and the non-visible wooden structure is produced in Canadian red cedar. There is full standing head-room of 1.9m. To port there is a well proportioned galley with hot and cold pressurised water. There is a double burner gas stove with an oven. The navigation area is to starboard, and the table serves as an additional counter space. There is an option to fit a refrigerator behind the navigation seat if required.

As you move up forward you enter the large heads compartment. It has a shower and big lockers. The owner's cabin is behind a sliding door; it has a wide double bed and lots of lockers. There is plenty of storage under the bunks. The aft cabin offers ample room and storage too. The table fitted between the two bunks opens up to provide a wash basin and underneath that a second head. It is said that the Dragonfly 1200 will make 15 knots in the right conditions.

Specification

LOA: 39ft 4in / 11.98m
LOA (folded): 44ft 7in / 13.50m
LWL: 7.81m
Beam (max): 28ft 2in / 8.60m
Beam (folded): 13ft 11in / 4.25m
Draught (max): 6ft 7in / 2.00m
Displacement: 2,273lbs / 5.000kg
Sail area: 1,010 sq ft / 94m2
Capacities:
Water: 150 litres
Fuel: 150 litres
Berths: 5
CE category: A (Ocean)

Design: Jens Quorning

Contact:
Multihull Promotions
Sandpipers
Smugglers Lane
Bosham
Chichester
West Sussex PO18 8QP
Tel: 01242 576533
Fax: 01273 576544

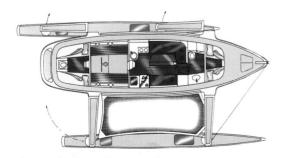

Dufour 40 - 39ft 4in

The **Dufour 40** offers a choice of four different layouts (see below). Version 1 offers two cabins with single heads, and volume that is out of the ordinary on a 40ft boat, a spacious cabin forward with an offset bed, and a large head compartment with separate shower.

Version 2 has two cabins with two heads. This version allows 4 people to live at sea while preserving their privacy.

Version 3 has three double cabins with one heads. Planned to accommodate 6 people, this version retains the advantage of the large cabin forward with its offset bed.

Version 4 has three cabins and double heads. This version allows 6 people to live at sea whilst preserving their privacy. The centre third of the boat remains the same whichever layout is chosen. This has an L shaped galley to port. The galley is not quite as large as some other 12m boats, but it is adequately equipped for cruising. Her beam is well aft where width is needed. She is fitted out in Moabi wood. To port is a shallow C-shape dinette with plenty of room round the table. A short settee opposite increases seating round the table. Stowage either side of the saloon is good. The saloon is well lit and ventilated. The heads compartment has a spacious feel, with an opening hatch and a mushroom ventilator. The two after cabins are much the same in layout and appearance. The navigation area has a large wraparound table with plenty of chart and instrumentation space.

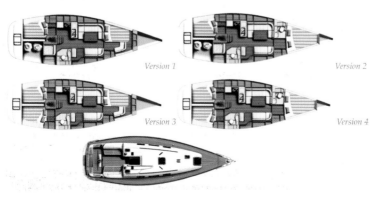

Version 1

Version 2

Version 3

Version 4

Specifications

LOA: 39ft 4in / 11.99m
LWL: 35ft 3in / 10.74m
Beam: 12ft 9in / 3.90m
Displacement: 16.102 / 17.300kg
Ballast: 2,700kg (5.940 lb)
Sail area: 958sq ft / 89 sq m
Berths: 4/8
Capacity:
Fuel: 35 gal / 160 litres
Water: 77 gal / 350 litres
Engine: Volvo 2040 40hp diesel
RCD Category: A

Contact:
Portfolio Marine
Beacon Quay
Torquay
Devon TQ1 2BG
Tel: 01803 380506
Fax: 01803 380507
Email: info@portfolio-marine.co.uk
www.portfolio-marine.co.uk

Price guide: £98.519 + VAT

Ronautica RO 400 - 39ft 5in

The RO 400 is a very modern looking yacht. She represents a new style of cruiser characterised by stylish lines, a fast hull, spacious interior, a large cockpit and distinctive rounded forms.

The interior is finished in cherry wood, headroom in the saloon is 1.95m. The large saloon table can be converted into a double berth in the owner or charter versions. Or there is a dedicated nav station in the racer version.

The chart table drops down as shown here, the galley contains a 2-ring cooker and oven and has plenty of drawers and storage. There are two aft cabins and one forward cabin. All cabins have a double berth and lockers. Headroom is 1.88m in the aft cabins and 1.91m forward.

The head is a complete bathroom with a marine toilet and shower unit. There is easy access to inlet and outlet seacocks. The compartment has pressurized water and an electric bilge pump for the shower tray.

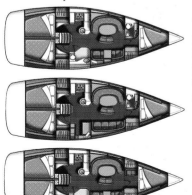

With her superior sailing performance, she can be easily handled by one or two people, with roomy accommodation for 6 or more. An ideal ocean cruiser.

Specifications

LOA: 39ft 5in / 12.05m
LWL: 38ft 5in /11.75m
Beam: 13ft 0in / 3,99m
Draft: 6ft 2in - 7ft 8in / 1.90m - 2,40m
Displacement: 15.432 lbs / 7.000kg
Ballast: 5.401 lbs / 2,450kg
Mainsail: 42sq m
Genoa: 38sq m
Spinnaker/Gennaker:
117 / 105sq m
CE Category: A

Contact:
South West
Yacht Brokers
Atlantic Quay
Richmond Walk
Plymouth PL1 4LN
Tel: 01752 551991
Fax: 01751551991
www.southwestyachts.co.uk

Price guide: £106.500   117

Huffler 40 Motor Sailer - 39ft 6in

The **Huffler 40** is a true motor sailer in the old tradition, combining the joy, excitement and grace of sailing with the comfort and security of a motor vessel. The Huffler, designed specifically for the builder by yacht designer Tony Tucker, is the latest in a long line of quality steel boats from Peter Nicholls. There is also a 35ft version available.

Down below the standard version accommodation has two self contained sleeping-cum-day cabins with toilet and shower facilities en suite. There is a folding table in the fore cabin. In the central saloon the dinette can be lowered to form a double berth. The spacious galley is finished in maple or cherry wood.

The Huffler's shallow draft with keel raised and self lowered mast allows exploration of shallow creeks, rivers and canals. The boat is robustly constructed from thicker than average steel plate. The dual steering position gives the comfort of a wheelhouse in bad weather with the advantage of an open air steering position on a sun deck, under an awning, when required. Despite her seemingly bluff bow, the boat does not slam into waves under sail or power, but lifts and rides over the crest with an easy motion.

Specifications

LOA: 39ft 6in
LWL: 35ft 6in
Beam: 11ft
Draft: 3ft 3in - 5ft (keel down)
Displacement: 11tonnes
inc 2 tonnes lead ballast
Mainsail: 31.8 sq m
Genoa: 36.4sq m
Mizzen: 7.6 sq m
Water capacity: 150 gals
Fuel capacity: 90 gals
Engine: Beta 2 803 6shp

Contact:
Peter Nicholls Yachtbuilders Ltd
Braunstone Marina
Trade Centre
Daventry Road
Braunstone
Northants NN11 7JH

Tel: 01788
Fax: 01788 899109
Email: peter@steelboats.com
www.steelboats.com

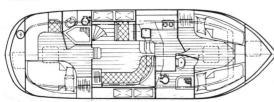

Price guide: £249.420 inc V

Etap 39s - 39ft 7in

The ETAP 39s, in common with all members of the Etap family, is unsinkable. She has a stylishly modern interior finish of mahogany treated with three coats of waterproof acrylic varnish.

All furnishings have solid mahogany frames. Or she can be delivered with a cherrywood interior. The floorboards are of maintenance free laminate with beech edging. Stainless steel inspection hatches provide easy access to the keel bolts and measuring equipment. The companionway has four curved aluminum treads coated with a nonslip finish. Headroom in the companionway area is 1.95m.

The saloon contains a large U-shaped sofa on the starboard side. A second seat is located amidships. A large table with a raised rim offers ample space for everyone on board. The galley is spacious and on the port side. It has a gimballed 2-burner gas oven. There is a large stowage capacity with cutlery drawer and bin-bag holder. Worksurfaces are finished in solid Corian. An insulated 125lt coolbox is provided. A 96 x 58cm chart table is located on the starboard side.

The front cabin has a large double berth and there is a washbasin with pressurized hot and cold water. Closable lockers are fitted along the hull sides. The aft cabin has a double skipper's berth 205 x 127cm. The heads compartment has a traditional marine toilet. The washbasin is fitted with a shower head and is fed by a pressurized hot and cold water supply. Headroom is 1.90m.

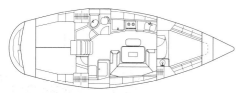

Specification

LOA: 39ft 7in / 11.88m
LWL: 38ft 1in / 11.60m
Beam: 12ft 7½in / 3.85m
Draught: 4ft 11in - 6ft 6in / 1.95 - 1.50m
Displacement: 15.418lbs - 14.978lbs / 6.800kg - 7.000kg
Sail area:
Mainsail: 444 sq ft / 41.20sq m
Genoa: 392sq ft / 36.40 sq m
Engine: 40hp / 29kW
CE category: A

Contact:
Kiss Solent Ltd
The Boatyard
Hythe Marina
Hythe Hants SO45 6DX
Tel: 02380 840 300
Fax: 02380 840 700

Price guide: £122.000 + VAT

Bavaria 38 Match - 39ft 8in

The Bavaria 38 Match is an elegant yacht with a high standard of workmanship on deck as well as below. The fine interior, with mahogany veneer and quality upholstery, creates a friendly, maritime atmosphere.

This cruiser-racer is available with two or three cabins, depending on the size of the family or the requirements of the owner. Whether it is for sailing, sun-bathing or cooking, the 38 Match offers plenty of space for a relaxed cruise on board. With a great deal of storage space, the yacht is also extremely well equipped for extended cruises.

The interior offers 3 cabins with 6 berths or 2 cabins with 4 berths plus the saloon with comfortable settees and a luxuriously styled table. There are sideboards with plenty of stowage space and lockers. The navigation area is well provided for with space to store charts and navigation instruments. The galley is equipped with two burners and an oven. There is an insulated cooling box, a stainless steel sink and good stowage with drawers. Dishes, pots and waste bin have good practical spaces below the galley unit. The heads compartment has easy-care synthetic surfaces. There are 6 hatches which open and 6 opening side windows.

Specification

LOA: 12.13m
LWL: 10.25m
Beam: 3.87m
Draught:
1.70m - 2.0m
Capacities:
Water: 300 lt
Fuel: 150 lt
Sail area:
Furling mainsail: 32.10 sq m
Battened mainsail: 37.60 sq m
Genoa: 45,80 sq m
Engine:
Inboard diesel 29hp
Berths:
Up to 6 in 3 cabins

Contact:
Opal Marine
Camper & Nicholsons
Marina
Mumby Road
Gosport
Hants PO12 1AH
Tel: 02392 583242
Fax: 02392 581028
www.opalmarine.co.uk

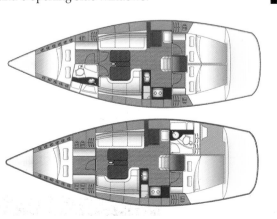

Price guide: £ on application

Ovni 385 - 39ft 8in

The Ovni 385 is a French boat, hand built in aluminium. The interior layout can be adapted to almost any requirement around the siting of the keelbox.

There are two basic alternatives, one with double cabins fore and aft, and the other has two forecabins and two aft cabins. There are single heads in both versions. The keelbox runs almost the full length of the saloon. It is incorporated as unobtrusively as possible into the table and a centre mounted storage unit. The location of the keelbox means that the saloon is well forward which leaves plenty of space for a large galley and a navigation area suiutable for a blue water cruiser. There is plenty of stowage space everywhere. The interior is fitted out with plenty of solid wood and well fitted vinyl head linings. Below you could almost feel you were in a wooden boat. There is a solid, light and airy feeling, the doors are all solid and are ventilated. The sole is in holly-splined teak with a plastic laminate, non-slip finish. The hull is fully lined.

In the saloon there are two settees 6ft 2in long. Headroom is 6ft 1in. The galley has lots of good stowage. A large icebox is included with plenty of work surfaces. The chart table is large, with useful stowage for books and plotting instruments. There is a door to the heads compartment which is generously proportioned. There is a wet hanging locker which has a hatch through to the cockpit locker. The forecabin has a V bunk 6ft 5in long and 5ft 8in wide at the shoulders. Headroom is 6ft 4in. The aft cabin has a large double bunk 6ft 7in x 5ft 10in.

Specification

LOA: 39ft 8in / 12.10 m
LWL: 31ft 3ins / 9.53 m
Beam: 12ft 6ins / 3.80 m
Ballast inc keel: 6650lbs / 3.020kg
Displacement: 18.694 lbs / 8.500kg
Draught: 1ft 9in - 6ft 9in / 0.52 - 2.05m
Sail areas: 893 sq ft / 83 sqm
Water: 93 gals / 423 lts
Fuel: 43 gals / 197 lts
Engine: Volvo 50hp

Contact:
Northsea Maritime Ltd
PO Box 5539
Southend-on Sea
Essex SS1 3TE
Tel/Fax: 01702 584 821
Email: info@northseamaritime.com

Price guide: £111.340 + VAT

Starlight 39 Mk 2 - 39ft 10in

The Starlight 39 Mk2 has a modern cruising interior with high quality teak joinery, featuring solid cappings to all locker and drawer openings. The layout offers space and comfort combined with practicality in a boat designed for offshore cruising.

The two settee berths serve as comfortable sea berths with lee cloths provided as standard. The owner's cabin is situated forward, with en suite heads and shower. A double guest cabin aft also has its own access to the aft day heads. The well fitted galley has double sinks, refrigerator and gimballed cooker with oven and grill. There is considerable stowage space outboard and below the worktop. A forward facing chart table with instrument console and comfortable seating ensures safe working in rough conditions.

An alternative layout is available for those who normally cruise with a small crew, which provides a larger owner's cabin. This is achieved by removing the forward heads compartment and replacing it with a vanity unit and wash basin. Additional stowage is provided by lockers above and below the work surface of the vanity unit. For those who prefer an alternative to the traditional teak, the interior joinery can be completed in American Cherry.

Specifications

LOA: 39ft 10in / 12.15m
LWL: 31ft 9in / 9.69m
Beam: 12ft 6in / 3.81m
Draught: Fin keel: 6ft 10in / 2.09m
Wing keel: 5ft 4in / 1.63m
Displacement:
19.749 lbs / 8.958kg
Ballast: 7.119 lbs / 3.229kg
Water: 50 imp gals / 227lts
Fuel: 40 imp gals / 182 lts
Engine: 35hp
Sail area: 748 sq ft / 69.54 sq m
CE Certification: A

Contact:
Rustler Yachts Ltd
Maritime Buildings
Falmouth Road
Falmouth Cornwall TR10 8AD
Tel: 01326 310120
Fax: 01326 314092
Email: info@rustler yachts.com
www.rustleryachts.com

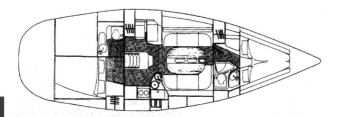

Price guide: £174.142

Elan 40 - *40ft*

Designed by New Zealander Rob Humphreys, the Elan 40 is available in 2 versions; the layouts are shown below. The 40 has a saloon with 1.98m headroom. There is a large U-shaped settee with cushions and backrests on the starboard side and a centreline settee on the port side. There is a large folding saloon table which can also be an auxiliary double bunk as an option. The forward cabin has a headroom of 1.89 m. The two aft cabins have double berths in each, with headroom of 1.92m. The galley has headroom of 1.92m. The cooker is gimballed with 3 rings and an oven. There is a 12v refrigerator. The double sink has a pressurized water system.

The navigation station has a chart table 750 x 600mm. The navigator's seat has storage under. There is a panel for navigation instruments with voltmeter for batteries, fresh water and fuel. The head has a wash basin with a pressurized water tap. Headroom is 1.88m. There are stowage lockers under the sink with access to seacocks.

Version 1

Version 2

Specification

LOA 12.20 m
Hull length 11.90 m
LWL 10.24 m
Beam 3.83 m
Draught 2.05 m / 2.40 m
Ballast 2555 kg / 2450kg
Weight 7900 kg
Engine 39 HP
Water capacity 235 lt
Fuel capacity 135 lt
Mainsail 41.40 sq m
Genoa 48.60 sq m
Spinnaker 116.70 sq m
Category CE A

Contact:
Elan Yacht Sales UK Limited
Swanick Marina
Southampton
Tel: 01489 885000
Fax: 01489 885509
email: sales@elanyachts.com

Price guide: £119.617 inc VAT

Beneteau 40.7 - 40ft 2in

The First 40.7 is a performance cruising yacht. The first step down the companionway reveals a resolutely marine atmosphere of beech wood furnishings, gentle curves, and lots of light.

The navigation station has a big chart table, bookshelf and lockers. The electronics panel is slightly curved so that all the instruments can be viewed at a glance. Behind the curved navigator's seat is a convenient locker for storage.

To port, the L-shaped galley is well planned for life at sea or in port. There is a stainless steel double sink with pressurised hot and cold water, big 12-volt refrigerator, gimballed oven cooker and plenty of lockers.

The saloon has plenty of space for the crew to sit comfortably round the inlaid table. There is a set of curved lockers/cupboards behind the two settees.

The heads compartment is to starboard, forward of the saloon. It is fully lined and fitted with a marine toilet, washbasin with shower unit, and a hanging locker and cupboard. The boat has 3 double cabins, all fitted with a hanging locker, cupboard and shelves. The forward cabin is ventilated by a large opening hatch and has its own entrance to the heads compartment. The two aft cabins have an opening hatch providing excellent ventilation. The mattresses of the double beds (2 m x 1.50 m) have been produced in two parts, so that leeboards can be installed.

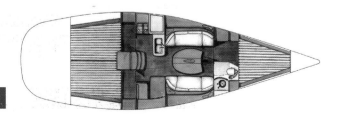

Specifications

LOA: 12.26m
LWL: 11.92m
Beam: 3.78m
Draught: 1.90 - 2.40m
Displacement: (approx.) 6 900kg
Berths: 6/8 pers.
Sail Area: (sqm) 98 sq m
Capacity: wate:r 300 lt fuel: 135 lt
CE Certification: A/12

Contact:
Ancasta International Boat Sales
Port Hamble
Satchel Lane
Hamble
Southampton SO31 4QD
Tel: 023 80 450 026
Email: Beneteau @ ancasta.co.uk
www.ancasta.com

Price guide: £125.000

Malo 39 - 40ft 2in

The **Malo 39,** has a spacious saloon with sofa on the starboard side and U-sofa on port side. There is a turnable cabin table with four flaps. There are various handrails to move about safely on board under sail. Headroom in saloon is 1,95 m.

The galley is L-shaped with bench lighting and good disposal areas of white laminate (with safety ledge all around, and a double bowl sink with mono-tap for hot and cold pressurized water. The stove has two burners and an oven; with gimballed suspension. There are cupboards and drawers, a well-insulated refrigeration box (80lt) with water-cooled compressor and full head-room.

The navigation area is situated on starboard forward of the head. It has a large navigation table with drawers and room for charts, and large detachable panels for individual positioning of instruments.

The head is centrally placed close to the companionway on the starboard side. The bulkheads in the head compartment are covered with white laminate. The washbasin has a monotap, extendable as shower. The shower tray empties via the electric drainage pump. There is a mirror on the bulkhead and a shower curtain in front of the door. The toilet connects with a holding tank that can either be emptied directly into the sea or pumped out through a connection on deck The aft cabin consists of a double berth and contains ample stowing space: hanging locker, locker with shelves and upper locker. There are two opening port lights, one of which in the cockpit side, allowing ventilation even in bad weather.

Specification

LOA: 40ft 2in / 12.24 m
LWL: 32ft 2in / 9.80 m
Beam: 12ft 4in / 3.76 m
Draught:
6ft 0in / 1.83 m
Displacement: 19.621.lbs / 8.9 ton
Engine: 56hp
Capacity:
Water: 120 US gals / 455 lts
Fuel: 74 US gals / 280 lts
Sail area:
Mainsail:
398.2 sq ft / 37.0 sq m

Contact:
Nordic Marine
Salterns Marina
Lilliput
Poole
BH14 8JR
Tel: 01202 700089
Fax: 01202 709072

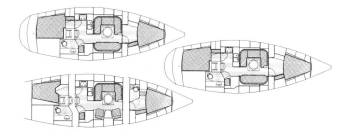

Najad 400 - 40ft 4in

The Najad 400 is the latest yacht which completes the upgrade of the entire fleet into the new design line developed in cooperation with Judel/Vrolijk & Co. The interior is handcrafted in unstained African mahogany, hand polished and varnished to a satin finish.

Each boat is built to order, with the possibility of combining other fixed layout alternatives. The spacious saloon has two settees surrounding the table, with bottle stowage in centre of table and ample overhead lights and reading lights for settees and berths. The companionway steps can be removed for easy access to the engine room. The L-shaped galley is located amidships allowing free passage between the cockpit and saloon. There are stainless steel twin sinks and a pressure system for hot and cold fresh water. There is a gimballed twin burner gas cooker with oven, with well insulated ice box, 100 lt, incuding a refrigeration unit. There is a waste basket fitted under the sink and an opening porthole above cooker. The navigation area is located amidships: forward facing navigation table with stowage for charts and drawers.

The heads compartment is amidships to starboard, with standing headroom approx. 1.95 m, with white laminated bulkheads, and a large wash basin built into the worktop. The aft cabin has a single berth on both sides with ample cupboards and a hanging wardrobe.

The forward cabin has two wide full size berths, with a wardrobe and settee on the port side and cupboards on the starboard side.

Specification

LOA: 40ft 4in / 12.20 m
LWL: 34ft 3in / 10.44 m
Beam: 12ft 7in / 3.85 m
Draught:
6ft 7in - 5ft 11in / 1.8 - 2.0 m
Displacement: 12.5 tonnes
Engine: 54.4 HP
Capacity:
Water: 132 gal / 600 lt
Fuel: 51 gal / 230 lt
Holding: 315 gal / 67 lt
Sail areas:
Mainsail:
420 sq ft / 39.0 sq m
Working jib:
377 sq ft / 35.0 sq m
Spinnaker:
1399 sq ft / 130.0 sq m

Contact:
Najad England
Hamble Point Marina, School Lane,
Southampton SO13 4NB
Tel: +44 2380 455 450
Fax: +44 2380 455 450
email: najadsales @btclick.com

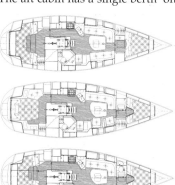

Price guide: 299.500 +

Catalina 400 - 40ft 6in

The Catalina 400. The most striking features of the cockpit are the twin wheels. Cruising sailors can enjoy the benefits of safety, visibility for the helmsman and easy stern access that were previously available only on grand prix and custom yachts. A large central cockpit table accommodates the entire crew for dining. Secure handrails, foot braces, and integrated fore and aft instrument clusters are also provided.

The accommodation is very comfortable. The aft cabin has private access to the head with stall shower, a queen size bed, great ventilation and lots of storage. The galley is impressive in a 40 footer. Molded counter tops, a front and top access refrigerator/freezer and a three burner stove with stainless steel stove hood create a pleasant, functional environment for the cook.

The main cabin is an inviting place to lounge with deep, comfortable seats and a large dining table. Many of the features most desired by cruisers, are built into the 400mkII. Large deep cycle battery banks, ample water, fuel, and waste tankage, a big anchor locker with a powerful windlass, high quality ports, hatches, and hardware are all standard.

Two cabin interior

Three cabin interior

Specification

LOA 40ft 6in
LWL 36ft 6in
Beam 13ft 6in
Draft Fin Keel 6ft 9in
Wing Keel 5ft 6in
Ballast Fin Keel 7,200lbs.
Wing Keel 8,000lbs.
Approximate Weight
Fin Keel 19,700lbs.
Wing Keel 20,500lbs.
Engine Diesel 4 cylinder 50 HP
Sail Area
(100% foretriangle) 808sq ft
I 52ft 8in
J 15ft 6in
P 47ft 0in
E 17ft 0in

Builder: Catalina Yachts USA
Contact: Windward Yachting, Northney Marina
Northney Road, Hayling Island, Hampshire PO11 0NH
Tel: 0870 350 1920
email: info@windwardyachting.co.uk
www.windwardyachting.co.uk

Price guide: £116.280 + VAT

127

Yachts currently out of production

The yachts in this section have all ceased production. But there are plenty of examples available on the used boat market. We have tried to give an accurate factual description of the boat.

An index size tab is printed in blue at the top right hand corner of the right hand page. The entire 'Out of Production Boats' section is marked as an index tab in blue on the left hand pages.

The information is presented in ascending size order.

The main photograph is usually of the boat at sea.

The smaller picture shows details of the interior.

When available a profile drawing of the boat is included with a drawing of the interior layout.

The Specification box gives dimensions as published in the builders' brochures. These were not always consistent in their form of presentation. Where information is missing it does not appear in the original brochures.

The Price guide is exactly what it says' a 'guide'. It is based on the average price of a used boat. Actual prices will vary depending on condition and other factors.

Please consult a marine surveyor to establish the condition of a boat you are interested in buying.

Freedom 21 - 21ft 8in

Specification

LOA: 21ft 8in
LWL: 19ft
Beam: 8ft
Draught: 2ft 6in
Displacement: 1.800lbs

Ballast: 750lbs
Sail areas:
main: 200sq ft
spinnake:r 265sq ft
Engine: Mariner 4hp or Tohatsu 4hp outboards

The **Freedom 21** was Designed by Gary Hoyt an ex advertising executive who has designed some radical and successful craft. She has the unstayed mast of a typical American Cat boat. She has a comparatively large sail area but it can be easily controlled by one person from the cockpit. The spinnaker is worked with the Hoyt 'gun mount' an unusual looking device that works well. The berths are roomy and comfortable. There is a simple sink unit and a curtain separates the head compartment from the saloon. The tandem wing keel was designed by Warwick Collins but it is not advisable to dry out with this configuration without the support of a wall.

Price guide: +/- £4.000

Seal 22 - 21ft 9in

Specification

LOA: 21ft 9in
LWL: 18ft 0in
Beam: 7ft 9in
Draught: 2ft - 3ft 10in
Displacement: 2.400lb
Sail areas:
Main 121sq ft
Racing Genoa: 142 sq ft
Cruising Genoa: 120 sq ft
Berths: 4/6

Designed by **Angus Primrose** and built by John Baker (Kenton Forge) Ltd. Production started in 1970 and continued until 1980. She was launched at the 1970 London Boat Show. She has always been a controversial boat with those who love her being enthusiastic and loyal devotees. She has some very different features, such as the sloping forward companionway. In 1972 the Mark II was introduced with the forecabin turning into space for the heads and stowage. Headroom is 4ft 5in. Accommodation for four was retained by moving the saloon berths under the cockpit seats. She has a lifting keel which is quite long and gives good directional stability.

Price guide: +/- £3.500

128

Splinter - 21ft 2in

The **Spinter** was designed in 1965 by Van de Stadt. She was built on Tyler mouldings by various companies. GS Marine, in Poole, Wm King, Burnham on Crouch, HH Marine, Horndean, BJ Marine, Dublin. Four berths. Had a great reputation for sailing ability after winning the Round the Island Race.

Specification

LOA: 21ft 2in
LWL: 17ft
Beam: 6ft 10in
Draught: Fin: 3ft 9in
Bilge: 2ft 6in
Displacement: 2800lbs
Ballast: 880lbs
Sail area: 190 sq ft

Price guide: +/- £3.000.

Jaguar 21 - 21ft 4in

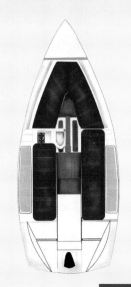

Jaguar 21. A lifting keel trailerable cruiser. The keel is flush with the bottom of the boat, so she sits upright if you take the ground. With the keel down she shows a good turn of speed with an exciting performance. Inside there are comfortable berths for four. There is a small single burner cooker next to the sink. The tinted windows provide plenty of light. Ideal as a weekender, she could be fitted out for longer passages and as a trailer sailer she can reach destinations denied by lack of time to bigger boats.

Specification

LOA: 21ft 4in
LWL: 16ft 11in
Beam: 8ft 3in
Draught:
Keel down: 4ft
Displacement:
2.550lbs
Ballast: 250lbs
Sail area: 200sq ft
Keel weight: 540lbs

Price guide: +/- £6.500

Jaguar 215 - 21ft 5in

Jaguar 215. Designed by John Mullins the Jaguar 21 has always had a good reputation on the used boat market. The interior accommodation is simple and works well. There is a hinged cover over the cooker which can also be used as a chart table. The cockpit is big enough for a crew of four. The photograph above is of a new boat they are now back in production built by Jaguar Yachts Ltd, 01255 677365.

Specification

LOA: 21ft 5in
LWL: 16ft 11in
Beam: 8ft 3in
Draught:
Keel down: 4ft
Keel up: 10in
Displacement:
2.550lbs
Ballast: 793lbs
Sail area: 200sq ft

Price guide: +/- £14.000.

Kingfisher 20 - 21ft 7in

The Kingfisher 20 was designed in 1959 by RAG Nierop and built by Westfield Engineering Ltd. Production carried on into the sixties and seventies, making her one of the most popular small twin bilge keel boats. She is rigged as a Bermudan masthead sloop. She can be cruised comfortably in coastal waters and is quite capable of cross-Channel passages in suitable weather. In 1969 she was developed to become the Kingfisher 20 Plus. She has a self draining cockpit and came with either a 6hp Johnson or 12hp Dolphin engine.

Specification

LOA: 20ft 7in
LWL: 18ft 6in
Beam: 6ft 11in
Draught: 2ft 4in
Displacement: 2700lbs
Ballast: 1100lbs
Sail area: 177sq ft
Capacities:
Fuel: 5 gallons
Water: 10 gallons
Berths: 4
Headroom: 4ft 10in
Construction: GRP

Price guide: +/- £3.000

Freedom 21 - 21ft 8in

Specification

LOA: 21ft 8in
LWL: 19ft
Beam: 8ft
Draught: 2ft 6in
Displacement: 1.800lbs

Ballast: 750lbs
Sail areas:
Main: 200sq ft
Spinnaker: 265sq ft
Engine: Mariner 4hp
or Tohatsu 4hp
outboards

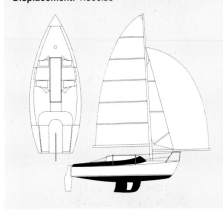

The Freedom 21 was Designed by Gary Hoyt an ex advertising executive who has designed some radical and successful craft. She has the unstayed mast of a typical American Cat boat. She has a comparatively large sail area but it can be easily controlled by one person from the cockpit. The spinnaker is worked with the Hoyt 'gun mount' an unusual looking device that works well. The berths are roomy and comfortable. There is a simple sink unit and a curtain separates the head compartment from the saloon. The tandem wing keel was designed by Warwick Collins but it is not advisable to dry out with this configuration without the support of a wall.

Price guide: +/- £4.000

Anderson 22 - 21ft 9in

Specification

LOA: 21ft 9in
LWL: 19ft 3in
Beam: 7ft 7in
Draught: 2ft min - 4ft 4in max
Displacement: 2500lbs
Ballast: 900lbs
Sail Area: 199sq ft
Construction: GRP

The Anderson 22 was designed in 1973 by Oliver Lee. A small but tough mini-cruiser which first appeared in 1974, she has comfortable accommodation with four berths. The boat has a lifting keel which is left partly outside of the hull when lifted. She has an excellent sea-keeping reputation with two transatlantic crossings to her credit. She is strongly rigged with a smallish sail area: a good starter boat. In 1982 the designer developed a larger sister, the Anderson 26 - production numbers were quite small.

Price guide: +/- £4.000

Seal 22 - 21ft 9in

Specification

LOA: 21ft 9in
LWL: 18ft 0in
Beam: 7ft 9in
Draught: 2ft - 3ft 10in
Displacement: 2.400lbs
Sail areas:
Main 121sq ft
Racing Genoa:
142 sq ft
Cruising Genoa:
120 sq ft
Berths: 4/6

The Seal 22 was designed by Angus Primrose and built by John Baker (Kenton Forge) Ltd. Production started in 1970 and continued until 1980. She was launched at the 1970 London Boat Show. She has always been a controversial boat with those who love her being enthusiastic and loyal devotees. She has some very different features, such as the sloping forward companionway. In 1972 the Mark II was introduced with the forecabin turning into space for the heads and stowage. Headroom is 4ft 5in. Accommodation for four was retained by moving the saloon berths under the cockpit seats. She has a lifting keel which is quite long and gives good directional stability.

Price guide: +/- £3.500

E Boat - 21ft 10in

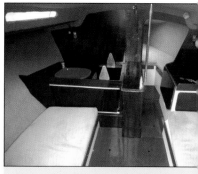

Specification

LOA: 21ft 10in
LWL: 18ft 1in
Beam: 9ft 1in
Draught:
Keel up / down:
0ft 10in / 4ft 6in
Displacement:
2.150lbs
Ballast: 700lbs
Sail area: 250 sq ft
Headroom: 4ft 7in
Engine:
4-6hp outboard

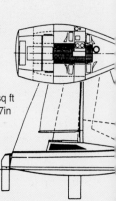

The E Boat was designed by Julian Everitt. Small, beamy, trailable and very roomy, there are not many production boats that meet that criteria. You can pick up a good used one for around £4500. Older boats are 20 years old and may need some TLC. She has a lifting keel. There is a bow well useful for anchor stowage. Her hull is very dished which gives her the comfortable interior. The saloon berths are 7ft long. There is an owners' association which organises events and publishes regular newsletters.

Price guide: +/- £4.500

Hurley 22 - 22ft

The **Hurley 22** was designed in 1966 by Ian Anderson. She is a safe boat for coastal cruising yet is more than able for serious offshore cruising. She has four berths, a chart table and a practical if small galley. She was still in production up to the late 1980s. Over 1500 were built and later versions using the same basic design with some modifications are known as the Hurley 22R. She has a long fin keel. A Dutch builder has also introduced a new model: the Hurley 800, much changed from the orginal Hurley concept. She is the epitome of a safe cruising boat.

Specification

LOA: 22ft
LWL: 17ft
Beam: 7ft 5in
Draught: 3ft 9in
Displacement: 3.900lbs

Price guide: +/- £6.500.

Foxterrier - 22ft 1in

The **Foxterrier** was designed in 1979 by Tony Dixon, the nephew of Uffa Fox and built by Copland Boats on the Isle of Wight. She has sensible accommodation and is a forgiving craft. She is more than capable of cross-channel crossings. The keel is housed in a knee high box. They are very roomy below and up to six people can sleep on full length berths. Mark II boats have an alternative layout with the quarter berths omitted to allow more cockpit stowage. A trailer sailer with the choice of inboard saildrive Volvo MB50 or up to 7hp outboards, there were approximately 100 boats built.

Specification

LOA: 22ft 1in
LWL: 19ft 4in
Beam: 8ft 2in
Draught: 4ft 1in
Displacement: 2.650lbs
Ballast: 1200lbs
Sail areas:
179 sq ft
Headroom: 5ft 3in
Berths: 4

Price guide: +/- £6.000

Limbo 6.6 - 22ft 3in

Specification

LOA: 22ft 3in
LWL: 17ft
Beam: 8ft 2in
Draught: 2ft 3in - 5ft
Displacement: 1950lbs
Sail area: 239 sq ft
Berths: 4
Headroom: 4ft 6in
Engine: 3-5hp outboard
Construction: GRP sandwich

The **Limbo 6.6** was designed by Andrew Stewart and built by Zygal Boats of Whitstable. She has a swing keel (a 850lb iron plate) but intrusion into the hull is minimal. She was available from 1979 until 1984 and124 were built. She has a large open cockpit with lots of working space. The maximum beam is further forward than most boats of her size. The boat has four berths, a simple galley and enough room for a chemical toilet. A larger version the Limbo 9.9 designed by Zygal Boats, appeared in 1982. She had an LOA of 32ft with a LWL of 27ft 6in and a beam of 11ft.

Price guide: +/- £4.000

Hunter Sonata - 22ft 7in

Specification

LOA: 6.9m
LWL: 5.5m
Beam: 2.5m
Draught: 1.4m
Displacement: 1115kg
Ballast: 440kg
Sail area: 18.21 sqm
Engine: Outboard
Water: 10 gallons
Headroom: 5ft 5in
Berths: 4

The **Hunter Sonata** was designed by David Thomas and built by Hunter Boats of Essex. A strict One Design, and 442 were built between November 1975 and June 1990. She became an RYA recognised National Class. Although she was designed for racing she is a very spacious 22 footer. For cruising she can take four full length berths. She also has a good galley and a heads compartment in the forecabin. There is a room for a chart table and plenty of room for stowage. She handles easily and is stable enough for comfortable family cruising.

Price guide: +/- £6.500.

Leisure 23 - 22ft 8in

The **Leisure 23,** designed by Frank prior and built by Cobramould/Brinecraft, was one of the most popular and well know small yachts ever built. She sells well as a used boat. The Leisure offers lots of space below and her freboard allows headroom of 5ft 10in. She has a generous galley taking up most of the port side with plenty of stowage space. There is an enclosed heads compartment and a cosy V berth up front. There is also a generous quarter berth, good for the navigator, by the companionway. There are plenty of deep lockers. She has a steady and comfortable motion at sea.

Specification

LOA: 22ft 8in
LWL: 20ft 0in
Beam: 7ft 10in
Draught: Fin: 3ft 11in
Twin: 2ft 8in
Displacement: 4.050lbs
Ballast: 1,950lbs
Sail area: 248sq ft
Headroom: 5ft 10in
Engine:
7-10hp outboard
or inboard

Price guide: +/- £5.000

Cobra 700 - 23ft

The **Cobra 700** was designed in 1982 by David Feltham as a modest budget, family cruiser. Built by Cobra Yachts in GRP. She has a maximum head-room of 6ft. Berths for four people in two cabins, and a separate heads compartment. Her high freeboard and good beam makes her a roomy 23 footer. The smallest of the Cobra range, many were built from kits, so quality standards are varied. She has an optional engine, up to 20hp. Her fuel capacity is 8 gallons and water 10 gallons.

Specification

LOA: 23ft
LWL: 18ft 4in
Beam: 8ft 9in
Draught: 3ft
Capacities:
Water: 10 gallons
Fuel: 8 gallons
Engine: Up to 20hp
Max headroom: 6ft
Berths: 4

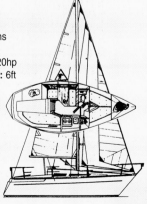

Price guide: +/- £9.000

Hunter 701 - 23ft

Specification

LOA: 23ft
LWL: 19ft 8in
Beam: 7ft 6in
Draught: 4ft
Displacement: 3000lbs
Sail area: 221sq ft
Headroom: 4ft 10in
Berths: 4

The **Hunter 701** was designed by Oliver Lee and built by Hunter Boats. There were 82 sold from September 1971 to September 1975. She has a hydraulic lifting keel. A cruising version has four berths for family accommodation. She resembles the earlier Hunter 19, the company's best seller (980 in ten years). Hunter Boats has been building boats for 30 years, over these years, they have won Awards for 'Best Production Boat of the Year', 'Yacht of the Year', 'Best Sailing Boat' ... and no fewer than four separate Design Centre Selections.

Price guide: +/- £3.500.

Pandora - 23ft

Specification

LOA: 21ft 10in
LWL: 18ft 9in
Beam: 6ft 11in
Draught: 3ft 9in
Ballast: 960lbs
Sail area: 216sq ft
Engine: Outboard
Headroom: 5ft 9in
Berths: 4

The **Pandora** was designed by Van De Stadt and built by Rydgeway Marine Ltd. There were hundreds of Pandoras built during the seventies. Maximum headroom is 5ft 9in. There are four berths. They were later uprated in 1974 and known as the Pandora International. She has a 3ft draught with bilge keels.

Price guide: +/- £3.000.

Samphire - 23ft

Specification

LOA: 22ft 7in
LWL: 17ft 11in
Beam: 7ft 9in
Draught: 2ft 11in
Displacement: 5.000lbs
Ballast: 1.950lbs
Sail area: 236 sq ft
Engine:
Volvo/Petter/Vire
usually 8-10hp

The **Samphire** was designed by David Cannell and built by North Sea Craft. She is a long keeled and heavy boat. Yachts like this are few and far between. The designer specified a substantial layup which incorporated woven rovings for extra strength. She is a bit like a smaller version of the Vertue. Her deep hull gives roomier accommodation than you might expect and she has ample stowage. If you are looking for something solid and safe she might well be the boat for you.

Price guide: +/- £5.500.

Foxhound - 23ft 9in

Specification

LOA: 23ft 9in
LWL: 18ft 1in
Beam: 8ft 3in
Draught:
Deep fin: 4ft 6in
Twin keels: 3ft 0in
Displacement:
2.800lbs
Ballast: 1.250lbs
Sail area: 260 sq ft
Engine: 7.5hp outboard
or Petter Mini six/
Vire 7hp inboard
Headroom: 5ft 2in

The **Foxhound** was designed by Uffa Fox in 1975 and built by Copland Boats. She received a mixed reception at her debut, but with the benefit of hindsight she does have a lot to offer. Her respectable performance and generous headroom in a high-volume hull plus generous stowage make her an attractive proposition. She has a wide cockpit for boats of her vintage. If you can find one in good condition and your surveyor gives her a good report, you will have found a boat with modern lines and a distinctive yellow hull.

Price guide: +/- £6.000.

Hurley 24/70 - 23ft 9in

Specification

LOA: 23ft 9in
LWL: 17ft 6in
Beam: 7ft 5in
Draught: 4ft 1in
Displacement: 5.040lbs
Ballast: 2.500lbs
Sail area: 216sq ft
Headroom: 5ft 11in

The Hurley 24/70 was designed by Ian Anderson in 1972. The Hurley 24/70 is based on the very popular Hurley 20. She has a restyled transom and a new coachroof. The options of bilge or fin keels were also offered. With her deep bilge she has good headroom of 5ft 11in. The saloon is spacious and light. There is a chart table and the bunks extend to 6ft 4in. The galley is a GRP moulding. Forward of of the berth on the port side is the heads. The forepeak has a double V berth with stowage underneath. The early boats had Mini-Petter 5hp engines installed.

Price guide: +/- £8.000.

Compac 23 - 23ft 11in

Specification

LOA: 23ft 11in
LWL: 22ft 0in
Beam: 7ft 10in
Draught: 2ft 3in
Displacement: 3.300lb
Ballast: 1.340lbs
Sail area: 250sq ft

The Compac 23 was designed by Clark Mills and built in the USA by Hutchins. She has the looks of a traditional and tough little cruiser. She is very attractive to look at, with bronze ports set in a low coachroof. The sink and cooker are designed to slide over the settee berths. Her forecabin is roomy and the heads compartment is separted from the saloon. She has a large open cockpit, ideal for day sailing. The original American rigging could be considered light by European standards, but imported models are likely to have been beefed-up for our more boisterous conditions.

Price guide: +/- £5.000

Husky 24 - 24ft

Specification

LOA: 24ft
LWL: 19ft 6in
Beam: 8ft 6in
Draught: 2ft 6in
Displacement: 6720lbs
Ballast: 1900lbs
Sail area: 220sq ft
Engine: BMC Captain diesel
Fuel: 25 gallons
Water: 25 gallons
Headroom: 6ft 3in
Berths: 4

The **Husky 24** was designed by CW Burnard and built by Yachthaven Ltd. First introduced in the early sixties. A robust looking motor sailer, she is a beamy masthead sloop. She has a shallow draft and easily handled rig. A family boat, she provides accommodation for four adults in two cabins. She has a separate heads compartment and a gas cooker. The boat was updated in 1966 increasing the fuel and water capacities. She later became the Husky Hustler in 1969 with upgraded accommodation for 6 and a centre cockpit.

Price guide: +/- £12.000.

Westerly GK24 - 24ft

Specification

LOA: 24ft
LWL: 19ft 8in
Beam: 9ft 4in
Draught: 5ft / 4ft 1in
Displacement: 3.800lbs
Ballast: 1.400lbs
Sail areas:
Main:140sq ft
100% jib: 150sq ft
Spinnaker: 538sq ft

The **Westerly GK24** was designed in 1974 by Laurent Giles/Chris Hawkins and built by Westerly yachts. She was designed with performance in mind and looks quite different to the Centaurs and Pageants from the same builder. She is also a popular cruising boat with her efficient internal layout. Her broad beam allows space for three people to sleep in the saloon. The galley is to port and has a two-burner cooker. There is plenty of stowage space although the headroom is restricted to a maximum of 4ft 8in.

Price guide: +/- £8.500.

Legend 240 - 24ft 1in

The Legend 240 was designed and built in the USA by the Hunter Marine Corporation. This boat is light enough to trail behind the family car. This is a difficult trick to bring off unless you can keep the weight down. The answer for this boat is to use water ballast. She is light and airy below and every inch of the space is used for occupation. Headroom is 4ft 7in. A basic galley, and a chemical toilet (beneath the foreberth) are included. A coolbox is fitted beneath the port seat.

Price guide: +/- £20.000

Specification

LOA: 24ft 1in
LWL: 22ft 1in
Beam: 8ft 3in
Draught:
Keel up: 1ft 6in
Keel down: 5ft 6in
Displacement: 2.300lbs
Water ballast: 1.300lbs
Sail area: 245 sq ft
Engine: 4-8hp outboard

Sadler 25 - 24ft 4in

The Sadler 25 was designed and built by David Sadler. This distinctive yacht with her blue hull always stands out. She is a popular boat and one of the prettiest. She has a deep cockpit with lots of locker space. The interior is bright and easy to keep clean. The berthing arrangements are conventional with a quarter berth extending under the cockpit. The saloon has a dinette format which can be converted into a double berth. There are two large cockpit lockers, a good place to keep fenders, dinghies etc.
There is an active Owner's association:
www.sadlerandstarlight.co.uk/docs/home.htm

Specification

LOA: 24ft 4in
LWL: 23ft 9in
Beam: 8ft 9in
Draught:
Deep fin: 4ft 8in
Shallow fin: 3ft 10in
Twin keels: 3ft 3in
C' plate: 2ft 3in/4ft 6in
Displacement: 4.500lbs
Ballast: 1.900lbs
Sail areas:
Mainsail: 132 sq ft
Genoa: 232 sq ft
Headroom: 5ft 2in
Berths: 4/5
Engine: Petter Mini Six and various outboards

Price guide: +/- £10.000

Yachting World 5 ton - 24ft 5in

Specification

LOA: 24ft 5in
LWL: 20ft 11in
Beam: 7ft 10in
Draught: 4ft 4in
Ballast: 1.9 tons iron
Sail area: 377 sq ft
Berths: 3

The Yachting World 5 tonner was designed by Robert Clark. The magazine *Yachting World* commissioned the designer to create a 5 ton cruising sloop in 1945. The idea was that drawings could be made available to their readers when scarce materials eventually became available after World War II. There were many built by professional and DIY owners. This 5-tonner is a pretty design, with elegant lines and a modest forward over-hang. Slightly shorter overall than a Laurent Giles Vertue, she is 8in (2.03m) beamier, and sets quite a bit more sail. She is best suited to being sailed by two people.

Price guide: +/- £8.000

Trapper 240 - 24ft 6in

Specification

LOA: 24ft 6in
LWL: 19ft 6in
Beam: 9ft 2in
Draught:
Keel up: 1ft 4in
Keel down: 5ft 5in
Displacement: 2.900lbs
Ballast: 1.00lbs
Sail area: 304 sq ft
Engine: 5-7 hp

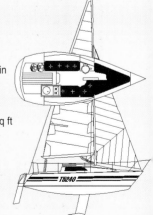

The Trapper 240 was designed by Ed Dubois and built by Trapper Yachts. She was launched in 1980 and initially built with a solid hull laminate, later they used a balsa sandwich. She has a lifting keel raised by block and tackle, and decent accommodation. She has a very broad transom. Headroom is 5ft 5in in the saloon. The galley slides out from the cockpit on the starboard side. It incorporates a two-burner cooker and good storage. The starboard berth is 7ft 10in long with the port side being 20ins shorter. The cockpit is comfortable with nicely angled mouldings.

Price guide: +/- £10.000.

Cobra 750 - 25ft

Specification

LOA: 25ft
LWL: 19ft 9in
Beam: 9ft 6in
Draught: Fin: 4ft 3in
Twin: 3ft 6in
Displacement: 2½ tons
Ballast: 1 ton
Sail area: Main: 120sq ft
No1 jib: 140sq ft

The **Cobra 750** was designed by David Feltham and built by Cobra Yachts. The designer set out to appeal to cruising families. They will find five berths including a sensible quarter berth on the starboard side. The interior is fitted out in teak. There is a walk through heads compartment on the port side, with a hanging locker opposite. A chart table is available on the starboard side next to the galley. Headroom measures 5ft 9in. There were a lot of home builds, so standards of finish will vary.

Price guide: +/- £9.000.

Folkboat - 25ft

Specification

LOA: 25ft
LWL: 19ft 8in
Beam: 7ft 2in
Draught: 3ft 11in
Displacement: 4.800lbs
Ballast: 2.750lbs
Berths: 4 in two cabins
Sail area: 280sq ft
Engine: 6hp outboard
Construction: Wood

The **Folkboat** was designed by Tord Sunden and a Swedish committee in the 1930s. They have been built in their hundreds by many builders. You can find them stripped out as racers or turned into cruising format. Surveys are a good idea as many have had the attention of enthusiastic amateur owners. But they are an attractive boat for family sailing. The design is still available see the entry in the 'Boats Currently in Production' section page 37.

Price guide: +/- £12.000.

Ocean 760 - 25ft

Specification

LOA: 25ft 0in
Beam: 8ft 4in
Draught: 1ft 2in -
4ft 6in
Displacement:
3.638lbs

Ballast:
internal: 882lbs
external: 154lbs
Sail area:
main: 156sq ft
jib: 86sq ft

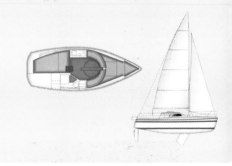

The **Ocean 760** was designed by Andrzej Skrzat. This boat was imported into the UK in 2001. Used versions are becoming available. She has spacious accommodation and is very nicely finished down below in light oak or mahogany. There is a big semi-circular table that sits on the centreboard case. Not a boat for overnight passages, she is more suitable for weekend day work. There is a good sized double berth up front. Under the cockpit there is another full sized double berth with built-in storage lockers. The coachroof lifts to provide an extra 7ins of headroom. She is designed as a trailer sailer but she is heavy enough to need a four wheel drive.

Tomahawk 25 - 25ft 4in

Specification

LOA: 25ft 4in
LWL: 20ft 0in
Beam: 8ft 6in
Draught:
Fin keel: 4ft 8in
Twin keel: 3ft 0in
Displacement:
5.66lbs
Ballast:
2.200lbs
Sail area:
Main: 137 sq ft
Genoa:
230 sq ft

The **Tomahawk 25** was launched and built by Marcon in 1970 this boat developed new possibilities available from GRP construction. All boats have a forecabin with two vee berths just under 6ft. The heads compartment is separate. There is enough space for a chart table. And headroom is 6ft in the main saloon. Some early boats have a dinette which can be converted to a berth. An inboard engine of around 9hp is usually fitted. She sails well and offers generous accommodation for a boat of this size.

Contessa 26 - 25ft 6in

Specification

LOA: 25ft 6in
LWL: 20ft 0in
Beam: 7ft 6in
Draught: 4ft
Displacement: 5.400lbs

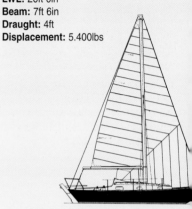

The Contessa 26 was designed by David Sadler and built by Jeremy Rogers. The design is a classic. She was developed with different layouts as her 13 year production run proceeded and 360 boats were built. Options included berths for up to five crew. The galley moved to the companionway with the chart table. The heads left the forecabin and became an enclosed compartment. She belongs to a range of boats under the Contessa range which are very popular in the used boat market.

Price guide: +/- £7.500

MG Spring - 25ft 6in

Specification

LOA: 25ft 6in
LWL: 22ft 9in
Beam: 9ft 0in
Draught: 3ft 0in
Displacement:
4.500lbs
Ballast: 1550lbs
Sail area: 398 sq ft
Headroom:
5ft 11in
Engine:
Volvo 2GM 10hp

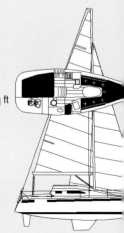

The MG Spring was designed by Tony Castro and built by Jaguar and Northshore. She was the original star of the TV soap *Howard's Way*. She has a fashionable sugar scoop transom with a fold-down ladder. She is big inside with nearly 6ft of headroom in the saloon. An open plan layout that has the galley to port and a chart table on starboard. She has a generous heads compartment. The aft cabin under the cockpit is vast. The centred table slides up and can be stowed under the deckhead. Her motion at sea is steady and she makes little leeway.

Price guide: +/- £13.500.

Harrison Butler Cyclone - 25ft 9in

Specification

Construction: Wood
LOA: 25ft 9in
LWL: 23ft 0in
Beam: 8ft 9in
Draught: 4ft 3in
Displacement: 5.8 tons
Keel Lead/Iron:
2.3/1.45 tons

The Harrison Butler Cyclone was designed by Thomas Harrison Butler. When he was born (early 20th century), yacht-designing was a self-taught and amateur leisure time activity and his practical experience of sailing in small boats with his family influenced his designs. His boats are for the fanatical lover of traditional wooden boats.

Price guide: +/- £25.000.

Legend 26 - 25ft 9in

Specification

LOA: 25ft 9in
LWL: 23ft 1¹/2in
Beam: 8ft 11¹/2in
Draught: Keel up: 1ft 9in
Keel down: 6ft 0in
Displacement
(Water ballasted) 5.000lbs
Sail area: 290 sq ft
Headroom: 5ft 8in
Engine: 8/9hp outboard

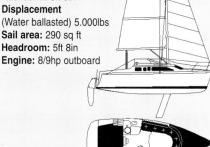

The Legend 26 was designed and built by Hunter Marine in the USA. She is a mass produced trailer sailer with water ballast. She appeals to first time buyers and others who are moving down from larger boats and who are looking for hassle-free sailing. She has a double berth in the forepeak. Windows make the interior light and airy. There is a galley including a large coolbox. She also has a chemical toilet in an enclosed heads. She is a big boat to trail every time you want to sail so most owners will probably settle for keeping her at home over winter. But you will certainly gain over the costs of hardstanding in a marina.

Price guide: +/- £17.000.

Mystere - 25ft 9in

The Mystere was designed by Frederick Parker and David Anderson. Built by Fairways Marine and Marine Construction (UK) Ltd. Launched in 1973 as a cruiser/racer, she was successful on the racing circuit and proved herself a speedy cruising yacht. There are four full berths and two smaller children's berths. She has a good-sized saloon, a smallish forecabin and a heads compartment. She is an elegant yacht. Her bigger sister, the Javelin (30ft) came from the same source.

Specification

LOA: 25ft 9in
LWL: 18ft 2in
Beam: 8ft 5in
Draught: 4ft 5in
Displacement: 4.900lbs
Ballast: 1950lbs
Sail area: 320sq ft
Fuel: 6 gallons
Water: 18 gallons
Headroom: 5ft 8in
Engine: Vire 6hp or Dolphin 12hp
Berths: 4-6

Price guide: +/- £9.000.

MacGregor 26 - 25ft 10in

The MacGregor 26 was designed and built by the MacGregor Yacht Corporation in the USA. An unusual boat. She is capable of 20 knots under power but is also equipped with sails for a more conventional cruising. These are very popular boats offering easy trailing, light weight and simple launching. She is spacious with six berths, a separate heads compartment. Standing headroom, a galley with a tiled worktop and inset sink, plus a single-burner cooker. She achieves stability by the use of water ballast plus a drop down plate. If you like the idea of a hybrid craft this could be the one for you. A later version is still in production, see page 36.

Specification

LOA: 25ft 10in
LWL: 23ft 0in
Beam: 7ft 10in
Draught:
Plate up: 0ft 9in
Plate down: 5ft 6in
Displacement:
Tank empty: 2.350lbs
Tank full: 3750lbs
Sail area: 357 sq ft

Price guide: +/- £19.000

Atalanta 26 - 26ft

The **Atalanta 26** was designed by Fairey Marine and Uffa Fox. Introduced in 1963. She was developed from the Uffa Fox WWII Airborne lifeboat. The unusual 'rolled' topside hull is fitted with double lifting keels. She has six berths and sitting headroom, unless you are more than 5ft 9in. Her interior could probably be described as simple. Nevertheless she is a distinctive boat and there are plenty still afloat. Be careful to have a potential buy surveyed as her hot moulded ply method of construction is expensive to work on.

Specification

LOA: 26ft 0in
LWL: 24ft 6in
Beam: 7ft 9in
Draught: 1ft 3in - 5ft 9in
Displacement: 4.480lbs
Ballast: 950lbs
Fuel: 11 gallons
Water: 12 gallons
Headroom: 5ft 9in
Berths: 6
Construction:
Hot moulded wood

Price guide: +/- £8.000.

Super Seal 26 - 26ft

The **Super Seal** was designed by Ron Holland and built by John Baker/GW Parker & Son, she was based on racing thinking and she has proved herself to many happy owners. She has a shallow hull and moderate beam so you might be surprised at how spacious she is below. There are six berths at least 6ft 3in long, a heads compartment, decent galley, a chart table to starboard and lots of stowage space. There is a keel case but it forms a partition between the heads and the entrance to the forecabin. Some Super Seals were built with fixed fin keels.

Specification

LOA: 26ft
LWL: 23ft 4in
Beam: 9ft 3in
Draught: Keel up: 1ft 1in
Keel down: 5ft 6in
Fixed Fin: 5ft 3in / 4ft 3in
Displacement:
Lifting keel: 5.000lbs
Ballast:
Lifting keel: 2.000lbs
Sail area: 406sq ft
Engine: 6-8hp
outboard
or 8-10 inboard
Headroom: 5ft 9in

Price guide: +/- £18.500.

Macwester 26 - 26ft

The **Macwester 26** was designed in 1964 by CSJ Roy and built by Macwester Marine Co Ltd, over 450 were built. She has good standing headroom under her high coachroof. There were variations on the interior; dinette or single straight berths. She has a separate heads and a good large forecabin. Seen by many as a good family boat, her shallow draught and bilge keels allow entrance to the quieter parts of our rivers and estuaries. The original design was updated as Series II in 1971, with an increase in sail area to 330 sq ft.

Specification

LOA: 26ft 0in
LWL: 21ft 0in
Beam: 9ft 2in
Draught: 2ft 9in
Displacement: 6.720lbs
Ballast: 2.265lbs
Sail area: 301sq ft
Water: 20 gallons
Fuel: 12 gallons
Headroom: 6ft
Berths: 4-5

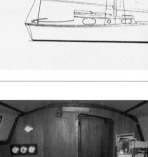

Price guide: +/- £7.000.

Mirage 26 - 26ft

The **Mirage 26** was designed by Walsh Wakefield Ltd and built by Thames Marine, there were about 60 Mirage 26s built. She has a high freeboard which means that she is roomy down below. A wide companionway adds to the sense of space. There is a table that folds back against the bulkhead. In the heads a sink hinges down over the toilet. With the benefit of a trotter box the starboard berth is 6ft 4ins long. There are three windows on each side, disguised by the dark acrylic cover. Nearly half of the boats built had fin keels. She looks a bit high for fast sailing but her looks belie her abilities.

Specification

LOA: 26ft 0in
LWL: 20ft 4in
Beam: 9ft 0in
Draught: Fin: 4ft 6in
Twin: 3ft 6in
Displacement:
5.600lbs
Ballast:
2.250lbs
Sail area:
300sq ft
Engine:
Yanmar/Volvo 7-8hp
Headroom: 6ft

Price guide: +/- £12.000.

Snapdragon 26 - 26ft

The **Snapdragon 26** was designed and built in 1965 by Thames Marine. A comfortable cruising yacht for the family. She is spacious below and has accommodation for up to five adults. Up front she has a toilet and a hanging locker which can be closed off with a door. There is a good sized dinette arrangement in the saloon which can be converted to a double bunk. The galley is supplied with a Formica worktop, sink unit and plenty of stowage space. She has good headroom for her size. She is not a particularly fast yacht, but cruising folk should not be daunted.

Price guide: +/- £8.000.

Specification

LOA: 26ft 0in
LWL: 21ft 8in
Beam: 8ft 6in
Draught: 2ft 6in
Displacement:
4.500lbs
Sail area: 255sq ft
Berths: 5
Headroom:
5ft 10in
Engine:
10hp Albin
or 8hp Sabb
Water:
12 gallons

Westerly Griffon - 26ft

The **Westerly Griffon** was designed by Ed Dubois for Westerly. She came after the popular Centaur. First launched in 1979 over 450 were sold. She is a safe sea kindly boat. Headroom throughout the saloon is 5ft 9in. There is a long settee to port, which extends back under the cockpit. She has plenty of stowage space under the seats. The table is sturdy and has a drop leaf. A retractable chart table is often available. The heads compartment is spacious with a slide-out sink. The toilet itself faces across the boat. The forecabin is large enough for dressing.

Specification

LOA: 26ft 0in
LWL: 21ft 7in
Beam: 9ft 3in
Draught:
Fin/Twin:
4ft 9in/3ft 3in
Displacement:
6.600lbs
Ballast: 2.717lbs
Sail area: 335sq ft

Price guide: +/- £17.500.

Etap 24i - 26ft 4in

The **Etap 24i** was built by Etap Yachting in Belgium. This is a performance boat. She is said by the builders to be unsinkable. She offers four berths big enough for six footers. For weekend cruising, there is enough space for a couple of adults and two children. The settee berths extend under the cockpit. The low coachroof does not allow standing headroom. The interior is finished to a high standard. The heads is fitted between the forward bulkhead and the V berth. There is plenty of space for stowage. The boat is still in production so if you are interested in a new one see page 38.

Price guide: +/- £41.000.

Specification

LOA: 26ft 3in
LWL: 22ft 0in
Beam: 8ft 2in
Draught:
Tandem keel: 3ft 0in
Fin keel: 4ft 11in
Displacement:
3.524lbs
Ballast: 1.101lbs
Sail area:
Main: 196 sq ft
Headsail: 131 sq ft
Berths: 4
Headroom:
5ft 4$^{1}/_{2}$ ins

Vancouver 27 - 27ft

The **Vancouver 27** was designed by Robert Harris, and first appeared in 1974. She is a seamanlike often used for short handed cruising. The first boat to this design was built for a Canadian couple to sail from Vancouver to New Zealand. She was the first production pocket ocean cruiser and she was a great success, with a number also built in the USA. Pheon Yachts built all the 27s for the European market with the majority on Northshore moulded hulls. She ceased production in 1986. Northshore made some changes and turned her into the Vancouver 28 which is still available, see page 44.

Specification

LOA: 27ft 0in
LWL: 22ft 11in
Beam: 8ft 8in
Draught: 4ft 6in
Displacement: 8.960lbs
Sail area: 356sq ft
Capacities:
Water: 50 gallons
Fuel: 28 gallons
Berths: 4-5
Max headroom:
6ft plus

Price guide: +/- £25.000.

Sabre 27 - 27ft 1in

The **Sabre 27** was designed by Alan Hill and built by Marcon. She was introduced in 1969 as a family cruising yacht. Inside she has a traditional feel: the saloon being seven foot wide has the feel of a larger yacht. Headroom is 6ft. Many boats were finished by owners, so the layouts may well be varied. Some will have an L shaped settee on starboard or a dinette. Two quarter berths are also a common choice. Heads compartments while on the small side are separated from the saloon. A sensible choice for young families.

Specification

LOA: 27ft 1in
LWL: 22ft 2in
Beam: 9ft 0in
Draught:
Fin keel: 4ft 8in
Twin keel: 3ft 0in
Displacement:
6.800lbs
Ballast: 2.800lbs
Sail area:
Main: 155sq ft
Genoa: 264sq ft

Price guide: +/- £12.500

Trapper 500 - 27ft 4in

The **Trapper 500** was designed by Cuthbertson & Cassian and built by Trapper Yachts in Canada, and Anstey Yachts in the UK. She is a tough boat capable of a fair pace. The saloon is roomy and welcoming. Perhaps the galley could be a bit larger but the same can't be said of the stowage. There are lockers beneath all the berths. The saloon table can be lowered to form an extra double berth. There is no aft cabin. Over 500 have been built. One thing to watch is the reversible rudder it can be swung through 360°. Early owners found it was much easier to sail with the rudder the right way round.

Specification

LOA: 27ft 4in
LWL: 22ft 2in
Beam: 9ft 2in
Draught: 4ft 9in
Displacement: 5.200lb
Ballast: 2.250lb
Sail area: 317sq ft
Engine: RCA Dolphin 12hp
Headroom: 5ft 10in

Price guide: +/- £15.000.

Fairey Fisherman - 27ft 5in

Specification

LOA: 27ft 5in
LWL: 25ft 0in
Beam: 8ft 9in
Draught: 2ft 3in
Displacement: 5.511lb
Ballast: 1.100lb
Engine: 45hp

The Fairey Fisherman was designed and built by Fairey Marine. Lots of space is what you get with this motor sailer. She's tough, squat and very chunky. But for all that she is a very popular boat, and owners tend to hang on to them. She has a flat floor that is wide, 6ft headroom and a view out through the large windows. There is a full length galley on the starboard, a large heads compartment, and a gigantic forecabin with two 6ft 6in by 2ft 6in berths. If you think this sounds more like a caravan, then you are exactly right, except that she floats and sails surprisingly well. If conditions require it you can always switch on the engine.

Price guide: +/- £8.000.

MG 27 - 27ft 6in

Specification

LOA: 27ft 6in
LWL: 23ft 6in
Beam: 10ft 0in
Draught:
fin: 5ft 5in
centreplate:
3ft 2in - 5ft 10in
twin: 3ft 7in
Displacement:
5.750lb
Ballast: 2.070lb
Sail area: 413 sq ft
Engine:
Volvo 2001
or 9hp Saildrive

The MG 27 was designed by Rob Humphreys and built by MG Yachts and Northshore. A lightweight and speedy yacht, she has speed and easy handling. OK she has light displacement but there is also a deep keel. One person can handle her with ease. Down below her saloon is a one piece moulding up to bunk height, which gives a production line feeling. Maximum headroom is 5ft 9in. The heads and galley are roomy. The aft cabin is partly beneath the cockpit but it is 7ft 5in long. The forecabin has a 6ft 2in V berth. Locker space is lacking.

Price guide: +/- £22.000.

Varne 27 - 27ft 9in

The **Varne 27** was designed by Duncan Stuart, and built by Varne Marine. She was introduced in 1973. A well planned cruiser/racer with a good spec. Performance and handling is good. A distinctive high bow and low top-sides add to the impression of a boat designed for speed. Late boats had a double forecabin. The saloon has a galley aft and only one quarter berth. Her builder did a good job and quality is not an issue. She has a large headsail and a small main.

Specification

LOA: 27ft 9in
LWL: 21ft 0in
Beam: 9ft 0in
Draught: 4ft 3in
Displacement: 5.090lb
Ballast: 2.690lb
Sail area: 344 sq ft
Headroom: 6ft 0in
Berths: 4-5
Engine: Farryman 12 hp

Price guide: +/- £15.000

Great Dane - 28ft

The **Great Dane** was designed by Klaus Baess and built by OR Anderson in Denmark. She was a popular transom sterned cruiser, introduced to the UK in 1964. Looking very like a Twister, she is a tough, capable and a good sea boat. Her interior contains five berths and the design is typical of the period. A tad small by today's standards, she is an easy and well mannered boat to sail and makes an excellent offshore cruiser.

Specification

LOA: 28ft 0in
LWL: 21ft 4in
Beam: 8ft 2in
Draught: 4ft 6in
Displacement: 8.500lb
Ballast: 3.900lb
Sail area: 395 sq ft
Fuel: 10 gallons
Water: 20 gallons
Headroom: 6ft +
Berths: 5
Engine:
Volvo Penta
MD2b 25 hp

Price guide: +/- £25.000.

Kelt 850 - 28ft

The Kelt 850 was designed by Giles Vaton and built by Kelt/Kirie in France. This is a boat with remarkable volume; she has a long waterline and full ends. She also has a drop keel which gives her a draught of only 2ft 2in. She has an open plan layout and an unusual U shaped bulkhead that provides seating around three sides of the saloon. An impressive chart table is to port and the heads to starboard. The keel case is hidden beneath the saloon table. The aft cabin is bright, lit by three ports. She was first seen in the UK in 1984.

Specification

LOA: 28ft 0in
LWL: 24ft 6in
Beam: 10ft 4in
Draught: fin: 5ft 4in
lifting keel: 2ft 2in - 5ft 11in
Displacement: 7.000lb
Ballast: 3.350lb
Sail area: 474 sq ft
Engine: Yanmar 10 or 20hp
Headroom: 6ft 0in

Price guide: +/- £18.000.

Stag 28 - 28ft

The Stag 28 was designed by Peter Milne and Edwin Meayers and built by the Salterns Yacht Agency. The design brief was to create a yacht with an exterior which would appeal to men and an interior for women. The result was a fine job. The boats have worn well. She has plenty of headroom at 6ft 5in. There are four permanent berths and the dinette to starboard can be converted as well. There is a decent chart table. The spacious forecabin could well be the chosen space for many in the crew. The interior is finished in teak and ash. Overall the quality is excellent.

Specification

LOA: 28ft 0in
LWL: 24ft 7½in
Beam: 9ft 10in
Draught: fixed keel: 4ft 5in
lifting keel: 3ft 0in - 6ft 11in
Displacement: 7.500lb
Ballast: 2.800lb
Sail area: 284 sq ft
Engine: Volvo MD7A 13hp
Headroom: 6ft 5in

Price guide: +/- £13.000.

Hunter Ranger - 28ft 2in

The Hunter Ranger was designed by David Thomas. She is a distinctive looking yacht, one of the few boats of this length with 6ft plus headroom. She looks and feels spacious below, helped by her slab sides, wide stern and high coachroof. She is open plan so the forecabin offers no privacy. The dinette seat is U shaped giving an unusual but useful seating arrangement. There is a good chart table and a practical peninsula galley. The gimballed cooker is positioned on the hull side. The heads is cleverly designed with good space and angled mirrors. The engine is easy to access.

Price guide: +/- £30.000.

Specification

LOA: 28ft 2in
LWL: 22ft 5in
Beam: 9ft 2in
Draught: 3ft 3in
Displacement:
2.54 tons
Ballast: 1.04 tons
Sail area:
Main: 205 sq ft
Jib: 101 sq ft
Berths: 6
Engine:
Yanmar 1GM10 9hp

Compromis 888 - 28ft 6in

The Compromis 888 was built by the Zaadnoodijk Yard in Holland. The first boat in the range appeared in 1987. Her sister ships are the 777 and 999. The Dutch have a reputation for building good seaworthy cruisers. These are no exception. The saloon is comfortable and based on the dinette plan. The table can be lowered to form a double berth. The galley is fitted with a two-burner gas cooker. The heads compartment has some ergonomic problems regarding space. Otherwise she meets Dutch standards very well.

Price guide: +/- £40.000.

Specification

LOA: 28ft 6in
LWL: 25ft 0in
Beam: 9ft 8in
Draught: 3ft 9in
Displacement: 7.496lbs
Ballast: 3.086lbs
Sail area: 483sq ft

Gib'Sea 284 - 28ft 6in

The **Gib'Sea 284** was designed by Philippe Briand and built by Gibert Marine SA in France. The 284 marked a change from the rounded hulls of the 304 and 264. This boat is more wedge shaped with a lean look. She is very much a French boat with a slippery hull. The fine bow does restrict space internally up front. Outside she has a wide open cockpit. She is a lively performer and would suit the small family looking for a three cabin layout in a coastal cruiser.

Specification

LOA: 28ft 6in
LWL: 24ft 3in
Beam: 9ft 3in
Draught:
Fin: 5ft 10in
Lifting keel: 2ft 4in - 5ft 1in
Displacement: 7.000lbs
Ballast: Fin: 2.800lbs
Lifting keel: 3.384lbs
Sail area: 516 sq ft
Engine: Yanmar 20hp
Headroom: 6ft 1in

Price guide: +/- £40.000

Sadler 290 - 29ft

The **Sadler 290** was designed by Stephen Jones and built by Rampart Yachts. She is a twin-keeled family cruising yacht, with lots of space down below. The broad stern gives plenty of room in the aft cabin. Headroom in the saloon is 6ft 3in and over 6ft in the heads and forecabin. The heads is placed forward of the saloon. The galley is positioned abaft the companionway, well out of the way and with lots of work top. Stowage is good throughout. Designed as a rational development of the popular twin keelers of the 70s and 80s, the 290 continued that tradition.

Specification

LOA: 29ft 0in
LWL: 25ft 11in
Beam: 10ft 8in
Draught: Deep fin: 5ft 8in
Shallow fin: 4ft 9in
Twin keels: 4ft 3in
Displacement: 10.500lbs
Sail area: 470sq ft
Engine: Beta 20hp
Headroom: 6ft 3in

Price guide: +/- £28.5000.

Sigma 292 - *29ft*

The **Sigma 292** was designed by David Thomas and built by Marine projects. The smaller of the famous Sigma family. They are good heavy weather boats and make an excellent sporty cruiser. The interior layout is very practical at sea. The galley is fitted as a peninsula unit, with the sink almost on the centreline. The chart table is to starboard and folds down over the saloon berth. The cockpit is deep as there is no aft cabin below. A pilot berth fits snugly out of the way of activity in the saloon. There were 30 boats built.

Price guide: +/- £20.000.

Specification

LOA: 29ft 0in
LWL: 23ft 0in
Beam: 10ft 1in
Draught:
5ft 10in
Displacement:
6.000lbs
Ballast: 2.700lbs
Sail area: 373 sq ft
Engine:
Volvo MD5A 9HP
Headroom: 5ft 9in

Hallberg Rassy 29 - *29ft 2in*

The **Hallberg Rassy 29** was designed by Olle Enderlein/ Christopher Rassy. A total of 571 of these yachts were built, and production finished in 1994. The saloon is cosy and inviting, with high quality mahogany and comfortable seating. She has a good sized galley with a proper cooker/oven, fridge and a deep double sink. The chart table is removable for access to the berth. The settee backs can be lifted up on hinges to increase the width of the berths. The heads are to port. Although she is a small yacht by ocean standards, she has a rugged feel and is perfectly capable of crossing the widest seas.

Price guide: +/- £35.000.

Specification

LOA: 29ft 2in
LWL: 23ft 9in
Beam: 9ft 3in
Draught: 5ft 3in
Displacement:
8.380lbs
Ballast: 3.860lbs
Sail area: 409sq ft
Capacities:
Water: 26.4 gallons
Fuel: 13.2 gallons
Engine:
18hp Volvo
Penta 2002
Saildrive

Vindo - 29ft 3in

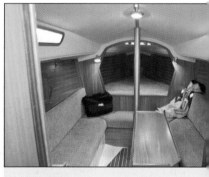

Specification

LOA: 29ft 3in
LWL: 22ft 0in
Beam: 9ft 1in
Draught: 4ft 3in
Displacement:
7.040lbs
Sail area: 344sq ft
Ballast: 3.300lbs

The Vindo was designed by Carl Andersson and built by Notesunds Varv AB, Sweden. This is a modern GRP yacht with the look of a traditional wooden boat. She was introduced in the early 1970s. The interior is traditional in style and the joinery is in mahogany and teak throughout. In the saloon there is an L shaped settee to starboard. The galley has lots of good storage and the chart table is large. In the forecabin there is light from two small windows. The Vindo is a nice proposition if you would love to own a wooden boat but don't have the time to maintain it. There were 300 built.

Price guide: +/- £30.000

Hanse 292/301 - 29ft 6in

Specification

LOA: 29ft 6in
LWL: 26ft 1in
Beam: 9ft 1¹/2in
Draught: Iron fin: 5ft 6in
Lead wing: 3ft 6¹/2in
Displacement:
Fin: 2.205lbs
Wing: 2.601lbs
Sail area: 464sq ft
Engine:
Volvo 2001 10hp
Headroom: 5ft 10in

The Hanse 292/301 was designed by Carl Beyer/Yachtzentrum Greifswald. This is a boat of Swedish origin, later built in East Germany. Two layouts were offered in the 30ft hull. The 292 has an open-plan design, whereas in the 301 there is a separate forward cabin. The joinery is teak faced. She is a boat with a good combination of speed, balance and easy handling. The boat was originally known as an Aphrodite 29, launched in the 80s. and finally ceased production. The moulds were bought by the new builders and the 292 first appeared at the Hamburg boat show in 1992. 200 boats have been sold.

Price guide: +/- £26.000.

Iroquois - 30ft

Specification

LOA: Mark 2:
30ft 0in
Mark 2A: 31ft 8in
LWL: 27ft 0in
Beam: 13ft 6in
Draught:
Centreboards
up: 1ft 4in
Centreboards
down: 5ft 0in
Displacement:
6.800lbs
Sail area:
345sq ft

The **Iroquois** was designed by Rod MacAlpine-Downie and built by Sail Craft, Brightlingsea. Some 300 of these multihulls were built between the late 1960s and the early 1980s. She is a genuine cruiser/racer with excellent accommodation. Both hulls have a single berth forward. The bridgedeck saloon is both spacious and very well lit. When you are in this cabin you are not down below as in a monohull. There is tons of storage making her particularly suitable for longer passages. The galley is positioned in the starboard hull. The cook gets an outside view and is on eye level with saloon.

Price guide: +/- £20.000.

Seadog - 30ft

Specification

LOA: 30ft 0in
LWL: 24ft 0in
Beam: 9ft 0in
Draught: 3ft 6in
Displacement:12.880lbs
Ballast: 3.920lbs
Sail area: 400sq ft
Capacities:
Water: 46 gallons
Fuel: 52 gallons
Berths: 5
Max headroom:
6ft plus
Engine:
Perkins 4.107

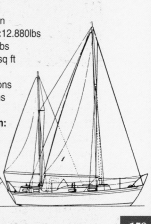

The **Seadog** was designed by RF Freeman and built by Reg Freeman (Yachts) Ltd. First introduced in 1964 she proved to be very popular. Developed over the years to become the Seadog Mk 4, by 1974 over 100 boats had been sold. The Seadog 30 is a very solid small centre-cockpit ketch-rigged cruiser - originally marketed as a motor-sailer, with fairly good sailing performance. She has a relatively shallow draught and the ability to take the ground if you have the triple keel version. Add masts in tabernacles so they can be lowered if necessary without outside assistance, and you have a genuinely go-almost-anywhere boat.

Price guide: +/- £27.000

Elan 295 - 30ft 2in

The **Elan 295** was designed by Rob Humphreys and built by Elan Marine, Slovenia. Looking a bit like a racer, she has a relatively narrow hull so her interior volume is likely to be restricted. To make up for this she is light and airy below. The L shaped galley is functional with dual sinks, and an opening port provides ventilation. There is an 18 gallon s/s water tank under each saloon berth, and the backrests hinge up for extra sleeping width. There is a fair sized aft cabin with a double berth. The heads compartment is to starboard by the companionway. The forecabin has a hanging locker and stowage under the berths.

Specification

LOA: 27ft 0in
LWL: 22ft 11in
Beam: 8ft 8in
Draught: 4ft 6in
Displacement: 8.960lbs
Sail area: 356sq ft
Capacities:
Water: 50 gallons
Fuel: 28 gallons
Berths: 4-5
Max headroom:
6ft plus

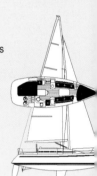

Price guide: +/- £40.000.

Dufour Arpege - 30ft 4in

The **Dufour Arpege** was designed by Michel Dufour. The cockpit is not large for a 30-footer, 6ft 4in long but reducing to 2ft 9in by the tiller caused by the narrow stern. She sails well though and is known as a seaworthy boat. The interior is quite different to many boats of her time. The layout has three separate sections. There are two quarter berths at the foot of the companionway plus the galley and chart table. The saloon can be closed off by double doors. The heads is forward of the saloon. Despite the fore-cabin being given over to storage the Arpege has six to seven berths.

Specification

LOA:
30ft 4in
LWL:
22ft 0in
Beam:
9ft 11in
Draught:
4ft 5in- 5ft 4in
Displacement:
8.000lbs
Sail area:
399sq ft

Price guide: +/- £12.000.

Macwester Wight - 30ft 6in

The **Macwester Wight** was designed and built by CSJ (Jim) Roy at Macwester Marine. The first Macwester was the 26 shown at the 1965 London Boat Show. The early boats were very heavily constructed. Later models were developed from the original 26 design. The Wight was stretched further and was offered in both aft and centre cockpit versions. She is predictable in the way she handles. The saloon is arranged on the dinette form on the starboard side. The galley is linear with a chart table to port. The aft cabin has two single bunks. The forecabin has two bunks, one higher than the other.

Price guide: +/- £16.000.

Specification

LOA: 30ft 6in
LWL: 26ft 0in
Beam: 9ft 5in
Draught: 3ft 3in
Displacement: 8.960lbs
Ballast: 2.725lbs
Sail area: 390sq ft

Legend 310 - 30ft 10in

The **Legend 310** was designed and built by Hunter Marine in the USA. How about this boat for a departure from conventional thinking? She has an enormous, almost circular cockpit, in addition to the overhead 'integrated arch'. Down below is a roomy and bright saloon with a very large galley. The aft cabin is the next star feature. It contains a vast double berth running athwartships beneath the cockpit sole. The heads is spacious and easy to clean. There is no dedicated chart table but it is suggested that you use the port saloon berth and swivel the table through 90°.

Price guide: +/- £46.000.

Specification

LOA: 30ft 10in
LWL: 28ft 0in
Beam: 10ft 10in
Draught:
Standard: 4ft 0in
Deep: 5ft 6in
Displacement: 8.500lbs
Ballast: 3.000lbs
Sail area: 523sq ft
Engine: Yanmar 2GM 18hp
Max headroom: 6ft 4in

Legend 326 - 30ft 10in

The **Legend 326** was designed and built by Hunter Marine in the USA. There are two double cabins in this boat. The galley, being on an American boat has an enormous coolbox, and is located on the starboard side. The separate and spacious heads compartment is to port. The starboard saloon seat is long (7ft 4in). The other to port is shorter and is expected to be have dual use at the chart table. The after cabin runs athwartships which saves on length. There is a escape hatch into the cockpit. Engine access is good, but stowage is possibly a bit on the light side.

Specification

LOA: 30ft 10in
LWL: 28ft 4in
Beam: 10ft 10in
Draught:
Fin: 5ft 10in
Twin: 4ft 4in
Displacement:
8.550lbs
Ballast:
fin/twin: 3.200lbs
Sail area: 540sq ft
Engine:
Yanmar 2GM 18hp
Headroom: 6ft 4in

Price guide: +/- £59.000.

Unna 31 - 30ft 10in

The **Unna 31** was built by Germany's db Yachtbau. Although she has a narrow beam, the interior feels spacious, with a functional layout for as many as six people. There is a substantial table with storage in its central section. Headroom in the saloon is 6ft 2in. There is a large and well planned heads compartment to starboard. The galley which offers more worktop space than usual is opposite the chart table. The aft cabin has plenty of space to move around the section under the cockpit sole which is 18ins.

Specification

LOA: 30ft 10in
LWL: 26ft 11in
Beam: 9ft 10in
Draught:
Deep fin: 5ft 11in
Shallow fin: 4ft 3in
Swing fin: 3ft 3in
Displacement: 7.497lbs
Ballast: 2.997lb
Sail area:
Mainsail: 265sq ft
No 3 Genoa: 215 sq ft
Engine:
Volvo Penta 2010 10hp

Price guide: +/- £53.000.

CR10 - 31ft

The CR10 was designed by CR Yachts/Hakan Sodergren in Sweden. The yacht interior is beautifully fitted out in mahogany, all carefully matched: no plastic bases here. The only interior mouldings are in the head, which is located by the companionway. Corian has been used in the galley, said to be the toughest and most hygenic material available. There are double sinks and plenty of storage. The nav area opposite faces outwards. The interior is of the highest quality. The aft cabin has a large double berth. The forecabin has two singles with hanging lockers on both sides.

Price guide: +/- £77.000.

Specification

LOA: 31ft 0in
LWL: 25ft 7in
Beam: 9ft 10in
Draught: 5ft 5in
Displacement: 8.818lbs
Ballast: 3.196lbs
Sail area: 532 sq ft
Engine:
Yanmar 2GM or 18hp Saildrive

Hanse 311 - 31ft

The Hanse 311 was designed by Judel/Vrolijk Engineering and built by Yachtzentrum in Germany. The spacious interior is fitted out in warm, mahogany faced marine ply. The headroom is 6ft 3in. The forward cabin is separated from the saloon by a door, and there is a large double-berth (6ft 6in long). The saloon has two straight settees separated by a table with storage in the pedestal, lockers and a bookshelf. There is also a chart table. The galley has a two burner gas cooker with oven, stainless steel round sink supplied with cold water by an electrical pressure system. On the port side there is a head with a marine toilet including a holding tank, and a sink supplied with cold water.

Price guide: +/- £50.000

Specification

LOA: 31ft 0in
LWL: 26ft 6in
Beam: 10ft 6in
Draught: 4ft 7in
Deep keel: 5ft 9in
Displacement: 8.490lbs
Sail area: Main: 306sq ft
Self tacking jib: 230 sq ft
Genoa: 349 sq ft
Spinnaker: 807 sq ft

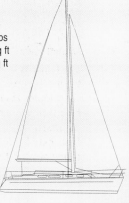

Hanse 315 - 31ft

Specification

LOA: 31ft 0in
LWL: 26ft 6in
Beam: 10ft 6in
Draught:
Deep fin: 5ft 9in
Shallow fin:
4ft 7in
Displacement:
8.509lbs
Ballast:
2.755lbs
Sail area:
536 sq ft
Engine: 18hp
Volvo 2020
Headroom:
6ft 2in

The Hanse 315 was designed by Judel & Vrolijk and built by Yachtzentrum in Germany. The Hanse 315 is also known as the 312, the yacht started life in Sweden. She is a fast passage-maker. Inside there is a conventional layout with settee berths over 6ft 2in long. The galley is to starboard and the nav station to port. The heads are located aft next to the companionway. The interior is bright mostly due to the use of white as the primary colour. Combined with red-stained mahogany she presents a pleasing appearance. The aft cabin berth is 6ft 5in wide by 5ft 4in. The forecabin has a double berth.

Price guide: +/- £49.500.

Maxi 95 - 31ft 2in

Specification

LOA: 31ft 2in
LWL: 25ft 7in
Beam: 10ft 6in
Draught: 4ft 11in
Displacement:
8.823lbs

The Maxi 95 was introduced in 1974 by Pettersen who were turning out 2000 boats each year at this time, there were 1600 built. She has spacious accommodation. a large deep cockpit in the centre with wheel steering. The separate aft cabin is entred from the cockpit. She has good performance. The saloon has two settee berths plus a large galley. The head is aft positioned by the companionway. The boat makes a good family cruiser and prices are fair. Check out her history and try to avoid ex charter craft.

Price guide: +/- £24.000.

Seaquest 320 - 31ft 3in

Specification

LOA: 31ft 4in
LWL: 27ft 0in
Beam: 10ft 6in
Draught: 6ft 5in
Displacement: 7.762lbs
Engine: Volvo Penta 2020 20hp

The **Seaquest 320** is a keel stepped fractional rigged sloop with swept back spreaders. The standard layout has 8 berths in three cabins. In the galley there is a stainless steel sink, a fully insulated coolbox and a Plastimo 2 burner gas stove with grill and oven. There is pressurised hot & cold water to heads in the shower and galley. Headroom is 5ft 9in. The aft cabin has two small double berths OK for children. The forward cabin is good. The interior finish is generally good. A fast boat as she is based on the Stephen Jones racing hull (SJ320). Easy to handle and stable under power or sail.

Price guide: +/- £70.000

Golden Hind - 31ft 6in

Specification

LOA: 31ft 6in
LWL: 26ft 9in
Beam: 9ft
Draught: 3ft 8in
Displacement: 11.603lbs

The **Golden Hind** was designed by Maurice Griffiths in the late 1960s. A shoal draught cruiser, very traditional, she is is as tough as she looks and makes an ideal sturdy offshore cruiser. She has a triple keel which helps her keep going in strong-wind conditions. Around 200 have been built by various yards, a few in wood but the majority in GRP. The interiors vary, but often they have a twin berth cabin up front, two berths in the saloon and some have a quarter berth. She has a good chart table and a practical galley. She can still be ordered today as a new boat at around £100.000. (Golden Hind Yachts)

Price guide: +/- £21.000.

Sadler 32 - 31ft 6in

The **Sadler 32** was designed as a development of the Contessa 32. She is possibly a better boat but not as successful commercially. She was launched in 1978 and in production until Sadler International took over in 1988. Up to then 294 had been built. Another 10 appeared after that. She has a conventional layout inside. The broad beam gives plenty of room for the galley and chart table. There is no aft cabin, but there is a sizeable quarter berth. There is a strong demand for these boats and a very lively Owners' Association.

Price guide: +/- £32.500.

Specification

LOA: 31ft 6in
LWL: 24ft 0in
Beam: 10ft 6in
Draught:
Deep fin: 5ft 6in
Shallow fin: 4ft 6in
Twin keels: 4ft 0in
Displacement:
10.000lbs
Ballast: 4.500lbs
Sail area:
Main: 215 sq ft
Genoa: 385 sq ft
Headroom: 6ft 2in
Engine:
Volvo 2018 (18hp)

Westerly Fulmar - 31ft 10in

The **Westerly Fulmar** was designed by Ed Dubois and built by Westerly Marine Construction. The Fulmar turned out to be one of their most popular models with over 450 built. Usually with fin keels although there are some bilge-keelers about. The interior has a traditional style with teak faced plywood and solid teak capping. Headroom is 6ft 1in at the aft end of the saloon. The U shaped galley has a large sink, an icebox, cooker with a two-burner hob. The heads compartment is to port, with headroom of 5ft 5in. All the berths are 6ft 3in long. Opposite the heads are two very large hanging lockers one of them situated in the forecabin. All in all she is an an excellent all-round cruiser. She has held her value so be prepared for hefty prices.

Specification

LOA: 31ft 10in
LWL: 26ft 0in
Beam: 10ft 11in
Draught:
4ft - 5ft 3in
Displacement:
9.900lbs
Ballast:
4.210 lbs
Sail area:
Main: 253 sq ft
No 1 Genoa:
313 sq ft
Capacities:
Water: 30 gallons
Fuel: 20 gallons
Engine:
Bukh 20hp

Price guide: +/- £40.000

Contessa 32 - 32ft

The **Contessa 32** was launched at the London Boat Show in 1972 where she won an award as boat of the year. She is a good looking boat with practical accommodation and good performance. Over 800 were built and they retain their value. She has 5-6 berths. The head is amidships with a hanging locker opposite. The galley is good and she has a dinette in the saloon. The chart table is located over the quarter berth. There is a strong class association and competitive racing events keep the name alive. There are plenty available.

Specification

LOA: 32ft 0in
LWL: 24ft 0in
Beam: 9ft 6in
Draught: 5ft 6in
Displacement: 9.520lbs

Price guide: +/- £33.000.

Nicholson 32 - 32ft

The **Nicholson 32** was first introduced in 1963 and remained in production for eighteen years until 1981, over 369 were built. She was one of the first boats to use GRP with extensive utilisation of interior mouldings. Her layout is designed for comfort and safety at sea. She has good headroom, five berths including a pilot. The galley is large. She is much sought after by experienced offshore sailors. Some changes were made during her production run. The Mark VIII of 1970 has a square doghouse windows. And in 1972 the Mark X has a single long window in the doghouse.

Specification

LOA: 32ft 0in
LWL: 24ft 0in
Beam: 9ft 3in
Draught: 5ft 6in
Displacement: 14.500lbs

Price guide: +/- £21.000.

Southerly 100 - 32ft

The **Southerly 100** was designed by Carter/Northshore 1983. A lifting keel which needs only 2ft of water to float sounds like a practical idea. The 100 was introduced in 1983 and has wheel steering. She has comfortable spacious accommodation which includes an L-shaped galley with lots of workspace. Next to the galley is a quarter berth. To starboard is a well ventillated heads. In front of the heads is the nav station and inside steering position. Headroom is over 6ft throughout the upper level, reducing to 6ft in the saloon. The starboard settee is straight and a good sea berth. The forecabin has two overlapping bunks. A good boat for a family or retired couple.

Price guide: +/- £45.000.

Specification

LOA: 32 0in
LWL: 25ft 0in
Beam: 9ft 11in
Draught:
Keel down: 5ft 10in
Keel up: 1ft 10in
Displacement:
9.500lbs
Ballast:
Plate:
2.774 lbs
Keel: 1.632 lbs
Sail area:
Main: 177sq ft
Genoa: 300 sq ft

Twins 36 - 32ft

The **Twins 36** was designed by Pat Patterson. The first version, the HT 26 was launched in 1971. Since then the marque has developed through several stages. She has a central cockpit which is well above the waterline and offers good protection from spray and excellent visibility. Sleeping berths are in the aft ends of both hulls. The galley is also located in the port hull. There are lots of variations in the layout chosen by previous owners. The central saloon has enough room for a good party. Given the vast interior volume the boat can be organised to cope with most stowage problems.

Specification

LOA: 36ft 0in
LWL: 32ft 0in
Beam: 19ft 0in
Draught: 3ft 0in
Displacement: 8.400lbs
Sail area:
Main: 243sq ft
Rolling Headsail: 218 sq ft
Engine: 30hp diesel + twin hydraulic drives.

Price guide: +/- £24.000.

Bénéteau 305 - *32ft 2in*

Specification

LOA: 32ft 2in
LWL: 30ft 8in
Beam: 10ft 8in
Draught:
Deep keel:
5ft 9in
Shoal draught:
4ft 6in
Displacement:
7.940 lbs
Ballast:
2.977 lbs
Sail area:
527 sq ft

The Bénéteau 305 was designed and built by Bénéteau in France. This boat has copious accommodation. Up to six people in two double cabins. The saloon is slightly constrained by the fine bow sections and the aft head and sleeping cabin. She has an island galley with twin sinks and a good worktop space. The saloon table has lots of storage in its central section. The forecabin is separated by a door. The aft cabin has a large locker in the transom. The head has lots of space and a wet locker. She looks like a performance boat with well laid out lines on deck, well designed cockpit, good stowage. And she is easy to handle.

Price guide: +/- £40.000

Barbican 33 - *32ft 8in*

Specification

LOA: 32ft 6in
LWL: 26ft 11in
Beam: 6ft 4in
Draught: Keel up 4ft 6in -
Keel down: 6ft 4in
Displacement: 5.75 tons
Ballast: 2.5 tons
Sail area: Main: 206sq ft
Genoa: 340 sq ft

The Barbican 33 was designed by Maurice Griffiths, this is a boat for cruising. She is shoal draught and there are bilge keel versions. It is probable that no two boats are the same inside. But it also likely that as the previous owners will have been sensible cruising folk, nothing so radical will have been done as to cause anxiety for a prospective purchaser.

Price guide: +/- £40.000.

Freedom 33 - 33ft

The Freedom 33 was designed and built by Freedom yachts in the USA. The free-standing rig is unusual; unstayed masts made of carbon-fibre or aluminium that bend in a gust. There are other advantages: saving of costs on expensive rigging, and less maintenance. The sail plan is efficient and friendly to the short-hander. She came with three different keel options: shoal, deep and shoal, and shoal with a ballasted centreplate. The boats are well built and owners have often kept them in top condition. They are seaworthy and with wheel steering. The cockpit is unusual but practical.

Price guide: +/- £40.000.

Specification

LOA: 33ft 0in
LWL: 34ft 9in
Beam: 11ft 0in
Draught:
Shoal/deep:
4ft 6in - 5ft 6in
Centreboard
up/down:
3ft 6in /6ft 0in
Displacement:
12.000lbs
Ballast: 3.800lbs
Sail area:
621 sq ft
Fuel: 25 gals
Water: 52 gals
Engine:
29 hp Volvo

Nauticat 33 - 33ft 2in

The Nauticat 33 was designed by Wilho Aarnipalo and described as the Grand Old Lady of the Nauticat fleet. Introduced into the UK in 1971. Now out of production after 1200 built, she has been replaced by the Nauticat 331. She is a chunky all weather motor-sailer. With her big engine and comfortable interior, she offers much to the dedicated cruising family. There are two steering positions, internal and external. She has wide decks and a side access wheelhouse. The interior has been fitted out with various options. The hull being voluminous has plenty of room for stowage.

Specification

LOA: 33ft 2in
LWL: 28ft 2in
Beam: 10ft 8in
Draught: 5ft 1in
Displacement: 17.000lbs
Sail area: 502 sq ft
Capacities:
Water: 88 gallons
Fuel: 132 gallons
Berths: 6
Max headroom:
6ft plus

Price guide: +/- £50.000

Westerly Storm - 33ft 2in

The Westerly Storm was designed by Ed Dubois. Westerlys have a well deserved reputation for being soundly built, therefore they hold their price in the used market. The Storm is no exception. She was launched at the Southampton Boat Show in 1986 and by the time production came to an end in 1993 a total of 171 had been built. The interior (designed by Ken Frievokh) is comfortable, practical and well finished. The galley, set quite high due to the dished hull, is to port and chart table to starboard. There is an aft cabin with large locker. The head is to starboard by the companionway. A good value family cruising boat with pedictable performance.

Price guide: +/- £34.000.

Specification

LOA: 33ft 2in
LWL: 27ft 0in
Beam: 11ft 7in
Draught: Fin:
5ft 6in
Displacement:
11.310lbs
Ballast:
4.210lbs
Sail area:
484sq ft
Engine:
Volvo 2020
Headroom:
6ft 1in

Gemini Cat - 33ft 6in

Designed by Tony Smith, built by Performance Cruising Inc in the USA. Inside she is roomy and being American the fridge is the largest you are likely to see on a boat. The interior moulding has oiled teak joinery. Storage is copious. Cats are sometimes thought of as having problems when it comes to mooring to marina berths and even piles. The Gemini has addressed this problem with a narrower beam than usual on European cats. This allows her down and up a normal slipway and makes her not that much wider than a monohull of similiar length.

Price guide: +/- £55.000.

Specification

LOA: 33ft 6in
LWL: 31ft 9in
Beam: 14ft 0in
Draught:
Centreboards
up: 1ft 6in
Centreboards
down: 5ft 5in
Displacement:
8.600lbs
Sail area:
581sq ft
Engine:
Westerbeke 27hp

MG 335 - 33ft 6in

The **MG 335** was designed by Tony Castro and built by Northshore. She is a beamy yacht with plenty of internal space. The galley and chart table are set amidships. There is an enormous locker on the starboard quarter and a shallower one to port. In the saloon there is plenty of light. The berths are angled which might prove slightly uncomfortable at night when trying to sleep. The aft cabin is of double bed proportions. On deck she provides plenty of comfort for the crew. The quarter decks give a well angled position for the helm. She moves beautifully whether racing or cruising.

Price guide: +/- £37.000.

Specification

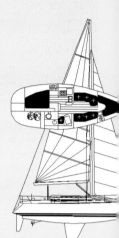

LOA: 33ft 6in
LWL: 27ft 8in
Beam: 11ft 3in
Draught:
Fin: 6ft 3in
Wing: 4ft 0in
Displacement:
8.900lbs
Ballast:
3.400lbs
Sail area:
652 sq ft
Engine:
18hp Volvo 2002

Moody 34 - 33ft 6in

The **Moody 34** was designed by Bill Dixon. Introduced in 1983 as a replacement for the Moody 33. She later became the 346. She is likely to be bought for her accommodation which is capacious. The saloon starts at the beamy part of the boat. Headroom ranges from 6ft 1in in the saloon to 4ft 8in in the tunnel to the gigantic aft cabin. The heads are to port and the galley to starboard, extending to the walkway under the cockpit. For general cruising she offers a lot. If you've not sailed a centre cockpit boat, then climb into this one and look down on most of the boats around you.

Specification

LOA: 33ft 6in
LWL: 27ft 1in
Beam: 11ft 8in
Draught: 5ft
Displacement:
11.200 lbs
Ballast: 5.080 lbs
Sail area: 514 sq ft
Berths: 6-7
Max headroom:
6ft 1in

Price guide: +/- £45.000.

Bavaria 32 - 33ft 9in

The Bavaria 32 was designed in 1999 the Bavaria 32 replaced the 31. She has much more internal volume and headroom. The saloon is light despite the relatively dark wood joinery. There's plenty of space to walk around the central table and the 6ft settees would make good sea berths. The galley is well planned with adequate storage. There is a large forward facing chart table. The heads compartment is large with a small hanging locker. An opening port gives harbour ventilation. When she was new you got a lot of boat for the money. Now it depends on the previous owner's investment in extras.

Price guide: +/- £50.000.

Specification

LOA: 33ft 9in
LWL: 27ft 9in
Beam: 11ft 0in
Draught:
Shoal keel:
4ft 11in
Deep keel:
5ft 11in
Displacement:
8.372 lbs
Sail area:
486sq ft

Legend 340 - 33ft 9in

The Legend 340: This American boat comes from Florida. She is luxuriously stylish with plenty of curves including a cockpit arch. The flowing lines take a dip around the stern. There is an athwartships aft cabin and the headroom is good. The galley is well equipped and is located on the port side of the companionway. The heads compartment is striking. Tons of space and well finished in every detail. The navigator sits on the end of the port settee, with the chart table facing aft with a hanging locker and instrument space. A powerful performance cruiser plus a comfortable home afloat. She is a fast and powerful boat.

Price guide: +/- £60.000

Specification

LOA: 33ft 9in
LWL: 28ft 7in
Beam: 11ft 8in
Draught:
Shoal: 4ft 6in
Deep: 6ft 0in
Displacement: 11.030 lbs
Ballast: 4.100lbs
Sail area: 682 sq ft

Hanse 341 - 33ft 11in

The Hanse 341 was designed by Judel & Vrolijk and built by Hanse Yachts in Germany. When she first appeared in 2003, her low price made her a popular choice as a starter yacht for a small family. The galley has two sinks a two burner cooker and a top-opening fridge. There are lots of drawers and lockers. There is a spacious forcabin which has a double berth with shelving and lockers, headroom is over 6ft. The V berth is well padded. The heads are spacious and equipped with a shower. There is a standard boat holding tank with a deck pump-out facility. The boat is easy to handle and the finish is good.

Price guide: +/- £60.000.

Specification

LOA: 33ft 11in
LWL: 29ft 2in
Beam: 11ft 2in
Draught:
Shoal/deep:
5ft 0in - 5ft 9in
Lifting keel:
3ft 4in - 6ft 2in
Displacement:
11.330lbs
Ballast:
4.004lbs
Sail area:
Main: 350 sq ft
Jib: 280 sq ft

Rival 34 - 34ft 0in

The Rival 34 was designed by Peter Brett and built by Southern Boat Building. She is highly rated by the Rival enthusiast: classic in style, seaworthy and well built. Her interior is traditional, which by today's standards might be called small. She still has room for six berths if you include the table lowered to form a double. The forecabin has two single berths there are two lockers. The heads compartment crosses the width of the boat. The saloon has two bunks which make good sea berths, and headroom is 1.85m near the main hatch. She will look after you at sea, a good cruising boat.

Specification

LOA: 34ft 0in
LWL: 24ft 10in
Beam: 9ft 8in
Draught:
Shoal keel:
4ft 8in
Deep keel:
5ft 10in
Displacement:
11.900 lbs
Sail area:
Main: 200 sq ft
Genoa: 360 sq ft

Price guide: +/- £43.000.

Frances - 34ft 3in

Specification

LOA: 34ft 3in
LWL: 28ft 4in
Beam: 10ft 7in
Draught: 4ft 10n
Displacement: 6.000lbs
Sail area: 568 sq ft

The **Frances** was designed by Chuck Paine and built by Victoria Yachts. She has a pilot house configuration. The advantage of weather protection and the ability to helm from outside are what the 34 offers. The inside steering position means that the helmsman and navigator can work together in relative peace and quiet. She is a good seaboat with accommodation comfortable enough for a family. The saloon is light and airy with galley to starboard and a dinette opposite. The forecabin has a double/vee berth. Heads are on the port side. She sails well and the engine is capable.

Price guide: +/- £84.000.

Feeling 1040 - 34ft 4in

Specification

LOA: 34ft 4in
LWL: 29ft 2in
Beam:11ft 10in
Draught: 5ft 10in
Displacement: 10.800 lbs
Sail area: Main: 276 sq ft
Genoa: 493 sq ft
Berths: 7-9
Max headroom: 6ft 4in

The **Feeling 1040** was designed by Philippe Harlé and built by Kirié in France. She was launched in the early 1980s. She has a generous beam and a wide stern. Her shallow cockpit gives good headroom in the aft cabin. The use of elm for the joinery gives a light and modern feel to the practical interior. The galley has a nice ergonomic wrapround shape. And the head also provides a space to wedge yourself in. There is a good sized chart table opposite the galley. She is a comfortable, fast and smart. Not quite as radical as some other French boats. But maybe she's the better for that.

Price guide: +/- £40.000.

Catalina 34 - 34ft 6in

The Catalina 34 was designed by Frank Butler and launched in 1986. This American boat builder has specialised in conservative family cruisers designed for long production runs and sold at a competitive price. There were 1600 of the 34 built. She has an open and spacious interior with a large galley, located amidships. She is really best for shortish trips; a weekend or maybe a week, she is light on stowage space. She is a comfortable boat for a family and a well balanced with gracious handling. A performance cruiser in a steady beamy hull.

Price guide: +/- £48.000

Specification

LOA: 34ft 6in
LWL: 29ft 10in
Beam: 11ft 9in
Draught: 5ft 2in
Displacement: 11.950 lbs
Sail area: 49.05 sq m
Capacities:
Water: 350 lts
Fuel: 114 lts
Berths: 7
Max headroom: 1.93m

Feeling 356 - 34ft 7in

The Feeling 356 was designed by Gilles Vaton & Patrick Roseo. A French boat with the option of a lifting keel, Kirié the builders have specialised in these since 1982. She is a sharp and modern looking boat. Her interior is roomy and bright with well finished elm joinery. The curved windows let in plenty of light. Headroom is good at 6ft 4in by the main hatch and ahead of the mast it reduces to 5ft 9in. The galley runs along most of the port side in the saloon. The keel case provides an extra worktop. The bottom of the hull is protected with a cast iron grounding plate on the lift keel version. She is good value for a family looking at modern fast yachts.

Specification

LOA: 34ft 7in
LWL: 29ft 2in
Beam: 11ft 6in
Draught:
Deep fin: 6ft 1in
Shallow fin: 5ft 7in
Lifting Keel:
2ft 6in - 6ft 11in
Displacement: 9.700lbs
Sail area: 607 sq ft
Engine: Yanmar 3GM 27hp

Price guide: +/- £50.000.

Island Packet - 35ft

The Island Packet was designed by Bob Johnson and built by Island Packet Yachts in the USA. She is a modern blue-water cruising yacht. The changes from an earlier generation include greater interior volume so the beam has become wider, and the freeboard higher. Her saloon is spacious and comfortable. There is a 4ft gap between the saloon seats, and 6ft 5in headroom. Her aft cabin is very big, as is her forecabin. The galley and heads are equally generous in spatial terms. As a liveaboard she must be a good bet.

Specification

LOA: 35ft 0in
LWL: 29ft 4in
Beam: 12ft 0in
Draught: 4ft 3in
Displacement:
16.000lbs
Sail area:
725 sq ft
Engine: 38hp

Price guide: +/- £149.000.

Jeanneau Sun 36 - 35ft

Designed in 1983 and built by the French Jeanneau yard. For a yacht that could be raced with confidence, she is also a practical cruising boat. Acommodation is good, there are two sizeable aft doubles, a smaller V berth up front and berths for four in the saloon. She has a broad stern with good sized lockers. The compact galley has twin sinks and a good sized cooker. The chart table is excellent. The heads compartment is forward of the saloon with a wet locker opposite. She handles well with a seamanlike cockpit. She has wide side decks.

Specification

LOA: 35ft 0in
LWL: 30ft 7in
Beam: 12ft 7in
Draught:
Fin: 6ft 3in
Lift up: 4ft 1in
Lift down: 6ft 11in
Displacement:
11.900 lbs
Sail area:
705 sq ft

Price guide: +/- £50.000.

Trapper - 35ft

The **Trapper** was designed by Paul Anstey/C&C Yachts. This Canadian yacht was the largest in the range. They are well finished boats built under licence by Trapper Yachts in the UK. She has a swing keel. Below she is traditional in layout with six berths. The saloon dinette table can be used as a double. She has a quarter berth rather than an aft cabin. The chart table has plenty of stowage. The heads is a comfortable size. Her shallow draught will allow you to explore the creeks and harbours out of reach to the deeper chaps.

Price guide: +/- £10.000.

Specification

LOA: 35ft 0in
LWL: 27ft 6in
Beam: 10ft 7in
Draught:
Lifting up: 4ft 3in
Lifting down: 6ft 9in
Displacement:
13.420lbs
Sail area:
Main: 245 sq ft
Genoa: 324 sq ft
Capacities:
Water: 40 gallons
Fuel: 15 gallons
Berths: 6
Engine:
Bukh 20

Warrior 35 - 35ft

The **Warrior 35** was designed by Angus Primrose and built by Morgan Giles, Trident Marine took over at a later stage. A centre cockpit yacht, she was launched in 1966. She has a 2 berth aft cabin entered from the cockpit. She was a popular boat in her day and rated highly as a performance and long distance cruiser. The saloon has a U shaped settee with a table to port. There is a good sized heads to port. Trident marine built 3 versions of the same Primrose designed hull: the Voyagers which are aft cockpit pilothouse or 'raised saloon' configuration, the Warrior which is centre cockpit and the Challenger which is aft cockpit.

Specification

LOA: 35ft 0in
LWL: 26ft 6in
Beam: 10ft 6in
Draught: 5ft 0in
Displacement: 5.4 tons
Ballast: 2.12 tons
Sail area:
Mainsail: 228 Sq ft
Working Jib: 209 Sq ft
Capacities:
Water: 60 gallons
Fuel: 27 gallons
Berths: 6
Max headroom:
6ft plus
Engine:
Perkins 4/107

Price guide: +/- £33.000

Nicholson 35 - 35ft 3in

The Nicholson 35 was designed and built by Camper & Nicholson. Introduced in 1970, she was still in production twenty years later. She was the big success of the Nicholson range, she was developed over the years culminating in the Mk 6. Strongly built, and very elegant, She is some people's idea of a 'Gentlemans Yacht'. The Mk1 had a 2 berth forecabin, a walk-through heads, and a saloon with a U shaped settee to port. She has a single settee opposite, a galley to port and a decent sized chart table to starboard. Her sail area was greatly increased over the years.

Specification

LOA: 35ft 3in
LWL: 26ft 9in
Beam: 10ft 5in
Draught: 5ft 6in
Displacement: 17.696 lbs
Sail area: 757 sq ft
Capacities:
Water: 80 gallons
Fuel: 40 gallons
Berths: 6
Max headroom: 6ft plus
Engine: Watermota Seapanther 25hp Petter 36 hp

Price guide: +/- £45.000

Rustler 36 - 35ft 4in

The Rustler was designed by Holman & Pye and built by Rustler Yachts. Possibly most famous as the boat chosen by HRH Princess Anne in 1992. The 36 is designed for long passages in safety and comfort. She has a traditional layout inside. She feels secure with good handholds throughout. The navigation station is excellent with lots of room for instruments. The open plan saloon is functional: a straight settee berth to starboard and a L shaped settee round the table. There have been many variations chosen by owners who could take advantage of the bespoke approach offered by the builders.

Specification

LOA: 35ft 4in
LWL: 26ft 11in
Beam: 11ft 0in
Draught: 5ft 6in
Displacement: 16.770lbs
Ballast: 7.603 lbs
Sail area: 693 sq ft

Price guide: +/- £90.000.

SHE 36 - 35ft 6in

Specification

LOA: 35ft 6in
LWL: 29ft 6in
Beam: 10ft 6in
Draught: 6ft 0in
Displacement:
14.780 lbs
Ballast:
6.375 lbs
Sail area:
625 sq ft
Capacities:
Water: 26 gallons
Fuel: 12 gallons
Berths: 6-7
Engine:
Bukh 20hp

The SHE 36 was designed by Sparkman & Stephens and built by South Hants Marine, launched in 1975. She makes an excellent cruising yacht. There have been various alternative interior layouts. The original SHE 36s had two pilot berths above the settees. There is a centrally mounted table big enough to seat 8 people. The galley is excellent with plenty of stowage space. The chart table is much larger than you will find on a new 36-footer. Her fine ends restrict the space on acommodation but she is a comfortable boat and will keep you feeling secure at sea.

Price guide: +/- £35.000.

Westerly 37 - 37ft 4in

Specification

LOA: 37ft 4in
LWL: 31ft 10in
Beam: 12ft 2in
Draught: 6ft 0in
Displacement: 18.941
Sail area: 871 sq ft
Capacities:
Water: 50 gallons
Fuel: 30 gallons

The Westerly 37 is a modern performance cruiser. The saloon is open and airy, with plenty of supplementary lighting. The settees make good sea berths. The well planned galley has a good worktop area and is to port of the companionway. The navigation station is opposite. There is plenty of space for a half folded Admiralty chart. There are two heads, one at each end. The forecabin is larger than average. The aft cabin has plenty of head space. She is a spacious boat with lots to comfort an anxious crew who value privacy.

Price guide: +/- £80.000.

Bavaria 37 - 37ft 10in

The **Bavaria 37** was launched in London in 2000. She ceased production in 1994. Her large cockpit and is available as either a two or three cabin layout. Her U shaped galley has plenty of stowage and two deep sinks. The heads are generous and there is a shower unit. There is a large chart table. She has 6 berths in three cabins. Her saloon is exceptionally spacious and comfortable. Unusually she has two armchairs on the port side. Her aft cabin is vast. There is a wide double bunk in the forecabin. She makes a very suitable family cruising boat.

Specification

LOA: 37ft 10in
LWL: 29ft 2in
Beam: 12ft 2in
Draught: 4ft 3in
Displacement: 11.819 lbs
Sail area: 682 sq ft

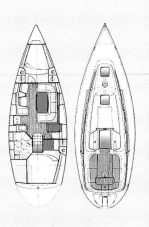

Price guide: +/- £72.000

Nautitect 395 - 39ft 3in

The **Nautitect 395** was designed by Alain Mortain and Yiannis Mavrikios. This French cat is built by Dufour. At the time of her build Dufour were turning out 40 cats a year. She has four cabins, ten berths, two heads, storage everywhere and enough room to swing several cats. The galley is practical and large, more like a kitchen at home. There is room for eight around the table, which is a natural space to spread out charts. There is also tons of deck space. She was priced competively against her main rivals in the UK. You can steer from both hulls.

Specification

LOA: 39ft 3in
Beam: 21ft 0in
Draught: 4ft
Displacement:
Sail area: 888 sq ft
Engines: 2 x 20 hp
Water: 110 gals
Fuel: 44 gals
Berths: 10

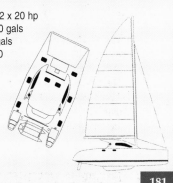

Price guide: +/- £80.000.

Najad 391 - 39ft 8in

The **Najad 391** has handcrafted, flush teak decks. Below deck layouts are basically the same as in many of the other Najad models. Standing headroom is approx. 1.93 m. The L-shaped galley is located amidships. There is a chart table with drawers and separate chart stowage under the deck. The heads compartment is amidships to starboard with standing headroom approx. 1.85 m. A passageway on the port side at the galley leads to the aft cabin. There are wide berths on each side, a wardrobe and a seat to starboard. The Najad 391 is designed to be a modern long distance cruiser with the highest sailing performance.

Price guide: +/- £200.000

Specification

LOA: 39ft 8in / 12.10 m
LWL: 33ft 2in / 10.10 m
Beam: 11ft 11in / 3.63m
Draught: 6ft 3in / 1.90m
Shallow draught: 5ft 6in / 1.69 m
Displacement: 10,000 kg / 10,0 t
Bolted lead keel: 4.200 kg / 4.2 t
Headroom in saloon:
6ft 4in / 1.93 m
Total height for transportation:
13ft 5in / 4.10 m
Engine:
Yanmar 4 JH3-TF.
Capacity:
Fuel: 60 gal
Water: 67 gal
Sail areas
Cruising:
780 sq.ft / 72.5 sq m
Fullbatten main:
420 sq.ft / 39.0 sq m
Working jib:
110% 377 sq.ft / 35.0 sq m

Catalac 12m - 40ft 10in

Specification

LOA: 40ft 10in
LWL: 36ft 0in
Beam: 17ft 3in
Displacement: 19.040 lbs
Sail area: 733 sq ft

The **Catalac 12m** is the flagship of the Catalac fleet. The 12m Catalac 41 is a large catamaran built on a production-line basis. There is a dual steering position. The interior position, to port of the main saloon. The external arrangement provides good visibility all round, easy sight of the internal instruments, and a second control unit for the Autopilot. The boat offers a seven berth layout. There is full standing headroom in both hulls and wheelhouse. The galley is located in the port hull. If you are looking for a large cat these boats are popular all over the world.

Price guide: +/- £70..000.

Freedom 21 - 21ft 8in

LOA: 21ft 5in - 21ft 9in

Specification

LOA: 21ft 8in
LWL: 19ft
Beam: 8ft
Draught: 2ft 6in
Displacement: 1,800lbs

Ballast: 750lbs
Sail areas:
main: 200sq ft
spinnaker 265sq ft
Engine: Mariner 4hp
or Tohatsu 4hp
outboards

The Freedom 21 was Designed by Gary Hoyt an ex advertising executive who has designed some radical and successful craft. She has the unstayed mast of a typical American Cat boat. She has a comparatively large sail area but it can be easily controlled by one person from the cockpit. The spinnaker is worked with the Hoyt 'gun mount' an unusual looking device that works well. The berths are roomy and comfortable. There is a simple sink unit and a curtain separates the head compartment from the saloon. The tandem wing keel was designed by Warwick Collins but it is not advisable to dry out with this configuration without the support of a wall.

Price guide: +/- £4,000

Seal 22 - 21ft 9in

Specification

LOA: 21ft 9in
LWL: 18ft 9in
Beam: 7ft 9in
Draught: 2ft - 3ft 10in
Displacement: 2,400lb
Sail areas:
Main 121sq ft
Racing Genoa:
142 sq ft
Cruising Genoa:
120 sq ft
Berths: 4/6

Designed by Angus Primrose and built by John Baker (Kenton Forge) Ltd. Production started in 1970 and continued until 1980. She was launched at the 1970 London Boat Show. She has always been a controversial boat with those who love her being enthusiastic and loyal devotees. She has some very different features, such as the sloping forward companionway. In 1972 the Mark II was introduced with the forecabin turning into space for the heads and stowage. Headroom is 4ft 5in. Accommodation for four was retained by moving the saloon berths under the cockpit seats. She has a lifting keel which is quite long and gives good directional stability.

Price guide: +/- £3,500

183

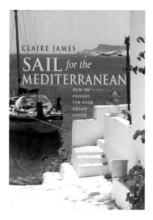
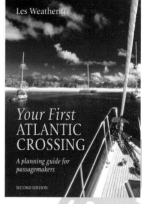

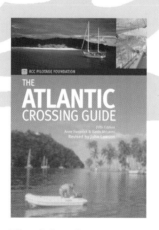
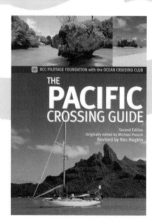

The following are Members
of the British Marine Federation

Advanced Laminates
(Full Member) (RMW Marine)
Contact
Richard Woof
Address
Rackfield Park
Uffculme
Devon
EX15 3AX
Telephone 01884 841880
Fax 01884 841780**Email**
richard@rmwmarine.com
Website www.rmwmarine.com

Advanced Marine Composites Ltd
(Probationary Member)
Contact
Peter Sylvester
Address
124 Bread Street
Beechingstoke
Wiltshire
SN9 6HW
Telephone 01380 860077
Fax 01672 851399**Email**
p.sylvester@virgin.net
Website www.powercat.co.uk

Anthony J Taylor
(Honorary Member)
Contact
Anthony Taylor
Address
18 Haven Crescent
Hill Head
Fareham
Hampshire
PO14 3JX
Telephone 01329 662127
Fax 01329 668900
Email Not available
Website Not available

Aqua Star Ltd
(Full Member)
Contact
Geoff Willson
Address
Ocean Yard
Bulwer Avenue
St Sampsons
Guernsey
GY2 4LE
Channel Islands
Telephone 01481 244550
Fax 01481 244711
Email aquastar@guernsey.net
Website
www.boatshow.com/aqua-starltd.

Aquafibre Mouldings Ltd
(Full Member)
(Aquafibre Ltd)
(Aquafibre)
Contact
Ben Mackintosh
Address
Wendover Road
Rackheath
Norwich
Norfolk
NR13 6LR
Telephone 01603 720651
Fax 01603 720654
Email info@aquafibre.co.uk
Website Not available

Ardfern Yacht Centre Ltd
(Full Member)
Contact
David Wilkie
Address
Ardfern
by Lochgilphead
Argyll
PA31 8QN
Telephone 01852 500247
Fax 01852 500624
Email office@ardfernyacht.co.uk
Website www.ardfernyacht.co.uk

Birchwood Marine
International Ltd
(Full Member)
Contact
Ian Willgress
Address
Fulwood Road
Huthwaite
Sutton in Ashfield
Nottinghamshire
NG17 2NB
Telephone 01623 515133
Fax 01623 440328
Email info@birchwoodmarine.com
Website
www.birchwoodmarine.com

Blondecell Ltd
(Full Member)
Contact
Gavin Brown
Address
Cracknore Industrial Park
Cracknore Hard
Marchwood
Southampton
Hampshire
SO40 4ZD
Telephone 023 80663437
Fax 023 8086 8799
Email Not available
Website www.blondecell.com

Bridgend Boat Company Ltd
(Full Member)
(Bridgend Boat Company)
Contact
Julie Hammonds
Address
Western Hanger
Lawrence Road
Mountbatten
Plymouth
Devon
PL9 9SJ
Telephone 01752 404082
Fax 01752 403405
Email bboatsco@aol.com
Website
www.bridgendboatcompany.co.uk

Broadblue Catamarans Ltd
(Probationary Member)
Contact
Stuart Davidsen
Address
Sealake Road
Oulton Broad
Suffolk
NR32 3LQ
Telephone 01502 518002
Fax 01502 518005
Email sails@broadblue.co.uk
Website www.broadblue.co.uk

Broom Boats Ltd
(Full Member)
(Broom)
Contact
Martin Broom
Address
Brundall
Norwich
Norfolk
NR13 5PX
Telephone 01603 712334
Fax 01603 714803
Email pauline@broomboats.com
Website www.broomboats.com

Camper & Nicholsons Yachting Ltd
(Full Member)
(Camper & Nicholsons Yachting)
Contact
Ian Crowden
Address
Mumby Road
Gosport
Hampshire
PO12 1AH
Telephone 023 92580221
Fax 023 92601145
Email Not available
Website Not available

Cara Marine
(Full Member)
Contact
Nevil Scott
Address
Church Road
Carrigaline
Cork
Eire
Telephone 00353 21 4373717
Fax 00353 21 4373726
Email info@caramarine.ie
Website www.caramarine.ie

Class Fibre Ltd
(Full Member)
Contact
Adam Crowther
Address
Unit 4/5 Oyster Haven
Haven Road
Colchester
Essex
CO2 8HT
Telephone 01206 867616
Fax 01206 867617
Email nigel@classfibre.co.uk
Website www.classfibre.co.uk

Colin Buttifant Yacht Builders
(Full Member)
Contact
Colin Buttifant
Address
Swallowtail Boatyard
Horsefen Road
Ludham
Gt Yarmouth
Norfolk
NR29 5QG
Telephone 01692 678066
Fax 01692 678067
Email
webmaster@swallowtailboats.co.uk
Website
www.swallowtailboats.co.uk

Corvette Marine Ltd
(Full Member)
Contact
R Nixon
Address
19 Station road
Reedham
Norwich
Norfolk
NR13 3TA
Telephone 01493 701260
Fax 01493 701455
Email sales@corvettemarine.co.uk
Website www.corvettemarine.co.uk

Dale Sailing Company Ltd
(Full Member)
(Dale Nelson)
Contact
R J Reynolds
Address
Brunel Quay
Neyland
Milford Haven
Pembrokeshire
SA73 1PY
Telephone 01646 603110
Fax 01646 601061
Email enquiries@dale-sailing.co.uk
Website www.dale-sailing.co.uk

David Hillyard Ltd
(Probationary Member)
(Aruncraft)
Contact
Simon Cullingford
Address
Rope Walk
Littlehampton
West Sussex
BN17 5DG
Telephone 01903 713327
Fax 01903 722787
Email hillyard@btclick.com
Website www.davidhillyard.co.uk

Devonport Royal Dockyard Ltd
(Full Member)
(DML)
(Devonport Yachts)
Contact
David Smeken
Address
Devonport Royal Dockland
Devonport
Plymouth
Devon
PL1 4SG
Telephone 01752 553311
Fax 01752 554883
Email yachts@devonport.co.uk
Website www.devonport.co.uk

Discovery Yachts Ltd
(Full Member)
Contact
John Charnley
Address
Harbour Close
Cracknore Industrial Park
Cracknore Hard
Marchwood
Southampton
Hampshire
SO40 4AF
Telephone 023 80865555
Fax 023 80865580
Email info@discoveryyachts.com
Website www.discoveryyachts.com

EC Landamore & Company Ltd
(Full Member)
Contact
Anthony J E Landamore
Address
Elanco Works
Wroxham
Norwich
Norfolk
NR12 8UH
Telephone 01603 782212
Fax 01603 784166
Email info@landamores.co.uk
Website Not available

Elan Yacht Sales UK Ltd

(Full Member)

(Previously known as Moody Yachts International Ltd)

Contact
Trevor Allen
Address
Swanwick Marina
Southampton
Hampshire
SO31 1ZL
Telephone 01489 576609
Fax 01489 885509
Email sales@elanyachts.com
Website www.elanyachts.com

Fairlie Restorations Ltd

(Full Member)

Contact
Duncan Walker
Address
Unit 4
Port Hamble
Satchell Lane
Hamble
Hampshire
SO31 4NN
Telephone 023 80456336
Fax 023 80456166
Email info@fairlierestorations.com
Website
www.fairlierestorations.com

Fairline Boats plc

(Full Member)

(Fairline Boats)

Contact
Derek Carter
Ken Wappat
Address
Barnwell Road
Oundle
Peterborough
Cambridgeshire
PE8 5PA
Telephone 01832 273661
Fax 01832 273432
Email bryanjones@fairline.com
Website www.fairline.com

Gibbs Technologies Ltd

(Full Member)

Contact
Tim Goodwin
Address
Avenue Road
Nuneaton
Warwickshire
CV11 4LY
Telephone 02476 388828
Fax 02476 388868
Email Not available
Website Not available

Golden Hind Marine

(Full Member)

Contact
Mark Urry
Address
2 Hybris Business Park
Crossways
Dorchester
Dorset
DT2 8BF
Telephone 01305 854938
Fax 01305 852713
Email Not available
Website
www.goldenhindmarine.com

Hardy Marine Ltd

(Full Member)

(Hardy Marine)

Contact
Debbie Williams
Address
Gaymers Way Industrial Estate
North Walsham
Norwich
Norfolk
NR28 0AN
Telephone 01692 408700
Fax 01692 406483
Email sales@hardy-marine.co.uk
Website www.hardy-marine.co.uk

Harley Racing Yachts Ltd

(Full Member)

Contact
Nigel Harley
Address
40 Sammuel Whites Industrial
Estate
Bridge Road
Cowes
Isle of Wight
PO31 7DU
Telephone 01983 280060
Fax 01983 280050
Email Not available
Website
www.harleyracingyachts.co.uk

HO Marine Support

(Probationary Member)

Contact
Nick Harvey
Address
55 Holly Hill Lane
Sarisbury Green
Southampton
Hampshire
SO31 7AE
Telephone 01489 579826
Fax 01489 579826
Email Not available
Website Not available

Hunton Powerboats

(Full Member)

Contact
P C T Warner
Address
2 Romsey Industrial Estate
Romsey
Hampshire
SO15 OHR
Telephone 01794 515236
Fax 01794 515238
Email sales@hunton.co.uk
Website www.hunton.co.uk

Jeremy Rogers Ltd

(Full Member)

(Jeremy Rogers Yachts)

Contact
Jeremy Rogers
Address
Laundry Lane
Milford on Sea
Hampshire
SO41 OWJ
Telephone 01590 645454
Fax 01590 642537
Email
jeremyrogersmbe@compuserve.com
Website www.jeremyrogers.co.uk

John Broom Boats Ltd

(Full Member)

Contact
J A Broom
Address
Brundall Gardens
Brundall
Norwich
Norfolk
NR13 3RG
Telephone 01603 712136
Fax 01603 712136
Email Not available
Website Not available

John Freeman Sales Ltd

(Full Member)

(Sheridan Marine)

Contact
A S Corless
Address
Moulsford
Oxfordshire
OX10 9HU
Telephone 01491 652085
Fax 01491 652990
Email info@sheridanmarine.com
Website wwwfreemancruisers.com

John Williams Boats
(Full Member)
Contact
John Williams
Address
The Staithe
Stalham
Norfolk
NR12 9DA
Telephone 01692 580953
Fax 01692 582132
Email johnwboats@aol.com
Website
www.johnwilliamsboats.co.uk

Latham's Boatyard Ltd
(Full Member)
(Grangeblue Ltd)
Contact
Paul Kendall
Address
Turks Lane
Sandbanks Road
Poole
Dorset
BH14 8EW
Telephone 01202 748029
Fax 01202 721601
Email Not available
Website
Not available

Luhrs Marine Ltd
(Full Member)
Contact
Stephen Cutsforth
Address
Osprey Quay
Portland Beach Road
Portland
Dorset
DT5 1RA
Telephone 01305 824600
Fax 01305 824603
Email info@luhrsmarine.co.uk
Website www.luhrsmarine.co.uk

MB Yachts Ltd
(Full Member)
Contact
Martyn Brake
Address
274 West Way
Broadstone
Poole
Dorset
BH18 9LL
Telephone 01258 861444
Fax 01202 692404
Email
enquiries@mbyachts.freeserve.co.uk
Website Not available

**Moody Service &
Construction Ltd**
(Full Member)
Contact
Graham Moody
Address
Swanwick Shore
Swanwick
Southampton
Hampshire
SO31 1ZL
Telephone 01489 885000
Fax 01489 885871
Email service@moody.co.uk
Website www.moody.co.uk

Multihull Centre
(Full Member)
Contact
Debbie Patterson
Address
Foss Quay
Millbrook
Torpoint
Cornwall
PL10 1EN
Telephone 01752 823900
Fax 01752 823200
Email sales@multihullcentre.co.uk
Website www.multihullcentre.co.uk

Multimarine Composites Ltd
(Full Member)
Contact
Darren Newton
Address
Foss Quarry
Millbrook
Torpoint
Cornwall
PL10 1EN
Telephone 01752 823513
Fax 01752 823179
Email info@multimarine.co.uk
Website www.multimarine.co.uk

Native Yacht Company Ltd
(Full Member)
Contact
Lisa Hodds
Address
Riverside Estate
Brundall
Norwich
Norfolk
NR13 5PW
Telephone 01603 716588
Fax 01603 716648
Email Not available
Website www.nativeyacht.co.uk

Newson Boatbuilders Ltd
(Full Member)
Contact
K Wood
Address
3 Sealake Road
Oulton Broad
Lowestoft
Suffolk
NR32 3LQ
Telephone 01502 574902
Fax 01502 574902
Email Not available
Website www.newson.co.uk

Norfolk Broads Direct Ltd
(Full Member)
Contact
Paul Greasley
Address
The Bridge
Wroxham
Norwich
Norfolk
NR12 8RX
Telephone 01603 782207
Fax 01603 784272
Email info@broads.co.uk
Website www.broads.co.uk

Norman Pearn & Company Ltd
(Full Member)
Contact
D Pearn
Address
Millpool Boatyard
Looe
Cornwall
PL13 2AE
Telephone 01503 262244
Fax 01503 262244
Email sales@looeboats.co.uk
Website www.looeboats.co.uk

Open World Yachts Ltd
(Probationary Member)
Contact
Simon Patterson
Address
The Saw Mill
Hawkshead
Cumbria
LA22 OPL
Telephone 015394 36660
Fax 015934 36670
Email info@openworldyachts.com
Website www.openworldyachts.com

Outhill Boatbuilders Ltd
(Full Member)
(Outhill Boatbuilders)
Contact
Bob Moulston
Address
Henley Road
Outhill
Studley
Warwickshire
B80 7DU
Telephone 01527 853798
Fax 01527 854510
Email outhillsales@aol.com
Website www.outhill.com

Ovington Marine Ltd
(Full Member)
Contact
David Ovington
Address
Tanners Bank
North Shields
Tyne and Wear
NE30 1JH
Telephone 0191 2580736
Fax 0191 2964707
Email mail@ovingtonmarine.co.uk
Website www.ovingtonboats.com

Oyster Marine Ltd
(Full Member)
(Oyster Marine)
Contact
Richard Matthews
Address
Foxs Marina
Ipswich
Suffolk
IP2 8SA
Telephone 01473 688888
Fax 01473 686861
Email yachts@oystermarine.com
Website www.oystermarine.com

Pearl Motor Yachts Ltd
(Full Member)
(Pearl Motor Yachts)
(Majorca Sea School)
Contact
Iain Smallridge
Address
19 Goldicote Business Park
Banbury Road
Stratford-upon-Avon
Warwickshire
CV37 7NB
Telephone 01789 740088
Fax 01789 748078
Email info@pearlmotoryachts.com
Website
www.pearlmotoryachts.com

Performance Sailcraft Europe Ltd
(Full Member)
(Laser Centre)
(Laser)
Contact
S Bowler
Address
Station Works
Long Buckby
Northamptonshire
NN6 7PF
Telephone 01327 841600
Fax 01327 841601
Email info@lasersailing.com
Website www.lasersailing.com

Picton Boats Ltd
(Full Member)
(Picton Boats)
Contact
J Picton
Address
Brymenyn Industrial Estate
Brymenyn
Near Bridgend
Glamorgan
CF32 9TZ
Telephone 01656 724444
Fax 01656 721709
Email Not available
Website www.pictonboats.com

Princess Yachts plc
(Full Member)
(Princess Yachts)
Contact
David King
Address
Newport Street
Plymouth
Devon
PL1 3QG
Telephone 01752 203888
Fax 01752 203777
Email
postmaster@princess-yachts.com
Website www.princess-yachts.com

Ribeye Ltd
(Full Member)
(Ribeye)
Contact
Charles Chivers
Address
Collingwood Road
Townstal
Dartmouth
Devon
TQ6 9JY
Telephone 01803 832060
Fax 01803 839090
Email charleschivers@ribeye.co.uk
Website www.ribeye.co.uk

Richard Faulkner Composites Ltd
(Full Member)
Contact
Richard Faulkner
Address
9 Hamble House Gardens
Hamble
Hampshire
SO31 4JG
Telephone 023 80457844
Fax 023 80457844
Email rfyachts@aol.com
Website Not available

Rossiter Yachts Ltd
(Full Member)
Contact
Charles Rossiter
Address
Rossiters Quay
Bridge Street
Christchurch
Dorset
BH23 1DZ
Telephone 01202 483250
Fax 01202 490164
Email rossiteryachts@hotmail.com
Website www.rossiteryachts.co.uk

Rustler Yachts Ltd
(Full Member)
Contact
Nick Offord
Address
Maritime Buildings
Falmouth Road
Falmouth
Cornwall
TR10 8AD
Telephone 01326 310120
Fax 01326 314092
Email nickofford@rustleryachts.com
Website Not available

Sealine International Ltd
(Full Member)
(Sealine Wine Bar)
Contact
Simon Houlder
Address
Whitehouse Road
Kidderminster
Worcestershire
DY10 1HT
Telephone 01562 749 142
Fax 01562 747709
Email simon.houlder@sealine.com
Website www.sealine.com

Seastream International Ltd
(Full Member)
Contact
Not available
Address
3 Shamrock Quay
William Street
Southampton
Hampshire
SO14 5QL
Telephone 023 8033 9040
Fax 023 8022 1009
Email sales@seastream.com
Website www.seastream.com

Shakespeare International
Marine Ltd
(Full Member)
Contact
Francis Whitley
Address
Station Road
Hartlebury
Hereford & Worcester
DY11 7YJ
Telephone 01299 250 685
Fax 01299 250 685
Email Not available
Website Not available

Sirius Yachts Ltd
(Full Member)
Contact
Bryan Jones
Address
Redstone Wharf
Sandy Lane
Stourport-on-Severn
Worcestershire
DY13 9QB
Telephone 01299 871048
Fax 01299 871048
Email bryan@siriusyachts.com
Website www.siriusyachts.com

Southampton Yacht Services Ltd
(Full Member)
Contact
Mandy Hatherley
Address
Saxon Wharf
Lower York Street
Northam
Southampton
Hampshire
SO14 5QF
Telephone 02380 335266
Fax 02380 634275
Email
mandyh@southamptonyachtservices.co.uk
Website
www.southamptonyachtservices.co.uk

Sunseeker International
Boats Ltd
(Full Member)
(Sunseeker)
(Sunseeker Champagne Bar)
Contact
Seth Marshall
Address
27-31 West Quay Road
Poole
Dorset
BH15 1HX
Telephone 01202 381111
Fax 01202 382222
Email
seth.marshall@sunseeker.com
Website www.sunseeker.com

Swancraft Cruisers
(Full Member)
Contact
A R Crampton
Address
Riverside Estate
Brundall
Norwich
Norfolk
NR13 5PL
Telephone 01603 712362
Fax 01603 712363
Email Not available
Website Not available

Thanetcraft Ltd
(Full Member)
Contact
John Armstrong
Address
29 Pope's Grove
Twickenham
Middlesex
TW1 4JZ
Telephone 020 8894 5218
Fax 020 8894 5218
Email sales@thanetcraft.com
Website www.thanetcraft.com

The Select Yacht Group
(Full Member)
(Cornish Crabbers)
(Hunter Boats)
(Red Fox Yachts)
Contact
Frank Colam
Address
Rock
Wadebridge
Cornwall
PL27 6NT
Telephone 01208 862666
Fax 01208 862 375
Email
frankcolam@selectyachts.co.uk
Website www.selectyachts.co.uk

Toughs Boatyard
(Full Member)
Contact
Bob Tough
Address
27 Ferry Road
Teddington
Middlesex
TW11 9NN
Telephone 020 8977 4494
Fax 020 8977 7546
Email johntough@btinternet.com
Website www.toughsboatyard.co.uk

Viking Mouldings
(Full Member)
Contact
David Underwood
Address
Unit 11
Ongar Road Trading Estate
Great Dunmow
Essex
CM6 1EU
Telephone 01371 875214
Fax 01371 873826
Email david@vikingmouldings.com
Website Not available

Windboats Marine Ltd
(Full Member)
Contact
T James
Address
Grange Walk
Wroxham
Norwich
Norfolk
NR12 8RX
Telephone 01603 782236
Fax 01603 784106
Email
trevorjames@windboats.co.uk
Website Not available

Wroxham Marine Ltd
(Full Member)
(Sheerline Motor Cruisers)
Contact
Peter Applegate
Address
c/o Highcraft
Griffin Lane
Thorpe St Andrews
Norwich
Norfolk
NR7 0SL
Telephone 01603 701100
Fax 01603 701100
Email
enquiry@sheerlinemotorcruisers.com
Website
www.sheerlinemotorcruisers.com

British Marine
Federation

The following are Members
of the British Marine Federation

A Blagdon Boatyard
(Full Member)
Contact
A Blagdon
Address
Richmond Walk
Devonport
Plymouth
Devon
PL1 4LN
Telephone 01752 561830
Fax Not available
Email
blagdonboatyard@btinternet.com
Website Not available

Alumacraft
(Seastrike Boats)
(Full Member)
Contact
D Irvine
Address
The Marina
Barns Lane
Stubbers Green
Aldridge
West Midlands
WS9 8BQ
Telephone 01922 458227
Fax 01922 744224
Email sales@seastrike.co.uk
Website www.seastrike.co.uk

Aqua Marine Ltd
(Full Member)
Contact
Michael Shackleton
Address
Units 14 & 15 Penton Hook Marina
Staines Road
Chertsey
Surrey KT16 8PY
Telephone 01932 570202
Fax 01932 570222
Email aok@aquamarine.uk.com
Website www.aquamarine.uk.com

Atlantic Boats Ltd
(Full Member)
(Maenporth Boats)
Contact
R Allen
Address
Maenporth
Falmouth
Cornwall TR11 5HN
Telephone 01326 251046
Fax 01326 251152
Email maenporthboatsuk@aol.com
Website Not available

Bell Boats Ltd
(Full Member)
Contact
J Bell
Address
Waterside
Brundall
Norwich
Norfolk
NR13 5PY
Telephone 01603 713109
Fax 01603 714141
Email Not available
Website Not available

Blue Boats
(Full Member)
(Powercat)
Contact
Barry Philpott
Address
Bryher Boatyard
Isle of Scilly
Cornwall
TR23 OPR
Telephone 01720 423095
Fax 01720 423011
Email sales@blueboats.co.uk
Website www.blueboats.co.uk

Blue C Marine Technology Ltd
(Full Member)
Contact
P Burborough
Address
Firs Industrial Est
Oldington Lane
Kidderminster
Worcestershire
DY11 7QN
Telephone 01562 746336
Fax 01562 746336
Email Not available
Website Not available

Boating World
(Probationary Member)
Contact
M S Hocking
Address
Landrake
Saltash
Cornwall
PL12 5ES
Telephone 01752 851679
Fax 01752 851515
Email boatingworld@supanet.com
Website www.boatingworldsw.co.uk

Bossoms Boatyard Ltd
(Full Member)
(Bossoms Boatyard)
Contact
Tom Ballance
Address
Binsey Lane
Medley
Oxford
Oxfordshire
OX2 ONL
Telephone 01865 247780
Fax 01865 244163
Email info@bossoms.co.uk
Website www.bossoms.com

BW Marine
(Full Member)
Contact
Peter Day
Address
Birchwood Cottages
Shaws Lane
Southwater Horsham
Sussex
RH13 7BX
Telephone 01403 730318
Fax 01403 730318
Email Not available
Website Not available

Capel Sailing
(Full Member)
Contact
C B Watts
Address
Five Oak Green
Tonbridge
Kent
TN12 6RB
Telephone 01892 832128
Fax Not available
Email Not available
Website
www.capelcanoesandsailing.co.u

CH Lavis & Son
(Full Member)
Contact
R E Lavis
Address
6 Camperdown Terrace
Exmouth
Devon
EX8 1EJ
Telephone 01395 263095
Fax 01395 263095
Email ronlavis@fsbdial.co.uk
Website Not available

Charo Boats Ltd
(Probationary Member)
Contact
Christopher Chawro
Address
Severn Cider
56 Brittania Gardens
Stourport-on-Severn
Worcestershire
DY13 9NZ
Telephone 01384 865172
Fax 01384 865172
Email Not available
Website Not available

Chippendale Craft Ltd
(Full Member)
Contact
E Bird
Address
Unit One
Rock Channel
Rye
Sussex
TN31 7HJ
Telephone 01797 227707
Fax 01797 227707
Email Not available
Website Not available

Churchouse Boats Ltd
(Full Member)
(McNalty Boats)
Contact
Stewart Brown
Address
Apsley Sawmill
Andover Road
Whitchurch
Hampshire
RG28 7SD
Telephone 01256 896292
Fax 01256 896292
Email sb@drascombe.org.uk
Website www.drascombe.org.uk

ClamBoat Ltd
(Full Member)
Contact
David Rolfe
Address
Albany House
Market Street
Maidenhead
Berkshire
SL6 8BE
Telephone 01628 421547
Fax 01628 421501
Email davidrolfe@clamboat.com
Website Not available

Clyde Technologies Marine Ltd
(Full Member)
Contact
James Boyle
Address
Fairlie Quay
Main Road
Fairlie
Ayrshire
KA29 0AS
Telephone 01475 744660
Fax 01475 744557
Email
sales@clyde-technologies.co.uk
Website
www.clyde-technologies.co.uk

Cockwells Modern & Classic Boatbuilding
(Full Member)
Contact
David Cockwell
Address
South West Shipyard
Ponsarden
Falmouth
Cornwall
TR11 2SE
Telephone 01326 377366
Fax 01326 377366
Email
davecockwell@btopenworld.com
Website Not available

Comet Dinghies
(Full Member)
Contact
Andrew Simmons
Address
Horsepond Meadow
South Molton
Devon
EX36 4EJ
Telephone 01769 574358
Fax 01769 574358
Email info@cometdinghies.com
Website www.cometdinghies.com

Conrad Natzio Boatbuilder
(Full Member)
Contact
J C Natzio
Address
The Old School
Brundish Road
Raveningham
Norwich
Norfolk
NR14 6NT
Telephone 01508 548675
Fax Not available
Email Not available
Website Not available

Craig Moore Marine Services
(Probationary Member)
Contact
Craig Moore
Address
40 West End
Langtoft
Peterborough
Lincolnshire
PE6 9LU
Telephone 01778 346008
Fax 01778 346008
Email Not available
Website Not available

Creative Marine
(Full Member)
Contact
Simon Read
Address
The Secret Boatyard
Barningham Barns
Matlaske
Norwich
Norfolk
NR11 7LE
Telephone 01263 570100
Fax 01263 570100
Email creative.marine@talk21.com
Website www.creativemarine.co.uk

Deft Developments Ltd
(Probationary Member)
Contact
Tim Lester
Address
11 Nightingale Road
Hampton
Middlesex
TW12 3HU
Telephone 020 89792128
Fax 020 89792128
Email tim_lester@defttech.co.uk
Website
www.deftdevelopments.co.uk

Elephant Boatyard Ltd
(Full Member)
Contact
Tom Richardson
Address
Lands End Road
Old Bursledon
Southampton
Hampshire
SO31 8DN
Telephone 023 8040 3268
Fax 023 8040 5085
Email
elephant@landsendrd.freeserve.co.uk
Website Not available

Evans Boatwork
(Full Member)
Contact
Colin Evans
Address
Unit 5
Havens Head Business Park
The Docks
Milford Haven
Pembrokeshire
SA73 3LD
Telephone 07815 075585
Fax 07967 303639
Email info@evansboatwork.co.uk
Website www.evansboatwork.co.uk

Explorer Boats Ltd
(Probationary Member)
Contact
B Atherton
Address
Falcongate
Dock Link
Wallasey
Wirral
Merseyside
CH44 3EQ
Telephone 0151 630 0466
Fax 0151 638 8129
Email sales@explorerboatsltd.co.uk
Website www.explorerboats.co.uk

FCS (Scotland) Ltd
(Full Member)
Contact
Steve Kelvin
Address
North Side Workshops
Grange Lane
Grangemouth Docks
Grangemouth
Falkirk
FK3 8UB
Telephone 01259 753605
Fax 01259 753605
Email steve.fcs@ukonline.co.uk
Website www.fcsscotlandltd.co.uk

Ferryman Boats
(Full Member)
Contact
Paul Ferry
Address
Balliniska Business Park
Springtown Industrial Estate
Londonderry
Northern Ireland
BT48 0LY
Telephone 028 71268766
Fax 028 71363405
Email Not available
Website Not available

Frank Halls & Son
(Full Member)
Contact
Christopher Halls
Address
Mill Lane
Walton on the Naze
Essex
CO14 8PF
Telephone 01255 675596
Fax 01255 677772
Email frankhalls@tiscali.co.uk
Website Not available

Fyne Boat Kits
(Full Member)
Contact
P S Stanistreet
Address
Ferry Road
Bowness-on-Windermere
Cumbria
LA23 3JH
Telephone 01539 444300
Fax 01539 447662
Email info@fyneboatkits.com
Website www.fyneboatkits.com

G J Boat Builders
(Full Member)
Contact
G S Packham
Address
5 Connaught Avenue
Gorleston-on-Sea
Norfolk
NR31 7LU
Telephone 01493 603 475
Fax Not available
Email gary@gjboats.com
Website www.gjboats.com

Giles Reinforced Plastics Ltd
(Full Member)
Contact
Mark Giles
Address
1 Hatch Way
Kirtlington
Oxford
Oxfordshire
OX5 3JS
Telephone 01869 347801
Fax do not use fax
Email anne.giles@tesco.net
Website Not available

Harry King and Sons
(Full Member)
Contact
G H King
Address
Kings Boatyard
Pin Mill
Ipswich
Suffolk
IP9 1JN
Telephone 01473 780285
Fax Not available
Email Not available
Website
www.harryking.maritimenet.co.uk

HE Hipperson Ltd
(Full Member)
Contact
J R Harrison
Address
The Quay
Gillingham Dam
Beccles
Suffolk
NR34 0EB
Telephone 01502 712166
Fax Not available
Email Not available
Website Not available

Heyland Marine
(Full Member)
Contact
Anthony G Harper
Address
Bourne End Marina
Wharf Lane
Bourne End
Buckinghamshire
SL8 5RR
Telephone 01628 528830
Fax 01628 819028
Email info@heylandmarine.com
Website www.heylandmarine.com

HJ Mears & Son
(Full Member)
Contact
P Mears
Address
The Harbour
Axmouth
Seaton
Devon
EX12 4AA
Telephone 01297 20964
Fax Not available
Email Not available
Website Not available

Honnor Marine Ltd
(Full Member)
(Original Devon Boats)
Contact
Bob Brown
Address
Unit 1
Caxton Street
Heywood
Lancashire
OL10 1AL
Telephone 01706 369084
Fax 01706 623189
Email info@honnormarine.co.uk
Website www.honnormarine.co.uk

Ice Marine Ltd
(Full Member)
(Ice Marine)
Contact
Oliver Selman
Address
PO Box 6352
Basingstoke
Hampshire
RG25 3RS
Telephone 01420 520770
Fax 01420 520117
Email info@icemarine.com
Website www.icemarine.com

James Reinman Marine Ltd
(Full Member)
(Shetland Boats)
Contact
James Reinman
Address
Grimstone End
Pakenham
Bury St Edmunds
Suffolk
IP31 2LZ
Telephone 01359 235255
Fax 01359 235251
Email sales@shetlandboats.co.uk
Website www.shetlandboats.co.uk

James Wharram Designs
(Full Member)
Contact
Ruth Wharram
Address
Greenbank Road
Devoran
Truro
Cornwall
TR3 6PJ
Telephone 01872 864792
Fax 01872 864791
Email wharram@wharram.com
Website www.wharram.com

JEP Marine
(Full Member)
Contact
John Pollitt
Address
Unit 4
Lamberhurst Farm
Dargate
Faversham
Kent
ME13 9EP
Telephone 01227 750585
Fax 01227 750585
Email
sales@jepmarine.demon.co.uk
Website Not available

JM Coulam Boatbuilders
(Full Member)
Contact
J Coulam
Address
3 Stirling Way
Northfields Industrial Estate
Market Deeping
Peterborough
Lincolnshire
PE6 8AS
Telephone 01778 348542
Fax 01778 380495
Email Not available
Website Not available

John Lack
(Full Member)
(Devon Yawl)
Contact
John Lack
Address
Flagstaff House
Coastguard Way
Mudeford
Christchurch
Devon
BH23 3NP
Telephone 01202 483191
Fax 01202 499669
Email Not available
Website Not available

John Williams Boats
(Full Member)
Contact
John Williams
Address
The Staithe
Stalham
Norfolk
NR12 9DA
Telephone 01692 580953
Fax 01692 582132
Email johnwboats@aol.com
Website
www.johnwilliamsboats.co.uk

Julian Mann, Boatbuilder
(Full Member)
Contact
J Mann
Address
Unit 3 The Greenway Building
Dartside Quay
Galmpton
Devon
TQ5 OGB
Telephone 01803 843877
Fax Not available
Email
julian@woodenboatrepairs.co.uk
Website
www.woodenboatrepairs.co.uk

Kittiwake Boats
(Full Member)
Contact
Roger Wilkinson
Address
56 Robin Lane
Lyme Green
Macclesfield
Cheshire
SK11 OLH
Telephone 01260 252157
Fax 01260 252157
Email roger@kittiwakeboats.co.uk
Website www.kittiwakeboats.co.uk

Lakeland Wooden Boats
(Full Member)
Contact
Kevin Halcrow
Address
2 Ghyll Brow
Brigsteer Road
Kendal
Cumbria
LA9 5DZ
Telephone 01539 727118
Fax no fax
Email
lakelandboats@the-internet-
pages.co.uk
Website Not available

LDC Racing Sailboats Ltd
(Full Member)
(LDC Racing Sailboats)
Contact
Martin Wadhams
Address
Trafalgar Close
Chandlers Ford
Eastleigh
Hampshire SO53 4BW
Telephone 023 80274500
Fax 023 80274800
Email info@ldcracingsailboats.co.uk
Website
www.ldcracingsailboats.co.uk

Mills Dockyard
(Full Member)
Contact
Stephen Mills
Address
Trent Lock
Nottinghamshire
NG10 2FY
Telephone 0115 9732595
Fax 0115 9732595
Email Not available
Website Not available

Morton Boats
(Full Member)
Contact
Peter Richards
Address
Eagle Road
Morton
Swinderby
Lincolnshire
LN6 9HT
Telephone 01522 868689
Fax 01522 869880
Email info@mortonboats.co.uk
Website www.mortonboats.co.uk

North Quay Marine
(Full Member)
Contact
Ted Spears
Address
North Quay House
1 North Quay
Conyer
Sittingbourne
Kent
ME9 9HL
Telephone 01795 521711
Fax 01795 521384
Email spearsboat@aol.com
Website Not available

Norwester Ltd
(Full Member)
(Character Boats)
Contact
Adrian Denye
Address
Unit 1 Rowlay Trading Estate
Allenby Road
Lytham St Annes
Lancashire
FY8 2DG
Telephone 01253 727004
Fax 01253 727004
Email Not available
Website www.characterboats.co.uk

Original Box Boat Co Ltd
(Full Member)
Contact
P J Strand
Address
Sweetwoods Park
Cowden
Edenbridge
Kent
TN8 7JN
Telephone 01342 850087
Fax 01342 850866
Email Not available
Website www.boxboat.com

Orkney Glass Fibre Ltd
(Full Member)
Contact
Brian Kynoch
Address
Scotts Road
Hatston Industrial Estate
Kirkwall
Orkney
KW15 1GR
Telephone 01856 872411
Fax 01856 879334
Email
sales@orkneyglassfibre.co.uk
Website
www.orkneyglassfibre.co.uk

Overton Marine Ltd
(Full Member)
Contact
Richard Godwin
Address
Overton Lodge
St Georges Road
Cheltenham
Gloucestershire
GL50 3EA
Telephone 01242 523371
Fax 01240 521938
Email admin@overton-bar.com
Website Not available

Oxfordia
(Probationary Member)
Contact
Diana Phillips
Address
55 Church Road
Wheatley
Oxford
Oxfordshire
OX33 1LU
Telephone 01865 439389
Fax 01865 873095
Email enquiries@oxfordia.co.uk
Website www.oxfordia.co.uk

Pascos Boatyard
(Full Member)
Contact
Julian Davy
Address
St Just-in-Roseland
Truro
Cornwall
TR2 5JD
Telephone 01326 270269
Fax Not available
Email lanzeague@aol.com
Website Not available

Performance Sailcraft Europe Ltd
(Full Member)
(Laser Centre)
(Laser)
Contact
S Bowler
Address
Station Works
Long Buckby
Northamptonshire
NN6 7PF
Telephone 01327 841600
Fax 01327 841601
Email info@lasersailing.com
Website www.lasersailing.com

Petticrows Ltd
(Full Member)
Contact
Sophia Hoj-Jensen
Address
The Quay
Burnham-on-Crouch
Essex
CMO 8AT
Telephone 01621 782115
Fax 01621 785389
Email petticrows@dial.pipex.com
Website Not available

Phantom Evolution Ltd
(Probationary Member)
Contact
John Evans
Address
Unit H4 Lambs Business Park
Tilburstow Hill Road
South Godstone
Surrey
RH9 8LJ
Telephone 01342 893418
Fax 01342 893796
Email Not available
Website Not available

Phoenix Fleet Ltd
(Full Member)
Contact
R F Richardson
Address
Repps Staithe Boatyard
Potter Heigham
Norfolk
NR29 5JD
Telephone 01692 670460
Fax Not available
Email Not available
Website Not available

Pippin Yachts Ltd
(Full Member)
Contact
K Scott
Address
Sutterton Entrerprise Park
Endeavour Way
Sutterton
Boston
Lincs
PE20 2AJ
Telephone 01205 461212
Fax Not available
Email pippin@pippin-yachts.com

Plancraft Marine
(Full Member)
Contact
Ron Buckingham
Address
Unit 4, Little Sheliwood Farm
Clayhill Road
Leigh,
Nr Reigate
Surrey RH2 8PA
Telephone 01306 611100
Fax 01306 611101
Email sales@plancraft.co.uk
Website www.plancraft.co.uk

Porter Brothers
(Marine & Industrial) Ltd
(Full Member)
Contact
Mike Porter
Address
1 Emsworth Yacht Harbour
Thorney Road
Emsworth
Hants
PO10 8BP
Telephone 01243 377522
Fax 01243 372929
Email porterems@aol.com
Website www.porters.org.uk

Portland Marine Ltd
(Full member)
Contact
Sebastian Gowar-Cliffe
Address
21-23 South Way
Southwell Business Park
Portland
Dorset
DT5 2NJ
Telephone 01305 861556
Fax 01305 861557
Email into@cirrusribs.com
Website www.cirrusribs.com

QB Marine (Marlin Boats)
(Full Member)
Contact
Chris Graham
Address
Saltmakers House
Hamble Point Marina
Hamble.
Southampton
Hants
SO31 4NB
Telephone 023 8045 8833
Fax 023 8045 8988
Email ribs@marlinboats.info
Website www.marlinboats.into

Reid Marine
(Full member)
Contact
Peter Reid
Address
Reid Street
Christchurch
Dorset
BH23 2BT
Telephone 01202 483333
Fax 01202 478863
Email reidmarine@reidsteel.co.uk
Website www.reidsteel.co.uk

Revenger Boat Company Ltd
(Full Member)
Contact
Mike Slogett
Address
Forward Buildings
46 Windsor Road
Slough
Berkshire
SL1 2EU
Telephone 01753 525496
Fax 01753 573955
Email revenger.rib@cwcom.net
Website www.revenger.co.uk

Sail and Oar
(Full member)
Contact
Julian Burn
Address
Unit 12 Brook House
Darlington
Totnes
Devon
T09 6DJ
Telephone 01803 866680
Fax 01803 863878
Email boatbuilder©sailoar.co.uk
Website www.sailoar.co.uk

Steve Sawford Marine Ltd
(Full Member)
Contact
Steve Sawford
Address
15 Drydens Close
Titchmarsh
Kettering
Northamptonshire
NN14 3DD
Telephone
01536 330477 (Daytime)
Email ssmarine@btinternet.com
Website www.sailingtorall.com

Sea Hopper Folding Boats
(Full Member)
Contact
Steven Rea
Address
3 Bagley Road
Rockwell Green
Wellington
Somerset
TA21 9PZ
Telephone 01823 665151
Fax 01823 660282
Email cherry.stevo@virgin.net
Website
www.seahoppertoldingboats.co.uk

South Holland Marine & Fabrication Ltd
(Full Member)
Contact
S Winfield
Address
Unit 3,
Poplars Farm
East Heckington,
Boston, Lincs
PE2O 30F
Telephone 01529 460758
Fax 01529 460758
Email
into@Southhollandmarine.com
Website www.shm.com

Specialized Marine Ltd
(Full Member)
Contact
Peter & Chris Turner
Address
1-3 Riverside Works
Coombe Street
Lyme Regis
Dorset
DT7 3PY
Telephone 01297 442694 (Office)
Fax 01297 442694
Emai
sales@specializedmarine.com
Website
www.specializedmarine.com

Sportique Ski Boats Ltd
(Full Member)
Contact
Mike & Yvonne Keeton
Address
Firebeacon Bridge
Firebeacon Lane
Covenham Louth
Lincolnshire
LN11 OPA
Telephone 01472 388296
Fax 01472 388944
Email mikosportique@aol.com
Website www.sportiqueboats.co.uk

Stowaway Boats Ltd
(Full Member)
Contact
M Walters
Address
12 High Street
Byfield
Northants
NN11 6XH
Telephone 01327 260600
Fax 01327 262512
Email cvs@globalnet
Website Not available

The Thames Electric Launch Company
(Full Member)
Contact
E Barrell
Address
P0 Box 3
Goring on Thames
Berkshire
RG12 1RL
Telephone 01491 873126
Fax 01491 872217
Email Not available
Website Not available

Thanetcraft Ltd
(Full Member)
Contact
John Arrmstrong
Address
24 Popes Grove
Twickenham
Middlesex
TW1 4JZ
Telephone 020 8894 5218
Fax 020 8894 5218
Email sales@thanetcratt.com
Website www.thanetcraft.com
www.jetsprintuk.com

Topper International Ltd
(Full Member)
Contact
Jason Fry
Address
Kingsnorth Technology Park
Wotton Road
Ashtord
Kent
TN23 6LN
Telephone 01233 629186
Fax 01233 645897
Email
jasontry@toppersailboats.com
Website www.toppersailboats.com

Trident - UK
(Full Member)
Contact
David Gebhard
Address
Trident Quay
5-6 South Shore Road
Gateshead
Tyne & Wear
NE8 3AE
Telephone 0191 490 1736
Fax 0191 478 2122
Email info@trident-uk.com
Website www.trident-uk.com

W Trout & Son Ltd
(Full Member)
Contact
Michael Trout
Address
Boathouse
Ferry Road
Topsham
Exeter
Devon
EX3 OJA
Telephone 01392 873044/875176
Fax 01932 875176
Email wtrout@tiscali.co.uk
Website Not available

Victor Boats
(Full Member)
Contact
Ms Kelly Cooke
Address
Unit 38 Longshot Lane
Bracknell
Berkshire
RG12 1RL
Telephone 01344 453210
Fax 01344 411359
Email agstructures@steelweb.co.uk
Website Not available

Warrior Boats
(Full Member)
Contact
Mrs Vivian Haynes
Address
Unit 24
Common Bank Ind Estate
Ackhurst Road
Chorley
Lancashire
PR7 1NH
Telephone 01257 277444
Fax 01257 276600
Email
warriorboats@tinyworld.co.uk
Website Not available

Watkin Boat Sales
(Full member)
Contact
Rob Parry
Address
Island Street
Salcombe
Devon
T08 8DP
Telephone 01548 843383
Fax 01548 843734
Email Not available
Website Not available

West Solent Boat Builders Ltd
(Full Member)
Contact
Mrs A Wreyford
Address
The Boatyard
Keyhaven
Milford-on-Sea
Lymington
Hants S041 OTR
Telephone 01590 642080
Fax 01590 645011
Email wsbb@beeb.net
Website Not available

John Williams Boats
(Full Member)
Contact
John Williams
Address
The Staithe,
Stalham
Norfolk
NR12 9DA
Telephone 01692 580953
Email Not available
Website
www.johnwilliamsboats.co.uk

Williams Marine
(Full member)
Contact
MD Hornsby
Address
1 Mill Lane
Chalgrove
Oxfordshire
OX44 75L
Telephone 01865 890558
Fax 01865 890355
Email
enquiries@williamsmarine.com
Website www.williamsmarine.com

Willow Bay Boats
(Full Member)
Contact
Phil Swift
Address
The Barn
Low House Farm
Lickbarrow Road
Cleabarrow
Windermere
Lancashire LA23 3NA
Telephone 015394 42741
Fax Not available
Email
wbb@pswift.freeserve.co.uk
Website
www.willowbayboats.co.uk

Wilstream Yachts (Tyne Slipway & Engineering Co Ltd)
(Full Member)
Contact
Johnathan Wilson
Address
Commercial Road
Temple Town
South Shields
Tyne and Wear
NE33 SPL
Telephone 0191 445 4893
Fax 0191 456 6396
Email
adventure@wilstreamyachts.com
Website www.wilstreamyachts.com

Wootton Bridge Industries Ltd
(Full Member)
Contact
P Webb
Address
9 Ashlake Farm Lane
Wootton Bridge
Isle of Wight
P033 4LF
Telephone 01983 280707
(workshop)
Fax 01983 280785
Email into@clinkerboat.com
Website www.clinkerboat.com

Working Sail
(Full Member)
Contact
Sara Powell
Address
11 New Street
Penryn
Cornwall
TR10 8EB
Telephone 01326 373645
Fax 01326 373645
Email info@workingsail.co.uk
Website Not available

Wraysbury Boathouse
(Full Member)
Contact
Tim O Keefe
Address
28 Old Ferry Drive
Wraysbury
Berkshire
TW19 5JT
Telephone 01784 482569
Email Not available
Website Not available

British Marine
Federation

The following are Members
of the British Marine Federation

**BMF - Association of Brokers
and Yacht Agents Ltd** (ABYA)
(Region and Group Association)
(YBDSA (Holdings) Ltd)
Contact
Jane Gentry
Address
The Glass Works
Penns Road
Petersfield
Hampshire
GU32 2EW
Telephone 01730 710425
Fax 0845 0900163
Email jane@ybdsa.co.uk
Website www.ybdsa.co.uk

Adrian Nicolle & Co Ltd
(Full Member)
(Nicolle Associates)
Contact
Adrian Nicolle
Address
Brooklands
Newbridge
Southampton
Hampshire
SO40 2NW
Telephone 023 8081 4156
Fax 023 80811144
Email info@nicolle-associates.com
Website
www.nicolle-associates.com

AM Dickie & Sons Ltd
(Full Member)
(Lagoon/Dickies Prestige)
(Dickies)
Contact
Peter Dickie
Address
36 Garth Road
Bangor
Gwynedd
LL57 2SE
Telephone 01248 363400
Fax 01248 354169
Email info@dickies.co.uk
Website www.dickies.co.uk

**Ancasta International
Boat Sales Ltd**
(Full Member)
(Bavaria Motor Boats (BMB))
(Lagoon)
(Beneteau)
Contact
Jocelyne Gerard
Address
Port Hamble
Satchell Lane
Hamble
Southampton
Hampshire
SO31 4QD
Telephone 023 8045 0008
Fax 023 8045 5415
Email marketing@ancasta.co.uk
Website www.ancasta.co.uk

Ardfern Yacht Centre Ltd
(Full Member)
Contact
David Wilkie
Address
Ardfern by Lochgilphead
Argyll
PA31 8QN
Telephone 01852 500247
Fax 01852 500624
Email david@ardfernyacht.co.uk
Website www.ardfernyacht.co.uk

BA Peters Plc
(Full Member)
(Opal Marine)
(Seasport)
(Rodman)
Contact
Brian Peters
Address
Chichester Marina
Birdham
Chichester
Sussex
PO20 7BG
Telephone 01243 511381
Fax 01243 511382
Email brianpeters@petersplc.com
Website www.petersplc.com

Berthon Boat Company Ltd
(Full Member)
Contact
Brian May
Address
The Shipyard
Lymington
Hampshire
SO41 3YL
Telephone 01590 673312
Fax 01590 676353
Email brian.may@berthon.co.uk
Website www.berthon.co.uk

Bray Marine Sales Ltd
(Full Member)
(Bray Marine Sales)
Contact
Dominic Smulders
Address
Bray Marina
Monkey Island Lane
Bray
Berkshire
SL6 2EB
Telephone 01628 773177
Fax 01628 660770
Email
braymarinesales@btopenworld.com
Website
www.thamesboatsales.co.uk

Cavendish White Ltd
(Full Member)
Contact
Michael White
Address
Lutidine House
Newark Lane
Ripley, Surrey
GU23 6BS
Telephone 020 7381 7600
Fax 020 7381 7601
Email mike@cavendishwhite.com
Website www.cavendishwhite.com

CEproof Ltd
(Full Member)
Contact
Peter Tier
Address
2 Mariners House
Copse Lane
Hamble
Hampshire
SO31 4QH
Telephone 023 8045 3245
Fax 023 8045 7456
Email petert@ceproof.com
Website www.ceproof.com

Charles Watson Marine Ltd
(Full Member)
Contact
Charles Watson
Address
3 The Square
Hamble
Southampton
Hampshire
SO31 4LS
Telephone 023 80456505
Fax 023 80457773
Email
cwatson@charles-watson.com
Website Not available

Clapson & Sons (Shipuilders Ltd)
(Full Member)
Contact
R Clapson
Address
South Ferriby Marina
South Ferriby
Barton On Humber
North Lincolnshire
DN18 6JH
Telephone 01652 635620
Fax 01652 660517
Email info@clapsons.co.uk
Website www.clapsons.co.uk

Dorset Yacht Company Ltd
(Full Member)
(Boston Whaler)
(Dorset Lake Shipyard)
Contact
Russell Culpan
Address
Lake Drive
Hamworthy
Poole
Dorset
BH15 4DT
Telephone 01202 674531
Fax 01202 677518
Email sales@bostonwhaler.com
Website www.bostonwhaler.co.uk

DS Maritime Ltd
(Full Member)
Contact
David Skellon
Address
Lou Mas de Lesper
23 Chemin du Castelet
06650
Le Rouret
France
Telephone 0033 9322 5727
Fax 0033 493 345573
Email Not available
Website Not available

Glasson Basin Yacht Co Ltd
(Full Member)
Contact
B Latham
Address
Glasson Dock
Glasson
Lancashire
LA2 0AW
Telephone 01524 751491
Fax 01524 752626
Email info@glassonmarina.com
Website www.glasson-marina.com

Global Yachts Ltd
(Probationary Member)
Contact
Mark Chapman
Address
Side Offices 1 & 2
Hamble Point Marina
School Lane
Hamble
Southampton
Hampshire
SO31 4NB
Telephone 023 80456788
Fax 023 80456798
Email info@global-yachts.co.uk
Website www.global-yachts.co.uk

Grand Soleil (UK) Ltd
(Full Member)
Contact
Richard Baldwin
Address
10 Saltmakers House
Hamble Point Marina
School Lane
Hamble
Southampton
Hampshire
SO31 4JD
Telephone 023 8045 5977
Fax 023 8045 5877
Email richard@grandsoleil.co.uk
Website www.grandsoleil.co.uk

Gweek Quay Boatyard
(Full Member)
Contact
Gilliam Emerson
Address
Gweek
Helston
Cornwall
TR12 6UF
Telephone 01326 221657
Fax 01326 221685
Email info@gweek-quay.com
Website www.gweek-quay.com

Harleyford Marine Ltd
(Full Member)
(Harleyford Marine)
(Boatshowrooms)
Contact
Colin Watts
Address
Shepperton Marina
Felix Lane
Shepperton
Middlesex
TW17 8NS
Telephone 01932 243722
Fax 01932 243152
Email colin@boatshowrooms.com
Website www.boatshowrooms.com

Kings Yacht Agency inc Alastair Easton & Partners
(Full Member)
Contact
Richard Seymour
Address
Shamrock Quay
William Street
Northam
Southampton
Hampshire
SO14 5QL
Telephone 023 8033 1533
Fax 01590 616318
Email brokerage@kingsyacht.com
Website www.kingsyacht.com

KJ Yacht Brokers
(Probationary Member)
Contact
Paul Knox-Johnston
Address
Southsea Marina
Fort Cumberland Road
Southsea
Hampshire
PO4 9RJ
Telephone 02392 864524
Fax 02392 862196
Email paul@kjyachtbrokers.com
Website www.kjyachtbrokers.com

Lochin Marine International Ltd
(Full Member)
Contact
Simon Thomas
Address
The Yacht Harbour
Newhaven
Sussex
BN9 9BY
Telephone 01273 512619
Fax 01273 512522
Email sales@lochin.com
Website www.lochin.com

Marine Sales UK Ltd
(Full Member)
(Marine Sales UK)
Contact
Louis Solomon
Address
Lake Shipyard
Hamworthy
Poole
Dorset
BH15 4DT
Telephone 001 941 5052524
Fax 001 941 5051214
Email ljsolomon@earthlink.net
Website www.marinesalesuk.com

Maritime Services (Int) Ltd
(Full Member)
Contact
I Biles
Address
1 Stone Lane
Gosport
Hampshire
PO12 1SS
Telephone 023 9252 4490
Fax 023 9252 4490
Email Not available
Website Not available

Medway Bridge Marina Ltd
(Probationary Member)
(Wellcraft)
Contact
Giles Billingsley
Address
Manor Lane
Rochester
Kent
ME1 3HS
Telephone 01634 843576
Fax 01634 843820
Email giles@medwaybridgemarina.co.uk
Website
www.medwaybridgemarina.co.uk

Mr TOD Craig
(Honorary Member)
Contact
TOD Craig
Address
Hillsbro
15 Ashcombe Avenue
Surbiton
Surrey
KT6 6PX
Telephone 020 83999412
Fax Not available
Email Not available
Website Not available

Narrowboat Surveys Ltd
(Full Member)
Contact
Paul Smith
Address
12 Canterbury Close
Studley
Warwickshire
B80 7JF
Telephone 01527 854039
Fax 01527 465360
Email
info@narrowboatsurveys.co.uk
Website
www.narrowboatsurveys.co.uk

Opal Marine Ltd
(Full Member)
(Opal Marine)
(Island Packet)
Contact
Julian Gowing
Address
Camper and Nicholson Marina
Mumby Road
Gosport
Hampshire
PO12 1AH
Telephone 023 9246 6075
Fax 023 9246 1838
Email
juliangowing@opalmarine.com
Website www.opalmarine.co.uk

Oyster Marine Ltd
(Full Member)
(Oyster Marine)
(Oyster Brokerage)
Contact
Richard Matthews
Address
Foxs Marina
Ipswich
Suffolk
IP2 8SA
Telephone 01473 688888
Fax 01473 686861
Email yachts@oystermarine.com
Website www.oystermarine.com

Patrick Boyd Multihulls Ltd
(Full Member)
(Patrick Boyd Multihulls)
Contact
Bill Bullimore
Address
Wicormarine
Cranleigh Road
Portchester
Hampshire
PO16 9DR
Telephone 01329 288257
Fax 01329 288259
Email
bill.bullimore@multihulls.co.uk
Website www.multihulls.co.uk

Penton Hook Marine Sales Ltd
(Full Member)
Contact
Chris Manners
Address
Penton Hook Marina
Staines Road Chertsey
Surrey KT16 8PY
Telephone 01932 570055
Fax 01932 570655
Email c.manners@talk21.com
Website
www.thamesboatsales.co.uk

Salterns Yacht Agency Ltd
(Full Member)
Contact
R Stokes
Address
Chichester Yacht Basin
Birdham
Chichester
Sussex
PO20 7EN
Telephone 01243 512745
Fax 01243 511382
Email Not available
Website Not available

South West Yacht Brokers Ltd
(Full Member)
(Class Yachts UK)
Contact
Alan Blackmore
Address
Atlantic Quay
Richmond Walk
Plymouth
Devon
PL1 4LN
Telephone 01752 551991
Fax 01752 551991
Email
alan@wswyachtbroker.demon.co.uk
Website Not available

Southern Motorboats Ltd
(Full Member)
Contact
Doug James
Address
Universal Marina
Crableck Lane
Sarisbury Green
Southampton
Hampshire
SO31 7ZN
Telephone 01489 565555
Fax 01489 565111
Email dj@medsale.net
Website Not available

Tewkesbury Marina Ltd
(Full Member)
Contact
S Morris
Address
Bredon Road
Tewkesbury
Gloucestershire
GL20 5BY
Telephone 01684 293737
Fax 01684 293076
Email
sales@tewkesbury-marina.co.uk
Website
www.tewkesbury-marina.co.uk

Toughs Boatyard
(Full Member)
Contact
Bob Tough
Address
27 Ferry Road
Teddington
Middlesex
TW11 9NN
Telephone 020 8977 4494
Fax 020 8977 7546
Email johntough@btinternet.com
Website www.toughsboatyard.co.uk

Virginia Currer Marine Ltd
(Full Member)
Contact
Virginia Currer
Address
1 Grove Close
Old Windsor
Berkshire
SL4 2LY
Telephone 01753 832312
Fax 01753 830130
Email vc@vcmarine.co.uk
Website www.vcmarine.co.uk

Wessex Marine
(Full Member)
Contact
David Adams
Address
Salterns Marina
Salterns Way
Lilliput
Poole
Dorset
BH14 8JR
Telephone 01202 700702
Fax 01202 916710
Email
enquiries@wessexmarine.co.uk
Website www.wessexmarine.co.uk

Williams & Smithells Ltd
(Full Member)
Contact
David Smithells
Address
Ocean Village Marina
3 Channel Way
Canute Road
Southampton
Hampshire
SO14 3TG
Telephone 023 8033 4445
Fax 023 8022 1675
Email
williamsandsmithells@btinternet.com
Website
www.williamsandsmithells.co.uk

Winters Marine Ltd (Lincombe)
(Full Member)
Contact
Tony Watson
Address
Lincombe Boatyard
Lincombe
Salcombe
Devon
TQ8 8NQ
Telephone 01548 843580
Fax 01548 843006
Email
tony.watson@lincombeboatyard.co.uk
Website
www.lincombeboatyard.co.uk

British Marine
Federation

The following are Members
of the British Marine Federation

Contact
David Banks
Address
372 Brook Lane
Sarisbury
Southampton
Hampshire
SO3 6ZA
Telephone 01489 582444
Fax 01489 589789
Email david@banks.co.uk
Website www.banks.co.uk

Arun Sails Ltd
(Full Member)
(Arun Sails)
(Rockall Sails)
Contact
Ivan Bole
Address
The Sail Centre
Southfield Industrial Park
Delling Lane
Bosham
West Sussex
PO18 8NW
Telephone 01243 573185
Fax 01243 573 032
Email arun@sailmakers.com
Website www.sailmakers.com

Bruce Banks Sails Ltd
(Full Member)
(Banks Sails)
Contact
David Banks
Address
372 Brook Lane
Sarisbury
Southampton
Hampshire
SO31 7ZA
Telephone 01489 582444
Fax 01489 589789
Email david@banks.co.uk
Website www.banks.co.uk

Dimension-Polyant (UK) Ltd
(Full Member)
Contact
Gary Owen
Address
Unit 11 Kingdom Close
Kingdom Business Park
Segensworth East
Fareham
Hampshire
PO15 5TJ
Telephone 01489 570551
Fax 01489 570451
Email Not available
Website Not available

Formula Yacht Spars Ltd
(Full Member)
Contact
Sandy Fielding
Address
Unit 8
Ampress Park
Lymington
Hampshire
SO41 8XN
Telephone 01590 610063
Fax 01590 610066
Email mail@formulaspars.com
Website www.formulaspars.com

Jeckells & Son Ltd
(Full Member)
Contact
Peter Jeckells
Address
Riverside Road
Wroxham
Nr Norwich
Norfolk
NR12 8UQ
Telephone 01603 784488
Fax 01603 783234
Email
jeckellsstrimmers@ukgateway.net
Website
www.jeckellstrimmerschandlers.co.uk

Jeckells of Wroxham Ltd
(Full Member)
(Jeckells -The Sailmakers)
Contact
Chris Jeckells
Address
Station Road
Wroxham
Norwich
Norfolk
NR12 8UT
Telephone 01603 782223
Fax 01603 784023
Email chris@jeckells.co.uk
Website www.jeckells.co.uk

Kemp Sails Ltd
(Full Member)
(Kemp Sails)
Contact
Linda Kemp
Address
Unit 2
Sandford Lane Industrial Estate
Wareham
Dorset
BH20 4DY
Telephone 01929 554308
Fax 01929 554350
Email linda@kempsails.com
Website www.kempsails.com

Ratsey Lapthorn Sailmakers Ltd
(Full Member)
Contact
M Ratsey-Woodroffe
Address
42 Medina Road
Cowes
Isle of Wight
PO31 7BY
Telephone 01983 294051
Fax 01983 294053
Email ratseysails@ratsey.com
Website
www.ratsey.com/ratseysails

W B Leitch & Son
(Full Member)
Contact
W B Leitch
Address
Garval Road
Tarbert
Argyllshire
PA29 6TR
Telephone 01880 820287
Fax 01880 820 596
Email leitchsails@aol.com
Website Not available

W G Lucas & Son Ltd
(Full Member)
(Lucas Sails)
Contact
Peter Lucas
Address
Portchester House
Hospital Lane
Portchester
Hampshire
PO16 9QP
Telephone 023 92373699
Fax 023 92373656
Email info@lucas-sails.com
Website www.lucas-sails.com

British Marine
Federation

The following are Members
of the British Marine Federation

**BMF - British Marine
Electronics Association**
(BMEA) (Region and Group
Association)
Contact
Tony Johns
Address
7 Eton Close
Weedon
Northamptonshire
NN7 4PJ
Telephone 01327 341 729
Fax 01327 341 004
Email secretary@bmea.org
Website www.bmea.org

Active Research Ltd
(Full Member)
Contact
Phil Whitehurst
Address
Unit 5
Wessex Trade Centre
Ringwood Road
Poole
Dorset
BH12 3PF
Telephone 01202 746682
Fax 01202 746683
Email phil@activer.com
Website www.actisense.com

Adverc BM Ltd
(Full Member)
(Adverc BM)
Contact
T Scarratt
Address
245 Trysull Road
Merry Hill
Wolverhampton
West Midlands
WV3 7LG
Telephone 01902 380494
Fax 01902 380435
Email techsales@adverc.co.uk
Website www.adverc.co.uk

Alpine Electronics of UK Ltd
(Associate Member)
(Alpine Electronics)
Contact
Graham Johnson
Address
Alpine House
Fletchampstead Highway
Coventry
Warwickshire
CV4 9TW
Telephone 01908 611556
Fax 01908 618420
Email
graham.johnson@alpineelectronics.co.uk
Website Not available

Amberley Marine Ltd
(Full Member)
Contact
Ray Brassington
Address
Hurley Cottage
Henley Road
Hurley
Berkshire
SL6 5LW
Telephone 01628 826104
Fax 01628 828322
Email amberleymarine@aol.com
Website
www.amberleymarine.co.uk

**Ampair (Doughty
Engineering Ltd)**
(Full Member)
(Ampair)
Contact
Mervyn Lister
Address
The Doughty Building
Crow Arch Lane
Ringwood
Hampshire
BH24 1NZ
Telephone 01425 480780
Fax 01425 479497
Email
mbl@doughty-engineering.co.uk
Website www.ampair.com

Atkinson Marine Ltd
(Full Member)
Contact
Nigel Atkinson
Address
4 South Street
Pennington
Lymington
Hampshire SO41 8ED
Telephone 01590 688389
Fax 01590 688868
Email info@atkinson-marine.co.uk
Website www.atkinson-marine.com

Autonnic Research Ltd
(Full Member)
Contact
Peter Ganderton
Address
Woodrolfe Road
Tollesbury
Essex
CM9 8SE
Telephone 01621 869460
Fax 01621 868815
Email info@autonnic.co.uk
Website www.autonnic.com

AW Marine
(Full Member)
Contact
A Williams
Address
Haslar Marina
Haslar Road
Gosport
Hampshire
PO12 1NU
Telephone 02392 501 207
Fax 02392 501 534
Email info@awmarine.com
Website www.awmarine.com

Axon Components Ltd
(Full Member)
Contact
B Vipond
Address
Unit 5 Blackburn Industrial Estate
Enterprise Way
Sherburn in Elmet
Leeds
Yorkshire
LS25 6NA
Telephone 01977 681781
Fax 01977 681688
Email
axoncomponents@tiscali.co.uk
Website Not available

British Marine Federation

The following are Members of the British Marine Federation

AH Moody & Son Ltd
(Full Member)
(AHM Electronics Ltd)
Contact
Phil Coundley
Address
Swanwick Shore
Swanwick
Southampton
Hampshire
SO3 1ZL
Telephone 01489 885000
Fax 01489 888871
Email grahammoody@moody.co.uk
Website www.moody.co.uk

Ali-It Marine Ltd
(Probationary Member)
Contact
Martin Hackett
Address
Unit 6
London Road Industrial Estate
Pembroke Dock
Pembroke
Pembrokeshire
SA72 6DU
Telephone 01646 622888
Fax 01646 686999
Email sales@ali-itmarine.co.uk
Website www.ali-itmarine.com

Alumacraft (Seastrike Boats)
(Full Member)
Contact
D Irvine
Address
The Marina
Barns Lane
Stubbers Green
Aldridge
West Midlands
WS9 8BQ
Telephone 01922 458227
Fax 01922 744224
Email sales@seastrike.co.uk
Website www.seastrike.co.uk

Amble Boat Company Ltd
(Full Member)
Contact
Nick Spurr
Address
The Boatyard Amble
Northumberland
NE65 0DJ
Telephone 01665 710267
Fax 01665 711354
Email info@ambleboat.co.uk
Website www.ambleboat.co.uk

Aqua Star Ltd
(Full Member)
Contact
Geoff Willson
Address
Ocean Yard
Bulwer Avenue
St Sampsons
Guernsey
GY2 4LE
Channel Islands
Telephone 01481 244550
Fax 01481 244711
Email aquastar@guernsey.net
Website
www.boatshow.com/aqua-starltd.

Arun Marine Design Ltd
(Full Member)
Contact
Graham Chatfield
Address
Arun Shipyard
Rope Walk
Littlehampton
West Sussex
BN17 5DH
Telephone 07850 734996
Fax 01903 725911
Email GMCatAMD@aol.com
Website Not available

Avon Inflatables Ltd
(Full Member)
(Avon Inflatables)
(Previously known as Avon)
Contact
Alan Morgan
Address
Dafen
Llanelli
Carmarthernshire
SA14 8NA
Telephone 01554 882000
Fax 01554 882039
Email info@avon-inflatable.com
Website www.avonmarine.com

Berthon Boat Company Ltd
(Full Member)
Contact
Brian May
Address
The Shipyard
Lymington
Hampshire
SO41 3YL
Telephone 01590 673312
Fax 01590 676353
Email projects@berthon.co.uk
Website www.berthon.co.uk

Blondecell Ltd
(Full Member)
Contact
Gavin Brown
Address
Cracknore Industrial Park
Cracknore Hard
Marchwood
Southampton
Hampshire
SO40 4ZD
Telephone 023 80663437
Fax 023 8086 8799
Email Not available
Website www.blondecell.com

Blue C Marine Technology Ltd
(Full Member)
Contact
P Burborough
Address
Firs Industrial Est
Oldington Lane
Kidderminster
Worcestershire
DY11 7QN
Telephone 01562 746336
Fax 01562 746336
Email Not available
Website Not available

Bonwitco
(Full Member)
Contact
Francis Wills
Address
Torr Quarry Industrial Estate
Near Kingsbridge
Totnes
Devon
TQ9 7QQ
Telephone 01548 521561
Fax 01548 521560
Email Not available
Website Not available

Bossoms Boatyard Ltd
(Full Member)
(Bossoms Boatyard)
Contact
Tom Ballance
Address
Binsey Lane
Medley
Oxford
Oxfordshire
OX2 ONL
Telephone 01865 247780
Fax 01865 244163
Email info@bossoms.co.uk
Website www.bossoms.com

Bramber Boat Trailers Ltd
(Full Member)
Contact
Terry Williams
Address
South View Road
Willand
Cullompton
Devon
EX15 2RU
Telephone 01884 820105
Fax 01884 820115
Email brambertrailers@aol.com
Website www.brambertrailers.com

Branson Boat Design Ltd
(Full Member)
Contact
J N Branson
Address
Unit 4A
Crowland Industrial Centre
Crease Drove
Crowland
Peterborough
Cambridgeshire
PE4 OBN
Telephone 01733 211966
Fax 01733 211966
Email
bransonboats@btinternet.com
Website Not available

Camper & Nicholsons
Yachting Ltd
(Full Member)
(Camper & Nicholsons Yachting)
Contact
Ian Crowden
Address
Mumby Road
Gosport
Hampshire
PO12 1AH
Telephone 023 92580221
Fax 023 92601145
Email Not available
Website Not available

Channelglaze
(Full Member)
Contact
Janet Pearson
Address
21a Rushey Lane
Tyseley
Birmingham
West Midlands
B11 2BL
Telephone 0121 7065777
Fax 0121 7067177
Email janet@channelglaze.com
Website www.channelglaze.com

Cheetah Marine Catamarans
(Full Member)
Contact
Keith Strevens
Address
Bonchurch
Ventnor
Isle of Wight
PO38 1RL
Telephone 0845 4506044
Fax 0845 5406043
Email sean@cheetahmarine.co.uk
Website www.cheetahmarine.co.uk

Chris Humphrey Boatbuilder
(Full Member)
Contact
C Humphrey
Address
Riverside
Teignmouth
Devon
TQ14 9PH
Telephone 01626 772324
Fax 01626 772324
Email Not available
Website Not available

Coastline Marine
(Full Member)
Contact
B Hallett
Address
Unit 7 Mercury Yacht Harbour
Satchell Lane
Hamble
Southampton
Hampshire
SO31 4HQ
Telephone 023 80453802
Fax 023 80457287
Email sales@coastlinemarine.co.uk
Website www.coastlinemarine.co.uk

Coupland Bell Ltd
(Probationary Member)
Contact
Mark Evans
Address
Barclays Venture Centre
University of Warwick Science Park
Sir William Lyons Road
Coventry
Warwickshire
CV4 7EZ
Telephone 01926 863563
Fax Not available
Email
mark.evans@couplandbell.com
Website www.couplandbell.com

Crayford Marine Ltd
(Full Member)
Contact
Alan Brooks
Address
Lyon Way
St Albans
Hertfordshire
AL14 OLQ
Telephone 01727 851222
Fax 01727 859222
Email crayfordse@aol.com
Website Not available

Cygnus Marine Ltd
(Full Member)
Contact
A T Clynick
Address
Britannia Yard
Penryn
Cornwall
TR10 9ER
Telephone 01326 372970
Fax 01326 374585
Email
info@cygnusmarine.demon.co.uk
Website www.cygnusmarine.com

Delta Power Services
(Full Member)
Contact
Charles Dyas
Address
Newby Road Industrial Estate
Hazel Grove
Stockport
Cheshire
SK7 5DR
Telephone 0161 456 6588
Fax 0161 456 6686
Email sales@deltapower.co.uk
Website www.deltapower.co.uk

Devonport Royal Dockyard Ltd
(Full Member)
(DML)
(Devonport Yachts)
Contact
David Smeken
Address
Devonport Royal Dockland
Devonport
Plymouth
Devon
PL1 4SG
Telephone 01752 553311
Fax 01752 554883
Email yachts@devonport.co.uk
Website www.devonport.co.uk

Ecocats Ltd
(Probationary Member)
Contact
Derick Reynolds
Address
1 The Green
Kingsand
Torpoint
Cornwall
PL10 1NH
Telephone 01752 822703
Fax Not available
Email info@ecocats.com
Website www.ecocats.com

Foxs Marina Ipswich Ltd
(Full Member)
(Fox's Yacht Sales)
Contact
J Munns
Address
The Strand
Wherstead
Ipswich
Suffolk
IP2 8SA
Telephone 01473 689111
Fax 01473 601737
Email
foxs.marina@oystermarine.com
Website Not available

Frank Halls & Son
(Full Member)
Contact
Christopher Halls
Address
Mill Lane
Walton on the Naze
Essex
CO14 8PF
Telephone 01255 675596
Fax 01255 677772
Email frankhalls@tiscali.co.uk
Website Not available

Goodchild Marine Services Ltd
(Full Member)
(Previously known as Aqua Bell)
Contact
Alan Goodchild
Address
Burgh Castle Yacht Station
Butt Lane
Burgh Castle
Great Yarmouth
Norfolk
NR31 9PZ
Telephone 01493 782301
Fax 01493 782306
Email info@goodchildmarine.co.uk
Website Not available

GRP Laminates Ltd
(Full Member)
Contact
Sally Lynskey
Address
Prospect Road
Cowes
Isle of Wight
PO31 7AD
Telephone 01983 200988
Fax 01983 200995
Email enquiries@grplaminates.com
Website www.grplaminates.com

Henshaw Inflatables Ltd
(Full Member)
(Henshaw Inflatables)
Contact
Chris Hornidge
Address
Southgate Road
Wincanton
Somerset
BA9 9RZ
Telephone 01963 33237
Fax 01963 34578
Email mail@henshaw.co.uk
Website www.henshaw.co.uk

Holyhead Marine Services Ltd
(Full Member)
Contact
J Colin York
Address
Newry Beach Yard
Holyhead
Anglesey
LL65 1YB
Telephone 01407 760111
Fax 01407 764531
Email
marine.services@holyhead.co.uk
Website www.holyhead.co.uk

Houdini Marine Windows
(Full Member)
Contact
Charlie Stewart
Address
Hallmark Industrial Estate
Southminster
Essex
CM0 7EH
Telephone 01621 773590
Fax 01621 773852
Email sales@houdini-marine.co.uk
Website www.houdini-marine.co.uk

ITT Jabsco Limited
(Full Member)
(Jabsco & Rule)
Contact
Geoff Sheddick
Address
Bingley Road
Hoddesdon
Hertfordshire
EN11 0BU
Telephone 01992 450145
Fax 01992 467132
Email
geoff.sheddick@fluids.ittind.se
Website www.jabsco.com

JS Mouldings Ltd
(Full Member)
Contact
J Shaw
Address
Unit 11 Essex Marina
Wallasea Island
Near Rochford
Essex
SS4 2HG
Telephone 01702 258267
Fax 01702 258267
Email Not available
Website Not available

Landguard Marine Ltd
(Full Member)
Contact
Philip Klein
Address
The Coach House
Norwich Road
Scole
Norfolk
IP21 4EE
Telephone 01379 741144
Fax 01379 741140
Email landguard@btconnect.com
Website www.landguardmarine.com

Lochin Marine International Ltd
(Full Member)
Contact
Simon Thomas
Address
The Yacht Harbour
Newhaven
Sussex
BN9 9BY
Telephone 01273 515085
Fax 01273 512522
Email sales@lochin.com
Website www.lochin.com

Marine GRP (UK) Ltd
(Probationary Member)
Contact
Carl Selwood
Address
16 Butcher Street
Old Portsmouth
Portsmouth
Hampshire
PO1 3BL
Telephone 07789 111115
Fax 02392 422889
Email enquiries@marine-grp.co.uk
Website www.marine-grp.co.uk

Marine Specialised Technology Ltd
(Probationary Member)
Contact
Philip Hilbert
Address
Unit 1 Atlantic Way
Brunswick Business Park
Liverpool
Merseyside
L3 4BE
Telephone 0151 708 4112
Fax 0115 708 4113
Email sales@mstltd.com
Website mstltd.com

Mike Derrett Marine
(Full Member)
Contact
Mike Derrett
Address
Stane Cottage
Watchouse Road
Stebbing Dunmow
Essex
CM6 3SP
Telephone 01371 856366
Fax 01371 856624
Email mderrett@compuserve.com
Website www.mikederrett.com

Milford Marina
(Full Member)
Contact
Adrian Owens
Address
The Docks
Milford Haven
Pembrokeshire
SA73 3AF
Telephone 01646 696300
Fax 01646 696302
Email marina@milford-docks.co.uk
Website www.milford-docks.co.uk

Ocean Dynamics International Ltd
(Full Member)
Contact
Shaun White
Address
Ocean Base
St Davids
Pembrokeshire
SA62 6RJ
Telephone 01437 721390
Fax 01437 720747
Email sales@oceandynamics.co.uk
Website www.ribworker.com

Orkney Boats Limited
(Full Member)
(Orkney Boats)
Contact
Richard Hay
Address
Unit 1
Ford Lane Business Park
Ford
Arundel
Sussex
BN18 0UZ
Telephone 01243 551456
Fax 01243 551914
Email Not available
Website www.orkneyboatsltd.co.uk

Peter Nicholls (Steel Boats)
(Full Member)
(Peter Nicholls Steel Boats)
Contact
Peter Nicholls
Address
Braunston Marina Trade Centre
Daventry Road
Braunston
Northamptonshire
NN11 7JH
Telephone 01788 891823
Fax 01788 899109
Email peter@steelboats.com
Website www.steelboats.com

Picton Boats Ltd
(Full Member)
(Picton Boats)
Contact
J Picton
Address
Brymenyn Industrial Estate
Brymenyn
Near Bridgend
Glamorgan
CF32 9TZ
Telephone 01656 724444
Fax 01656 721709
Email Not available
Website www.pictonboats.com

RLL Boats
(Full Member)
Contact
R Boyce
Address
Unit 1 Broadmead Lane Ind Est
Broadmead Lane
Keynsham, Bristol
Gloucestershire
BS31 1ST
Telephone 01179 869860
Fax 01179 869872
Email Not available
Website www.rllboats.co.uk

R W Davis & Son Ltd
(Probationary Member)
Contact
Phil Trotter
Address
Junction Dry Dock
Saul
Gloucestershire
GL2 7LA
Telephone 01452 740233
Fax 01452 741307
Email sales@rwdavis.co.uk
Website www.rwdavis.co.uk

Ribcraft Ltd
(Full Member)
Contact
R M Gardner
Address
Edward Close
Houndstone Business Park
Yeovil
Somerset
BA22 8RU
Telephone 01935 411846
Fax 01935 411870
Email sales@ribcraft.co.uk
Website www.ribcraft.co.uk

Ribtec Ltd
(Full Member)
(Ribtec)
Contact
Tim Wilks
Address
Collingwood Road
Townstal
Dartmouth
Devon
TQ6 9JY
Telephone 02380 633700
Fax 02380 633885
Email timwilks@ribtec.co.uk
Website www.ribtec.co.uk

Scorpion RIBs Ltd
(Full Member)
Contact
Graham Jelley
Address
Haven Quay
Mill lane
Lymington
Hampshire
SO41 9AZ
Telephone 01590 677805
Fax 01590 671911
Email sales@scorpionribs.com
Website www.scorpionribs.com

Sea Otter Workboats Ltd
(Full Member)
(Sea Otter Boats)
Contact
Ray Shepherd
Address
Adelphi Way
Ireland Industrial Estate
Stavely
Chesterfield
S43 3LS
Telephone 01246 470005
Fax 01246 470006
Email
rshepherd@seaotterboats.co.uk
Website www.seaotterboats.co.uk

Seaglaze Marine Windows Ltd
(Full Member)
(Seaglaze Marine Windows)
Contact
Richard Clayton
Address
Wendover Road
Rackheath
Norwich
Norfolk
NR13 6LH
Telephone 01603 720 745
Fax 01603 721770
Email richard@seaglaze.co.uk
Website www.seaglaze.co.uk

Seaward Marine Ltd
(Full Member)
Contact
Alison Kimber
Address
1 Prospect Road
Cowes
Isle of Wight
PO31 7AD
Telephone 01983 280333
Fax 01983 295095
Email admin@seawardboat.com
Website www.seawardboat.com

Stormcats Ltd
(Probationary Member)
Contact
Angus Newman
Address
Surnaig Farm
Lagavulin
Isle of Islay
Argyllshire
PA42 7DX
Telephone 01496 300129
Fax 01469 300129
Email gus@stormcats.co.uk
Website www.stormcats.co.uk

Thanetcraft Ltd
(Full Member)
Contact
John Armstrong
Address
29 Pope's Grove
Twickenham
Middlesex
TW1 4JZ
Telephone 020 8894 5218
Fax 020 8894 5218
Email sales@thanetcraft.com
Website www.thanetcraft.com

Three C's Marine Ltd
(Full Member)
Contact
S Curtis
Address
Stone Pier Boat Yard
Warsash
Southampton
Hampshire
SO31 9FR
Telephone 02380 453148
Fax 01489 559119
Email
sales@cougar-powerboats.com
Website Not available

Tiger Marine Ltd
(Probationary Member)
Contact
Charles Eld
Address

3 Church Farm Close
Standlake
Witney
Oxfordshire
OX29 7SN
Telephone 01785 780 741
Fax 01785 780 742
Email charleseld@tigermarine.co.uk
Website Not available

Toughs Boatyard
(Full Member)
Contact
Bob Tough
Address
27 Ferry Road
Teddington
Middlesex
TW11 9NN
Telephone 020 8977 4494
Fax 020 8977 7546
Email johntough@btinternet.com
Website www.toughsboatyard.co.uk

Trans-Web Ltd
(Associate Member)
Contact
Graham Collins
Address
72 - 76 Manchester St
Oldham
Lancashire
OL9 6EF
Telephone 0161 627 0022
Fax 0161 627 3784
Email sales@trans-web.co.uk
Website Not available

Tremlett Boat Sales Ltd
(Full Member)
Contact
Diana Tremlett
Address
Odhams Wharf
Topsham
Exeter
Devon
EX3 0PD
Telephone 01392 873680
Fax 01392 876277
Email Not available
Website Not available

VT Halmatic Ltd
(Full Member)
Contact
Sebastian Freeman
Address
Portchester Shipyard
Hamilton Road
Portsmouth
Hampshire
PO6 4QB
Telephone 023 9253 9600

Fax 023 9253 9601
Email seb.freeman@halmatic.com
Website www.vtplc.com/halmatic

Wynstruments Ltd
(Full Member)
Contact
Antony Parker
Address
Wynn House
Lansdown Estate
Cheltenham
Gloucestershire
GL51 8PL
Telephone 01242 232266
Fax 01242 231131
Email sales@wynn.co.uk
Website www.wynn.co.uk

BOAT NAME	LOA	PRICE	PAGE No:
Hawk 20	20ft	£16600.00	14
Horizon Cat	20ft	£23000.00	15
Red Fox 200	20ft.3in	£22207.00	16
Pippin 20	20ft 8in	£16350.00	17
Jeanneau Sun 2000	21ft 6in	£10706.00	20
Etap 21i	21ft 6in	£14175.00	19
Beneteau First 211	21ft.6in	£21500.00	18
Cornish Crabber 22 Gaff Cutter	22ft	£46412.00	21
Viva 700	22ft.9in	£21153.00	22
Yarmouth 23	23ft	£48255.00	23
Europa TS 230	23ft 2in	£17745.00	24
Parker 235	23ft 5in	£22000.00	25
Com-Pac 23/3	23ft 11in	£23795.00	26
Jeanneau 26	24ft 1in	£28380.00	27
Corsair 24	24ft 5in	£32700.00	28
RO265	24ft 6in	£39950.00	30
Ranger 245	24ft 6in	£40664.00	29
Beneteau 25	24ft 7in	£14773.00	31
Com-Pac 25	25ft	£38245.00	32
Fisher 25	25ft 3in	£73381.00	33
Benetea 260	25ft 6in	£37500.00	34
Sportina 760	25ft 6in	£35500.00	35
MacGregor 26	26ft	£19990.00	36
Nordic Folkboat	26ft	£23500.00	37
Etap 24i	26ft.3in	£23450.00	38
Etap 26i	27ft 8in	£37500.00	42
Odin 820	26ft 9in	£23860.00	39
Channel 27	26ft 9in	£50225.00	41
Hunter Channel 27	26ft 9in	£50225.00	40
Hunter Pilot 27	26ft 9in	£60391.00	41
Corsair 28	28ft	£53500.00	43
Vancouver 28	28ft	£72659.00	44
Jeanneau 29.2	28ft 11in	£35372.00	45
Beneteau First 27.7	29ft	£45500.00	46
Sadler 290	29ft	£62195.00	47
Com-Pac 27/2	29ft 7in	£64595.00	48
Legend 306	29ft 11in	POA	49
Dragonfly 920	30ft 2in	£71750.00	50
Elan 31	30ft 2in	£59702.00	51
Etap 30i	30ft 7in	£50500.00	52

BOAT NAME	LOA	PRICE	PAGE No:
Channel 31	30ft 9in	£78603.00	53
Hanse 312	31ft	£54990.00	55
Global Midget	31ft	£75594.00	54
Jeanneau Odyssey 32	31ft 5in	£46065.00	56
Hallberg Rassy 31	31ft 7in	£74000.00	57
Nauticat 321	32ft 1in	£100900.00	58
Etap 32s	32ft 3in	£63000.00	59
DazCat	32ft 5in	POA	60
Beneteau Clipper 323	32ft 8in	£60000.00	61
Najad 331	32ft 8in	POA	62
RO340	32ft 9in	£72980.00	63
Elan 333	32ft 9in	£72489.00	63
Parker 335H	33ft 9in	£78000.00	65
Event 34	33ft 9in	£72244.00	66
Hallberg Rassy 34	33ft 9in	£92250.00	67
Legend 33	33ft 9in	POA	68
Ovni 345	34ft 1in	£90200.00	69
Catalina 320	34ft 3in	£591000	70
Vancouver 34	34ft 3in	£103251.00	71
Vancouver 34P	34ft 3in	£122438.00	72
Fisher 34	34ft 4in	£142890.00	73
Dufour 34	34ft 9in	£62723.00	74
Etap 34s	34ft 10in	£74600.00	75
Nordship 35	35ft	£118103.00	79
Hunter Mystery 35	35ft 2in	£89693.00	76
Jeanneau Odyssey 35	35ft 3in	£62570.00	77
Southerly 110	35ft 6in	£99713.00	81
Legend 36	35ft 6in	POA	80
Rustler 36	36ft	£114450.00	78
Corsair 36	36ft	POA	82
Dufour Classic 36	36ft 1in	£68949.00	83
Ovni 36	36ft 1in	£103655.00	84
Starlight 35 mk2	36ft 1in	£124500.00	85
Nauticat 35	36ft 3in	£137900.00	86
Catalina 36 mkII	36ft 4in	£74460.00	87
Feeling 36	36ft 5in	£110000.00	88
Sweden 370	36ft 7in	POA	89
Nauticat 37	36ft 8in	£169900.00	90
Beneteau Clipper 373	36ft 9in	£96500.00	91
Hanse 371	36ft 11in	£84990.00	93
Etap 37s	36ft 11in	£90500.00	92
Elan 37	37ft	£93840.00	94
Southerly 115	37ft	£135061.00	96
Fisher 37	37ft	£189137.00	95

BOAT NAME	LOA	PRICE	PAGE No:
Hallberg Rassy 37	37ft 2in	£136300.00	97
Malo 36	37ft 3in	£157500.00	98
Jeanneau Odyssey 37	37ft 4in	£71749.00	99
Najad 373	37ft 8in	POA	100
Island Packet 370	37ft 10in	POA	101
Nordship 38	38ft	£111804.00	103
Broadblue Catamaran 38	38ft	£151500.00	102
Vancouver 38	38ft	£169618.00	104
Vancouver 38P	38ft	£191705.00	105
Legend 386	38ft 3in	POA	106
Feeling 39	38ft 4in	£108100.00	107
Athena 38	38ft 5in	£150000.00	108
Nauticat 39	38ft 9in	£171950.00	110
Nauticat 38	38ft 9in	£176900.00	109
Crabber Pilot Cutter 30	39ft	£102992.00	111
Lavezzi 40	39ft	£180000.00	112
Sweden 390	39ft	POA	113
Salona 40	39ft 3in	£99285.00	114
Dufour 40	39ft 4in	£98519.00	116
Dragonfly 1200	39ft 4in	£227500.00	115
Ro 400	39ft 5in	£106500.00	117
Huffler Motor Sailer	39ft 6in	£249240.00	118
Etap 39s	39ft 7in	£122000.00	119
Ovni 385	39ft 8in	£111340.00	121
Bavaria 38 Match	39ft 8in	POA	120
Starlight 39 Mk2	39ft 9in	£174142.00	122
Elan 40	40ft	£119617.00	123
Beneteau 40.7	40ft 2in	£125000.00	124
Malo 39	40ft 2in	POA	125
Najad 400	40ft 4in	POA	126
Catalina 400	40ft 6in	£116280	127

BOAT NAME	LOA	PRICE £	PAGE No:
Jeanneau Sun 2000	21ft 6in	£10706.00	20
Etap 21i	21ft 6in	£14175.00	19
Beneteau 25	24ft 7in	£14773.00	31
Pippin 20	20ft 8in	£16350.00	17
Hawk 20	20ft	£16600.00	14
Europa TS 230	23ft 2in	£17745.00	24
MacGregor 26	26ft	£19990.00	36
Viva 700	22ft 9in	£21153.00	22
Beneteau First 211	21ft 6in	£21500.00	18
Red Fox 200	20ft 3in	£22207.00	16
Horizon Cat	20ft	£23000.00	15
Etap 24i	26ft 3in	£23450.00	38
Nordic Folkboat	26ft	£23500.00	37
Com-Pac 23/3	23ft 11in	£23795.00	26
Odin 820	26ft 9in	£23860.00	39
Jeanneau 26	24ft 1in	£28380.00	27
Corsair 24	24ft 5in	£32700.00	28
Jeanneau 29.2	28ft 11in	£35372.00	45
Sportina 760	25ft 6in	£35500.00	35
Benetea 260	25ft 6in	£37500.00	34
Etap 26i	27ft 8in	£37500.00	42
Com-Pac 23/3	23ft 11in	£23795.00	26
RO265	24ft 6in	£39950.00	30
Ranger 245	24ft 6in	£40664.00	29
Beneteau First 27.7	29ft	£45500.00	46
Jeanneau Odyssey 32	31ft 5in	£46065.00	56
Cornish Crabber 22 Gaff Cutter	22ft	£46412.00	21
Yarmouth 23	23ft	£48255.00	23
Channel 27	26ft 9in	£50225.00	40
Hunter Channel 27	26ft 9in	£50225.00	41
Etap 30i	30ft 7in	£50500.00	52
Corsair 28	28ft	£53500.00	43
Hanse 312	31ft	£54990.00	55
Catalina 320	34ft 3in	£59100.00	70
Elan 31	30ft 2in	£59702.00	51
Beneteau Clipper 323	32ft 8in	£60000.00	61
Hunter Pilot 27	26ft 9in	£60391.00	41
Sadler 290	29ft	£62195.00	47
Jeanneau Odyssey 35	35ft 3in	£62570.00	77
Dufour 34	34ft 9in	£62723.00	74
Etap 32s	32ft 3in	£63000.00	59
Com-Pac 27/2	29ft 7in	£64.595.00	48

BOAT NAME	LOA	PRICE £	PAGE No:
Dufour Classic 36	36ft 1in	£68949.00	83
Jeanneau Odyssey 37	37ft 4in	£71749.00	99
Dragonfly 920	30ft 2in	£71750.00	50
Event 34	33ft 9in	£72244.00	66
Elan 333	32ft 9in	£72489.00	63
Vancouver 28	28ft	£72659.00	44
RO340	32ft 9in	£72980.00	64
Fisher 25	25ft 3in	£73381.00	33
Hallberg Rassy 31	31ft 7in	£74000.00	57
Catalina 36 mkII	36ft 4in	£74460.00	87
Etap 34s	34ft 10in	£74600.00	75
Global Midget	31ft	£75594.00	54
Parker 335HS	33ft 5in	£78000.00	65
Channel 31	30ft 9in	£78603.00	53
Hanse 371	36ft 11in	£84990.00	92
Hunter Mystery 35	35ft 2in	£89693.00	76
Ovni 345	34ft 1in	£90200.00	69
Etap 37s3	6ft 11in	£90500.00	93
Hallberg Rassy 34	33ft 9in	£92250.00	67
Elan 37	37ft	£93840.00	94
Beneteau Clipper 373	36ft 9in	£96500.00	91
Dufour 40	39ft 4in	£98519.00	116
Salona 40	39ft 3in	£99285.00	114
Southerly 110	35ft 6in	£99713.00	81
Nauticat 321	32ft 1in	£100900.00	58
Crabber Pilot Cutter 30	39ft	£102992.00	111
Vancouver 34	34ft 3in	£103251.00	71
Ovni 36	36ft 1in	£103655.00	84
Ro 400	39ft 5in	£106500.00	117
Feeling 39	38ft 4in	£108100.00	107
Feeling 36	36ft 5in	£110000.00	88
Ovni 385	39ft 8in	£111340.00	121
Nordship 38	38ft	£111804.00	103
Rustler 36	36ft	£114450.00	78
Catalina 400	40ft 6in	£116.280.00	127
Nordship 35	35ft	£118103.00	79
Elan 40	40ft	£119617.00	123
Etap 39s	39ft 7in	£122000.00	119
Vancouver 34P	34ft 3in	£122438.00	72
Starlight 35	36ft 1in	£124500.00	85
Beneteau 40.7	40ft 2in	£125000.00	124
Southerly 115	37ft	£135061.00	96
Hallberg Rassy 37	37ft 2in	£136300.00	97
Nauticat 35	36ft 3in	£137900.00	86
Fisher 34	34ft 4in	£142890.00	73

BOAT NAME	LOA	PRICE £	PAGE No:
Athena 38	38ft 5in	£150000.00	108
Broadblue Catamaran 38	38ft	£151500.00	102
Malo 36	37ft 3in	£157500.00	98
Vancouver 38	38ft	£169618.00	104
Nauticat 37	36ft 8in	£169900.00	90
Nauticat 39	38ft 9in	£171950.00	110
Starlight 39 Mk2	39ft 9in	£174142.00	122
Nauticat 38	38ft 9in	£176900.00	109
Lavezzi 40	39ft	£180000.00	112
Fisher 37	37ft	£189137.00	95
Vancouver 38P	38ft	£191705.00	105
Dragonfly 1200	39ft 4in	£227500.00	115
Huffler Motor Sailer	39ft 6in	£249240.00	118
Bavaria 38 Match	39ft 8in	POA	120
Corsair 36	36ft	POA	82
DazCat	32ft 5in	POA	60
Island Packet 370	37ft 10in	POA	101
Legend 306	29ft 11in	POA	49
Legend 33	33ft 9in	POA	68
Legend 36	35ft 6in	POA	80
Legend 386	38ft 3in	POA	106
Malo 39	40ft 2in	POA	125
Najad 331	32ft 8in	POA	62
Najad 373	37ft 8in	POA	100
Najad 400	40ft 4in	POA	126
Sweden 370	36ft 7in	POA	89
Sweden 390	39ft	POA	113

Yachts out of production - by ascending LOA

NAME OF BOAT	FT	INCHES	METRES	AVERAGE PRICE +/-	PAGE NO:
Splinter	21	2	6.45	£3,000.00	129
Jaguar 21	21	4	6.50	£6,500.00	129
Jaguar 215	21	5	6.53	£14,000.00	130
Kingfisher 20	21	7	6.58	£3,000.00	130
Freedom 21	21	8	6.60	£4,000.00	131
Seal 22	21	9	6.63	£3,500.00	132
Anderson 22	21	9	6.63	£4,000.00	131
Hurley 22	22	0	6.70	£6,500.00	133
E-Boat	21	10	6.70	£4.500.00	132
Foxterrier	22	1	6.73	£6,000.00	133
Limbo 6.6	22	3	6.78	£4,000.00	134
Leisure 23	22	8	6.90	£5,000.00	135
Hunter Sonata	22	7	6.90	£6.500.00	134
Pandora	23	0	7.01	£3,000.00	136
Hunter 701	23	0	7.01	£3,500.00	136
Cobra 700	23	0	7.01	£9,000.00	135
Samphire 23	23	0	7.01	£5,500.00	136
Hurley 24.70	23	9	7.20	£8,000.00	138
Foxhound	23	9	7.25	£6,000.00	137
Compac 23 (Finistere)	23	11	7.29	£5,000.00	138
Westerly GK24	24	0	7.31	£8,500.00	139
Husky 24	24	0	7.31	£12,000.00	139
Legend 240	24	1	7.34	£20,000.00	140
Yachting World 5 tonner	24	5	7.44	£8,000.00	141
Trapper 240	24	6	7.47	£10,000.00	141
Cobra 750	25	0	7.62	£9,000.00	142
Ocean 760	25	0	7.62	£20,000.00	143
Folkboat (modified)	25	0	7.62	£12.000.00	137
Tomahawk 25	25	4	7.70	£10.000.00	143
Contessa 26	25	6	7.80	£7,500.00	144
Etap 26	25	5	7.80	£14,000.00	152
MG Spring	25	6	7.80	£13,500.00	144
Mystere	25	9	7.85	£9,000.00	146
Harrison Butler Cyclone II	25	9	7.85	£25,000.00	145
Legend 26	25	9	7.85	£17,000.00	145
MacGregor 26	25	10	7.87	£19,000.00	146
MacWester 26	26	0	7.92	£7,000.00	148
Atlanta 26	26	0	7.92	£8,000.00	147
Snapdragon 26	26	0	7.92	£8,000.00	149
Mirage 26	26	0	7.92	£12,000.00	148

NAME OF BOAT	FT	INCHES	METRES	AVERAGE PRICE +/-	PAGE NO:
Westerly Griffon	26	0	7.92	£17,500.00	149
Super Seal 26	26	0	7.92	£18,500.00	147
Etap 24i	26	4	8.02	£41,000.00	150
Hunter Ranger	26	6	8.08	£30,000.00	155
Sabre 27	27	0	8.22	£12,500.00	151
Vancouver 27	27	0	8.22	£25,000.00	150
Fairey Fisherman	27	5	8.35	£8,000.00	175
MG 27	27	6	8.38	£22,000.00	152
Varne 27	27	9	8.46	£15,000.00	153
Great Dane 28	28	0	8.50	£25,000.00	153
Stag 28	28	0	8.53	£13,000.00	154
Trapper 500	28	0	8.54	£15,000.00	151
Kelt 850	28	4	8.65	£18,000.00	154
Compromis	28	6	8.69	£40,000.00	155
Sigma 292	29	0	8.80	£20.000.00	157
Sadler 290	29	0	8.84	£28.500.00	156
Hallberg Rassy 29	29	2	8.90	£35,000.00	157
Dufour Arpege	29	6	8.99	£12,000.00	160
Hanse 292	29	6	8.99	£26,000.00	158
Iroquois	30	0	9.14	£20,000.00	159
Seadog	30	0	9.14	£27.000.00	159
Elan 295	30	2	9.20	£40,000.00	160
MacWester Wight	30	6	9.30	£16,000.00	161
Legend 310	30	10	9.40	£46.000.00	162
Unna 31	30	10	9.40	£53.000.00	162
Hanse 311	31	0	9.44	£50,000.00	163
Hanse 315	31	0	9.45	£49,500.00	164
CR 310	31	0	9.45	£77,000.00	163
Maxi 95	31	2	9.50	£24,000.00	165
Seaquest 320	31	3	9.52	£62,000.00	165
Golden Hind	31	6	9.60	£21,000.00	165
Sadler 32	31	6	9.60	£32,500.00	166
Legend 326	30	10	9.63	£59,000.00	161
Westerly Fulmar	31	10	9.70	£40,000.00	164
Nicholson 32	32	0	9.75	£21,000.00	167
Contessa 32	32	0	9.75	£33,000.00	167
Twins 36 (Cat)	32	0	9.75	£24.000.00	167
Southerly 100	32	0	9.75	£45.000.00	168
Barbican 33	32	8	9.95	£40,000.00	169
Freedom 33	33	0	10.00	£40,000.00	170
Nauticat 33	33	2	10.10	£50,000.00	170
Westerly Storm	33	2	10.11	£34,000.00	171
Moody 34	33	6	10.21	£45,000.00	172
MG 335	33	6	10.21	£37,000.00	172

NAME OF BOAT	FT	INCHES	METRES	AVERAGE PRICE +/-	PAGE NO:
Gemini (Cat)	33	6	10.21	£55,000.00	171
Bavaria 32	33	9	10.28	£50,000.00	173
Legend 340	33	9	10.28	£60,000.00	173
Hanse 341	33	11	10.34	£60,000.00	174
Rival 34	34	0	10.36	£43,000.00	174
Frances 34	34	3	10.40	£84,000.00	175
Feeling 1040	34	4	10.46	£40,000.00	176
Catalina 34	34	6	10.52	£48,000.00	176
Feeling 356	34	7	10.54	£50,000.00	143
Beneteau 35	34	9	10.60	£40,000.00	169
Jeanneau Sun 36	35	0	10.67	£50,000.00	177
Island Packet 350	35	0	10.67	£149,000.00	178
Trapper	35	0	10.67	£10,000.00	178
Warrior 35	35	0	10.67	£33,000.00	178
Nicholson 35	35	3	10.70	£45,000.00	179
Rustler 36	35	4	10.79	£90,000.00	179
SHE 36	35	6	10.80	£35,000.00	180
Westerly 37	37	4	11.38	£80,000.00	180
Bavaria 37	37	10	11.45	£72,000.00	181
Nautitect 395	39	3	11.96	£80,000.00	181
Najad 391	39	8	12.10	£200,000.00	182
Catalac 12m	40	10	12.45	£70,000.00	152

NAME OF BOAT	FT	INCHES	METRES	AVERAGE PRICE -/+	PAGE NO:
Kingfisher 20	21	7	6.58	£3,000	130
Pandora	23	0	7.01	£3,000	136
Splinter	21	2	6.45	£3,000	129
Hunter 701	23	0	7.01	£3,500	136
Seal 22	21	9	6.63	£3,500	131
Anderson 22	21	9	6.63	£4,000	131
Freedom 21	21	8	6.60	£4,000	131
Limbo 6.6	22	3	6.78	£4,000	134
E-Boat	21	10	6.70	£4.500	132
Compac 23 (Finistere)	23	11	7.29	£5,000	138
Leisure 23	22	8	6.90	£5,000	135
Samphire 23	23	0	7.01	£5,500	136
Foxhound	23	9	7.25	£6,000	137
Foxterrier	22	1	6.73	£6,000	133
Hurley 22	22	0	6.70	£6,500	133
Hunter Sonata	22	7	6.90	£6,500	134
Jaguar 21	21	4	6.50	£6,500	129
MacWester 26	26	0	7.92	£7,000	148
Contessa 26	25	6	7.80	£7,500	144
Atlanta 26	26	0	7.92	£8,000	147
Fairey Fisherman	27	5	8.35	£8,000	175
Hurley 24.70	23	9	7.20	£8,000	138
Snapdragon 26	26	0	7.92	£8,000	149
Yachting World 5 tonner	24	5	7.44	£8,000	141
Westerly GK24	24	0	7.31	£8,500	139
Cobra 700	23	0	7.01	£9,000	135
Cobra 750	25	0	7.62	£9,000	142
Mystere	25	9	7.85	£9,000	146
Sadler 25	24	4	7.41	£9.000	140
Tomahawk 25	25	4	7.70	£10,000	143
Trapper	35	0	10.67	£10,000	178
Trapper 240	24	6	7.47	£10,000	141
Dufour Arpege	29	6	8.99	£12,000	160
Folkboat (modified)	25	0	7.62	£12,000	137
Husky 24	24	0	7.31	£12,000	139
Mirage 26	26	0	7.92	£12,000	148
Sabre 27	27	0	8.22	£12,500	151
Stag 28	28	0	8.53	£13,000	154
MG Spring	25	6	7.80	£13,500	144
Etap 26	25	5	7.80	£14,000	152

NAME OF BOAT	FT	INCHES	METRES	AVERAGE PRICE -/+	PAGE NO:
Jaguar 215	21	5	6.53	£14,000	130
Trapper 500	28	0	8.54	£15,000	151
Varne 27	27	9	8.46	£15,000	153
MacWester Wight	30	6	9.30	£16,000	161
Legend 26	25	9	7.85	£17,000	145
Westerly Griffon	26	0	7.92	£17,500	149
Kelt 850	28	4	8.65	£18,000	154
Super Seal 26	26	0	7.92	£18,500	147
MacGregor 26	25	10	7.87	£19,000	146
Legend 240	24	1	7.34	£20,000	140
Sigma 292	29	0	8.80	£20,000	157
Iroquois	30	0	9.14	£20,000	159
Ocean 760	25	0	7.62	£20,000	143
Golden Hind	31	6	9.60	£21,000	166
Nicholson 32	32	0	9.75	£21,000	167
MG 27	27	6	8.38	£22,000	152
Maxi 95	31	2	9.50	£24,000	165
Twins 36 (Cat)	32	0	9.75	£24,000	168
Great Dane 28	28	0	8.50	£25,000	153
Harrison Butler Cyclone II	25	9	7.85	£25,000	145
Vancouver 27	27	0	8.22	£25,000	150
Hanse 292	29	6	8.99	£26,000	159
Seadog	30	0	9.14	£27,000	159
Sadler 290	29	0	8.84	£28.500	156
Hunter Ranger	26	6	8.08	£30,000	155
Vindo	29	3	8.91	£30,000	158
Sadler 32	31	6	9.60	£32.500	166
Contessa 32	32	0	9.75	£33,000	167
Warrior 35	35	0	10.67	£33,000	178
Westerly Storm	33	2	10.11	£34,000	171
Hallberg Rassy 29	29	2	8.90	£35,000	157
SHE 36	35	6	10.80	£35,000	180
MG 335	33	6	10.21	£37,000	172
Barbican 33	32	8	9.95	£40,000	169
Beneteau 35	34	9	10.60	£40,000	169
Compromis	28	6	8.69	£40,000	155
Elan 295	30	2	9.20	£40,000	160
Feeling 1040	34	4	10.46	£40,000	176
Freedom 33	33	0	10.00	£40,000	170
GibSea 284	28	6	8.68	£40,000	156
Westerly Fulmar	31	10	9.70	£40,000	164
Etap 24i	26	4	8.02	£41,000	150
Rival 34	34	0	10.36	£43,000	174
Moody 34	33	6	10.21	£45,000	172
Nicholson 35	35	3	10.74	£45,000	179

NAME OF BOAT	FT	INCHES	METRES	AVERAGE PRICE -/+	PAGE NO:
Southerly 100	32	0	9.75	£45,000	168
Legend 310	30	10	9.40	£46,000	162
Catalina 34	34	6	10.52	£48,000	176
Hanse 315	31	0	9.45	£49,500	164
Bavaria 32	33	9	10.28	£50,000	173
Feeling 356	34	7	10.54	£50,000	143
Hanse 311	31	0	9.44	£50,000	163
Jeanneau Sun 36	35	0	10.67	£50,000	177
Nauticat 33	33	2	10.10	£50,000	170
Unna 31	30	10	9.40	£53,000	162
Gemini (Cat)	33	6	10.21	£55,000	171
Legend 326	30	10	9.63	£59.000	161
Hanse 341	33	11	10.34	£60,000	174
Legend 340	33	9	10.28	£60.000	173
Seaquest 320	31	3	9.52	£62.000	165
Catalac 12m	40	10	12.45	£70,000	152
Bavaria 37	37	10	11.53	£72,000	181
CR 310	31	0	9.45	£77,000	163
Nautitect 395	39	3	11.96	£80,000	181
Westerly 37	37	4	11.38	£80,000	180
Frances	34	3	10.43	£84,000	175
Rustler 36	35	4	10.79	£90,000	179
Island Packet 350	35	0	10.67	£149,000	178
Najad 391	39	8	12.09	£200,000	182

Acknowledgments

Grateful acknowledgment is made to the following:

David Harding for his photographs of out of production yachts.

Alastair Garrod for his line drawings of out of production yachts.

Sailing Today magazine for their photographs and line drawings of out of production yachts.

Robin Blain for his loan of historical reference material.

Mark Grimwade for his loan of historical reference material.

Conversion formulae

To convert:

Inches to millimetres

Multiply 1 inch x 25.4
example 12inches x 25.4 = 304.8mm

Millimetres to inches

Multiply 1 millimetre x 0.0394
example 0.0394mm x 304.8mm = 12.00 inches

Feet to metres

Multiply 1 foot x 0.305
example 25 ft x 0.305 = 7.625 metres

Metres to feet

Multiply 1 metre x 3.281
example 7.625 x 3.281 = 25ft